CORPORATE ELITES AND THE REFORM OF PUBLIC EDUCATION

Edited by
Helen M. Gunter, David Hall, Michael W. Apple

First published in Great Britain in 2017 by

Policy Press
University of Bristol
1-9 Old Park Hill
Bristol
BS2 8BB
UK
t: +44 (0)117 954 5940
pp-info@bristol.ac.uk
www.policypress.co.uk

North America office:
Policy Press
c/o The University of Chicago Press
1427 East 60th Street
Chicago, IL 60637, USA
t: +1 773 702 7700
f: +1 773-702-9756
sales@press.uchicago.edu
www.press.uchicago.edu

© Policy Press 2017

British Library Cataloguing in Publication Data
A catalogue record for this book is available from the British Library

Library of Congress Cataloging-in-Publication Data
A catalog record for this book has been requested

ISBN 978-1-4473-2680-9 hardcover
ISBN 978-1-4473-3518-4 ePub
ISBN 978-1-4473-3517-7 Mobi
ISBN 978-1-4473-2682-3 epdf

The right of Helen M. Gunter, David Hall and Michael W. Apple to be identified as editors
of this work has been asserted by them in accordance with the Copyright, Designs and
Patents Act 1988.

Cover design by Policy Press
Front cover image: Eyewire
Printed and bound in Great Britain by CPI Group (UK) Ltd,
Croydon, CR0 4YY
Policy Press uses environmentally responsible print partners

Contents

Foreword

Romuald Normand

Education and elite reproduction are central themes in the sociological tradition. From Pareto's (1991) famous theory on the circulation of elites to Pierre Bourdieu's (1998) critique of the Nobility State, sociologists have evidenced the power and domination relationships as well as the structuration of social classes behind the meritocratic justification of school selection. Sociologists of education have taken a more recent interest in these themes, and this area of research has been considerably updated due the emergence of a globalised cosmopolitan class which challenges the usual standards of social reproduction by the education system. The rise of global mobility, combined with the development of 'world-class' schools transform issues of school competition, and create new inequalities between working-class and upper-class students. This edited volume by Helen Gunter, David Hall and Michael Apple offers an eye-opening investigative approach to this new field of research that demonstrates the global reach of the corporate elite through the marketisation/privatisation of education and the influence of business and philanthropy networks in the public education sector.

As Stephen Ball and Deborah Youdell wrote (2008), the privatisation of public education reshapes the boundaries between the public and the private in two ways: as 'endogenous' privatisation, it imports ideas, techniques and practices from the private into the public education sector to reproduce business models; as 'exogenous' privatisation, it opens public education to the private sector in order to make profits and replace some services. Exogenous privatisation is characterised by the externalisation of services in school transportation, catering, digital technologies, textbooks, cleaning services and extracurricular activities. These services are sold to schools, leading to the integration of the market within the public education sector. This can be described as a 'McDonaldisation', 'Coca-Colisation' or 'Microsoftisation' of the educative sphere. Moreover, as they push a common neoliberal agenda on policy makers, business leaders and philanthropists cooperate through global powerful networks to promote school choice, public–private partnerships, the diversification of school provision and statuses, the introduction of digital technologies and other commercial products (Ball, 2012).

The Right's systematic critique of public education laid the groundwork for this neoliberal indoctrination. Michael Apple convincingly showed that the critique of US public schools was supported by a New Right rhetoric that gained legitimacy during the presidential mandates of Reagan and Bush (Apple, 2006). Beyond religious and moral conservatism, the support to school choice and vouchers, in the US as well as in England, has been the Trojan horse of the neoliberal ideology. New Right think-tanks have disseminated official discourses to groom the public for a critique of public education based on abusive conclusions, rumours and false reports (Berliner and Glass, 2014; Chitty, 1989). Therefore, it paved the way for the diversification of school status and provision, in which representatives of business and religious groups rushed to develop initiatives from Microsoft to Edison programmes, from charter schools in the US to academies in England.

Several contributors to this book show that this movement has become global. The education service industry and private consultancies have contributed to the corporatisation of public education through strategies of marketisation and commodification that benefit a minority of people and social groups. Thus corporate elites, structured in power networks and relationships, disseminate a neoliberal ideology and an entrepreneurial spirit under the guise of private and philanthropic funding, while actually restricting the democratic governance of schools and legitimising consumerist and individualistic practices. The dismantling of public institutions and the transfer of expertise to agencies, think-tanks and consultancy groups increase the corporatisation of national and local governments.

What are the consequences of these changes for public education? Several authors in the book show that corporatisation impacts on school and university organisations, professional cultures, as well as teaching and learning conditions. It has resulted in the daily normalisation of practices through the delivery of marketised services, packaged programmes, digital technologies and instrumental devices in leadership. The spirit of capitalistic and managerial ideology has pervaded the entire educative sphere, up to the definition of the skills that students must acquire to become 'entrepreneurs'. School policy has become a matter of business and charity, as local communities – and society as a whole – are losing the ownership of grassroots projects and of their collective future. This privatisation does not only consist in restructuring the organisation of schools; indeed, it has also brought about the depoliticisation of the school system's principles as the concepts of equality and fairer allocation of funds are disregarded in favour of freedom and charity. Segregation and poverty issues are concealed behind the ideas of incentives and competition praised by economists.

The book documents a combination of a variety of trends in this corporatisation of education services. Consultancy groups like McKinsey & Company are particularly active at global level. They deliver advice and services to multiple governments and agencies throughout the world in the form of 'best practices' aimed at making schools better, more efficient and more equal. The critique of bureaucracy is used to legitimate managerial technologies and *doxa* for privatisation through narratives and success stories borrowing their language and ideology from business (Bourdieu, 2000).

Another trend has been the spread of elite schools, which aim to provide high standards in teaching and learning experiences for students. Under cover of class solidarity, sustained by 'world-class' programmes to reassure upper-class families, these schools maintain social barriers, while enhancing a variety of economic, cultural and social capitals for their students. This emerging elite is prepared to face global mobility and competition, and to profit from an education leading them to occupy the most powerful and prestigious positions in society. In these new social spaces, the new cosmopolitan corporate ruling class is progressively being built, nurturing the 'new spirit of capitalism'. The business model (Walmart, Google, and so on) – with its techniques of supply chain, quality approaches, client focus groups, leadership – is extended to school management, to justify the improvement of student skills. Entrepreneurship has become the ultimate yardstick by which to judge individual commitment, teamwork and empowerment, and by which people are considered to be serving the aims of the community or of society.

Under these circumstances, how is it even possible to resist this global societal movement, particularly as it becomes a reference for international organisations? The digitalisation of society and the adjustment to global competition are often argued to be ineluctable forces, legitimising the restructuring of education systems and professions for the sake of the survival of public education. Consequently, the ties between education systems and societies weaken, whereas individualisation and consumerism are presented as the future. Ultimately, there is an anomic risk of weakening social solidarity and increasing ghettoisation and apartheid within education systems.

The editors and co-authors in this collection remind us that education is a collective good that should not be divided between multiple private interests. More broadly, the book highlights the ways in which elite schools and corporate networks at global level contribute to increasing the inequality gap between those who profit from mobility and accumulation of wealth, and those who are maintained in deprived neighbourhoods where public education services are scaled back even as they face social misery and great poverty.

The sociological critique is needed to unveil these risks of social fragmentation, but also to raise awareness among policy makers of the necessity to shape new forms of social solidarity and social mix in schools, instead of subjecting them to a global competition dictated by international surveys and rankings. What is at stake is promoting social justice and school democratisation without giving in to the easy, utopian solutions drawing from economisation and the market. This book will surely interest anyone engaged in everyday efforts to reinvent democratic and civic education and to find alternatives to neoliberal globalisation.

References

Apple, M.W. (2006) *Educating the "right" way: Markets, standards, God, and inequality*. New York: Routledge.

Ball, S.J. (2012) *Global Education Inc.: New policy networks and the neo-liberal imaginary*. Routledge.

Ball, S.J. and Youdell, D. (2008) *Hidden privatisation in public education*. Brussels: Education International.

Berliner, D.C. and Glass, G.V. (eds) (2014) *50 Myths and Lies that Threaten America's Public Schools: The real crisis in education*. New York, NY: Teachers College Press.

Bourdieu, P. (1998) *The State Nobility: Elite schools in the field of power*. Stanford, CA: Stanford University Press.

Bourdieu, P. (2000) *Pascalian Meditations*. Cambridge: Polity Press.

Chitty, C. (1989) *Towards a New Education System: The victory of the new right?* Lewes: Falmer Press.

Pareto, V. (1991) *The Rise and Fall of Elites: Application of theoretical sociology*. New Brunswick, NJ: Transaction Publishers.

Notes on contributors

Michael W. Apple is John Bascom Professor of Curriculum and Instruction and Educational Policy Studies at the University of Wisconsin, Madison, US. He has written extensively on the relationship among culture, power and education, and on understanding and interrupting conservative movements in education. Among his recent books are: *Educating the 'right' way*; *Can education change society?*; *Power, knowledge, and education*; and *Official knowledge* (3rd edn).

Patricia Burch is Associate Professor in the Rossier School of Education at the University of Southern California, US. Her research explores the interactions of public education and private markets and the policy and equity implications of these dynamics. She is the author of: *Hidden markets: The new education privatization* (New York: Routledge); *Equal scrutiny: Privatization and accountability in digital education* (Cambridge: Harvard Education Press) with Annalee Good; and *Mixed methods research for policy and program evaluation* (Thousand Oaks: Sage) with Carolyn Heinrich.

Steven J. Courtney is Lecturer in Management and Leadership in the Manchester Institute of Education, University of Manchester, UK. His principal research interests are in the relationship between education policy, especially concerning structural reform, and the identities and practices of those leading schools. His most recent publications are: 'Mapping school types in England' in the *Oxford Review of Education*; and 'Corporatised leadership in English schools' in the *Journal of Educational Administration and History*. He is the recipient of the American Educational Research Association Division A 2016 Outstanding Dissertation Award for his doctoral thesis.

James R. Duggan is Research Fellow in the Faculty of Education at Manchester Metropolitan University, UK. His research interests are in public sector transformation with a particular focus on leadership and collaboration.

Tanya Fitzgerald is Professor of History of Education and Head of School, Humanities and Social Sciences, at La Trobe University, Australia. Her primary field of research is the history of women's higher education, higher education policy and leadership. She serves on a number of international editorial boards and is one of the series editors of *Perspectives on Leadership in Higher Education* (Bloomsbury). She has been the Chief Editor of *History of Education Review* (2002–12) and co-editor of the *Journal of Educational Administration and History* (with Helen M. Gunter, 2007–17). She is the elected President of the Australian and New Zealand History of Education Society (2015–17).

Nurdiana Gaus is Doctor of Higher Education Policy and Management in the School of Social Welfare (STIKS), Makassar, Indonesia. Her main research interests are in higher education policy with a specific focus on neoliberalism and professional identity. Her most recent publication is: 'Performance indicators in Indonesian university: the perception of academics' (*Higher Education Quarterly Journal*, 2016).

Helen M. Gunter is Professor of Educational Policy and Sarah Fielden Professor of Education in the Manchester Institute of Education, University of Manchester, UK, and is a Fellow of the Academy of Social Sciences. She co-edits the *Journal of Educational Administration and History*. Her work focuses on the politics of education policy and knowledge production in the field of school leadership. Her most recent books are: *Leadership and the reform of education* (Policy Press, 2012); *Educational leadership and Hannah Arendt* (Routledge, 2014); and *An intellectual history of school leadership practice and research* (Bloomsbury Press, 2016).

David Hall is Professor of Education Policy and Founding Head of the Manchester Institute of Education, University of Manchester, UK. His research has focused on the contemporary working lives of education professionals, with a particular interest in the development of professional identities during periods of rapid reform. His work has been funded by organisations including the Joseph Rowntree Foundation and the Economic and Social Research Council.

Rob Higham is Senior Lecturer in the Department of Learning and Leadership at the UCL Institute of Education, London, UK. His main research interests are in education policy, quasi-markets, school networks and educational leadership, about which he has published widely. He is currently co-leading the Nuffield Foundation funded project *Understanding the 'self-improving' school-led system: An analysis of hierarchy, markets and networks in England*.

Leonel Lim is Assistant Professor of Curriculum, Teaching and Learning at the National Institute of Education, Singapore. His research focuses on curriculum theory and the politics of education, with specific interests in the relations between ideology and curriculum, state power, elite schooling and the sociology of curriculum. In 2014, he was the recipient of the American Educational Research Association's Outstanding Dissertation Award in the field of curriculum studies. He is the author of *Knowledge, control and critical thinking in Singapore* (Routledge, 2015) and the co-editor (with Michael W. Apple) of *The strong state and curriculum reform* (Routledge, 2016). He currently serves as Associate Editor for *Critical Studies in Education* and *Pedagogies: An International Journal*.

Ruth McGinity is Lecturer in Educational Leadership and Policy in the Manchester Institute of Education, University of Manchester, UK. Her main research interests focus on critical educational policy studies. She uses socially critical theories to illuminate power relations and the associated inequities that emerge as a result of neo-conservative and neoliberal social and educational policy agendas. Her most recent publication is: 'Conceptualizing teacher professional identity in neoliberal times: resistance, compliance and reform', *Education Policy Analysis Archives* (2015, with David Hall).

Romuald Normand is Fulbright Fellow and Professor of Sociology in the Faculty of Social Sciences, Research Unit SAGE: Societies, Actors and Government of Europe, at the University of Strasbourg, France. He is convenor of the network 'Sociologies of European Education' in the European Association of Educational Research, and a member of the editorial board of the *British Journal of Sociology of Education*. His research interests are on European policies/politics in education, new public management, and higher education. He has co-edited, with Martin Lawn, *Shaping of European education* (Routledge, 2014).

Howard Prosser is Lecturer in the Faculty of Education, Monash University, Australia. His research interests include sociology of education, social and political theory, and the history of ideas. He co-edited *In the realm of the senses: Social aesthetics and the sensory dynamics of privilege* (Springer, 2015).

Andrew L. LaFave is a PhD candidate in Urban Education Policy in the Rossier School of Education at the University of Southern California, US. His research explores the ways that private markets interact with public education and how the contracts that govern these interactions function. His subsidiary interests include the economics of education, organisational management and innovations in qualitative methodology.

Kenneth J. Saltman is Professor in the Educational Leadership and Policy Studies PhD Programme at the University of Massachusetts Dartmouth, US. A number of concerns appear throughout his work, including the threats posed to democratic life and culture posed by the corporatisation and militarisation of schools and society, the possibilities and promises of critical pedagogy and theory, and the necessity of taking seriously the educative force of culture for educational policy and associated living. His newest book is *Scripted bodies: Corporate power, smart technologies, and the undoing of public education* (Routledge, 2016). He is the author most recently of *The politics of education: A critical introduction* (Routledge, 2014); *Toward a new common school movement*, co-authored with Noah DeLissovoy and Alexander Means (Routledge, 2014); and *Neoliberalism, education, terrorism: Contemporary dialogues*, co-authored with Jeffrey Di Leo, Henry Giroux and Sophia McClennen (Routledge, 2014).

Eleni Schirmer is a PhD candidate in Educational Policy Studies and Curriculum and Instruction, at University of Wisconsin-Madison, US. Her research interests are the political economy of education and social movements therein. She is preparing a dissertation about intersections between teachers' unions and racial justice movements. Former co-president of the Teaching Assistants' Association, the nation's oldest graduate employee union, her writing has appeared in *Jacobin, The Progressive, Labor Notes* and *Education Review.*

Kristin Sinclair is a doctoral candidate at the University of Maryland, College Park, US. Her research critically examines how teachers, schools and education reflect, contribute to, and/or challenge social inequalities related to race, class and gender, with a particular eye towards community and place-based education. Her scholarly work includes a forthcoming article in the *Peabody Journal of Education* on the impact of de-unionization on teachers' classroom practices and work lives in post-Act 10 Wisconsin.

Jahni M.A. Smith is a PhD candidate studying Urban Education Policy in the Rossier School at the University of Southern California, US. She is an international scholar with interests in K-12 education policy, economics of education, and understanding market-based reforms in education with specific attention to equity and equality.

John Smyth is Visiting Professor of Education and Social Justice, University of Huddersfield, UK. He was Research Professor of Education, Federation University Australia, and is Professor Emeritus of Flinders University, and of Federation University Australia. He is a former Senior Fulbright Research Scholar, the recipient of several awards from the American Educational Research Association, and a Fellow of the Academy for Social Science in Australia. His most recent book is *Critical educational research: A conversation with the research of John Smyth* (with Down, McInerney and Hattam; Peter Lang, 2014). His research interests include policy sociology, policy ethnography, social justice and sociology of education.

Katy Swalwell is Assistant Professor in the School of Education at Iowa State University, US. Her research focuses on how social justice education is enacted in the social studies curriculum and elite educational settings. One of her most recent publications is 'Mind the civic empowerment gap: Economically elite students and critical civic education' in *Curriculum Inquiry* (2015). She also authored the award-winning book *Educating activist allies: Social justice pedagogy with the suburban and urban elite* (Routledge, 2013).

Andrew Wilkins is Reader in Education Governance at the University of East London, UK. His research focuses on theories and practices of statecraft, statehood and state power in the context of studies of educational governance. He is a member of the Economic and Social Research Council Peer Review College, Fellow of the Royal Society for the encouragement of Arts, Manufactures and Commerce (RSA), Fellow of the Higher Education Academy, co-convenor of the BERA SIG Social Theory and Education, and Associate of the Robert Owen Centre for Educational Change, University of Glasgow, UK. His most recent publication is *Modernising school governance: Corporate planning and expert handling in state education* (Routledge, 2016).

INTRODUCTION

Scoping corporate elites and public education

Helen M. Gunter, Michael W. Apple and David Hall

Introduction

Public service education has been hard won but is not yet fully achieved in many countries around the world – and where it is seemingly in place, it is not secure and is being actively privatised. In this book we not only report research about how and why this is happening, but we also specifically focus on the contribution of corporate elites to the ideas, conditions and materiality of the reform of public education. Such corporate elites do not usually have a personal or family stake in schools for the masses, because their purchasing power is greater than those they are acting as benefactors for. Indeed, as Dorling (2014b) reports, 'in the US, the wealthiest 1 per cent of the population now takes 20 per cent of all income before tax. In the UK, that figure stands at around 15 per cent' (pp 36-8). Such corporate elites are not only very wealthy, but are globally mobile and networked, and can locate across national boundaries in ways that disconnect their lives from the realities of those who support, access and rely on public services.

Elites studies has not been a strong feature of social sciences research (see Savage and Williams, 2008a), but a range of recent texts suggest that there is a serious problem with inequality and the power structures and processes that construct and sustain it (Wilkinson and Picket, 2009; Judt, 2010; Stiglitz, 2013; Dorling 2014a; Jones, 2014). Such concerns are evident within public education, where the causal relationship between poverty and educational underachievement in affluent countries is regarded as an endemic problem located in commodification and trade (Raffo et al, 2010).

Elites studies in educational policy research is also limited. Work has taken place on the economising of education policy (Ball, 2007, 2012a; Burch, 2009; Lundhal, 2011; Norris, 2011), philanthropy (Ball, 2008; Scott, 2009; Saltman, 2010), the networking role of elites (Ball and

Junemann, 2012; Gunter, 2012; Spring, 2012; Au and Ferrare, 2015), and the type and impact of elites education (Kynaston, 2014; Kenway and Koh, 2015; van Zanten et al, 2015; Ye and Nylander, 2015). Elites studies is a site where the complexities of what is unfolding is being identified as being in need of a range of in-depth studies (Buckley and Burch, 2011). Additionally, investigative journalists are making public the destructive impact of corporate structures and practices on public education (for example Beckett, 2007), and parents and community activists are challenging consumerism by raising questions about access and the quality of schooling for their children and the community (for example Benn, 2012). There are now a series of accounts illuminating the 'hoaxes' (Ravitch, 2014), 'big lies' (Gorski and Zenkov, 2014) and 'myths' (Benn and Downs, 2016) that have been constructed to justify reform, with counter-narratives that are showing the quality of public education (Lubienski and Lubienski, 2014).

The research reported in this book adds to this growing body of work, by recognising emerging forms of *corporatised governance*. We do this by providing a series of global-local essays that present data and analysis about how and why stratified and influential corporate elites are impacting on the local provision of education services in ways that serve capital accumulation. We begin by examining the reforms made to public education, before going on to outline who we mean by corporate elites and how and why governance within and for public education is being corporatised. We then introduce the particular research reported by our co-authors, particularly by outlining the contribution that these projects are making to charting, understanding and explaining the changes being made to the idea, reality and sustainability of public service education.

Reforming public education

The idea and reality of public education, based on the right to local services that are free at the point of access and delivery, is undergoing major changes globally and nationally (Apple, 2006a; Ball, 2007, 2012a; Rizvi and Lingard, 2010). Approaching the complexity of such change is best undertaken through identifying two interrelated interventions designed to economise and corporatise schools and higher education *within* and *outside* the public system:

- *Within* the public system through turning schools and higher education into businesses: income streams are based on competition to attract students, crowd sourcing for learning resources and bidding for projects. Reforms can be best understood through site-based management, where for example schools were given their own budgets and the right to hire and fire staff, such as *Tomorrow's Schools* in New Zealand from 1989 where middle tier local democracy was removed (Minister of Education 1988), and *Local Management of Schools* in England from 1988 where Coopers and Lybrand (1988) recommended delegation from the local authority and imagined the school as a site of "good management" based on performance objectives (p 7).

- *Outside* of the public system through enabling entry and exit by providers: families can exit through home schooling, and/or can access new types of schools, colleges and universities that enter into the market place. For example, the state can fund education through formulas, loans, scholarships and vouchers, and may allow for-profit education. Free Schools for profit were set up in Sweden from 1992; in the US Charter Schools were set up from 1991; and in England Academy Schools from 2000 and Free Schools from 2010 have been established. (Gunter, 2011)

This restructuring has not only enabled a shift in ownership, but has generated major changes to the purposes of education and schools/universities, along with the curriculum and pedagogy, and the composition and identity of the education profession. Professional practice has been recultured around the technology of organisational effectiveness combined with meeting consumer needs, where high-stakes outcome measures (testing in schools, retention and graduation numbers in higher education) have focused attention on data collection, management and analysis, and this is linked to performance audits that generate rewards or contract termination. Integral to this is the emphasis on controlling and building the business through leadership, where the ideas from the corporate world – such as Collins' (2001; undated) prescription about getting the right people on and off 'the bus' – have come to dominate priorities (Gray and Streshly, 2008; Courtney and Gunter, 2015). The public service, trained and accredited teacher and research professionals are being performance managed into corporate thinking, language and practices, and are being replaced by corporate-ready personnel who are organisationally efficient and effective through corporate experiences.

Public education is becoming *commodified* as a product to be bought and sold; *demanded*, where parents, children and young adults are enabled to understand that they need to choose one product rather than another; *supplied*, where the workforce meets demand

and so generates profit; and *marketised*, where commercial exchange relationships are extended to previously publicly owned services. This can be illuminated by changes to and within public education in a range of countries, where Ball (2007) identifies an 'Education Services Industry' (p 10). For example, Burch (2009) examines the role of educational management organisations (EMOs) in the US, which provide services that previously local public administration did: 'these firms typically assume full responsibility for all aspects of school operations, including administration, teacher training, building maintenance, food service, and clerical support' (p 4). The survival of such schools in the marketplace is based on testing, where companies such as Pearson are actively involved in the structuring of teaching and in outcomes (Junemann and Ball, 2015). Gutiérrez (2014) provides evidence about how the focus on testing means that private consultants are bought in to give advice on how to improve test results, by focusing on 'bubble kids' or those on pass-fail borderline (p 17) (see also Gunter and Mills, 2017). The role of ICT is integral to such changes; Spring (2012) provides evidence of how online learning in virtual classrooms enables hardware and software sales.

Interestingly, research into the reforms in the US show that the changes do not always deliver in ways expected and they destroy what is regarded as precious (Ravitch, 2010). Nevertheless, the layering and accumulation of change, and the influence of particular policy actors, has enabled two main outcomes: first, the normalisation of education as a business within and outside public administration:

> Mandatory comparative testing is now so institutionalized that it will be very difficult to remove. The need to be competitive, to be seen as business-like, to employ the strategies of business in restructuring public institutions such as schools, and thus to be seen as lean and efficient and to incorporate managerial ideologies and technical resources to support all of this – all these things seem to have been cemented in place. (Apple, 2009, pxi)

And second, the purposes of education have changed from a shared experience to a templated audit with data-determined judgements about pass and fail:

> the digital mind of ICT managers tends to see school as institutions composed of data while not seeing the holistic context of students' lives such as their families,

neighborhoods, and income levels. If data shows a decline in test scores, the data manager sees it as a school and individual student problem and might not blame the social world of the student. (Spring, 2012, p 25)

This is illuminative of a major shift in the role of the state, towards what the neoliberal analyst Bobbitt (2002) identifies as the market state, where the family is the site of choice for and about education as a private good (see Tooley, 2000). For example, the form of education couture promised by the market impacts on the practice of identity:

> Personalisation is a much deeper type of marketisation, one which goes beyond mere 'choice' of structures, and instead purports to bring user and provider together into a continuing and personalised 'co-producer' relationship. And this co-production – this 'prosumption' – may result in a re-production in the sense that new configurations and flexibilities among professionals become necessary to meet the personalised needs of the user. (Hartley, 2012, p 107, emphasis in original)

There is a form of privatisation that is not only about the reworking of the school and university as an organisation, institution and within a system, but is also a form of depoliticisation, where issues that used to be public are now increasingly private, and so only matter when the individual and the family bring them into the consumer exchange relationship with producers (see Courtney and Gunter, 2017).

The notion of the public is being reworked from a shared concern around equitable access and provision towards the aggregation of consumer choices. This shift is seen as beneficial by those who support deregulation to enable families to have new freedoms, but is seen as problematic for families who have needs that may not be commercially viable (for example special needs, languages) and where pro-marketeers outline how such needs should be met by charity (see Tooley, 2000). Neoliberals are doing a good deal of work around this matter, not least in creating the knowledge claims to support how the market does – and will – work regarding fully marketised services. For example, while reforms are taking place to the voucher system in Chile (Carrasco et al, 2015) and the evidence suggests that advocates should remain cautious about the causal link between vouchers and student outcomes (Barrow and Rouse, 2008), this does not prevent the theoretical and policy case to be made. Croft et al (2013) argue for more choice and competition within the state system, where vouchers can be spent at state and private schools. Indeed, the question asked by Barrow and Rouse (2008) is: if rich can opt out, then why can't the poor? Considerable attention is being given to how lower-income families can afford to pay for private education (Tooley, 2000; Banchero, 2012).

The unfolding and often contraditory reform process within public service education in affluent countries is linked to corporate elites either directly through their funding, ideas and personal practices, or indirectly through how others act to enable such interests. And yet it is also important to recognise that not everything can be causally linked, or even given recognition. We now move on to this matter.

Corporate elites

Spring (2012) following Rothkopf (2008) argues that there is an identifiable but fluid 'superclass' of about 6,000 people, 'which includes all the world's billionaires, heads of major global corporations and financial companies, political and military leaders of globally influential countries, and major religious leaders' (p 5). Corporate reforms are therefore not only direct through ownership of wealth accumulation technologies but also through webs of association and integration, whether this is through the funding of politics, the purchasing of corporate products, and/or accessing investment portfolios by established institutions. Such corporate elites are anchored within nation states (as well as tax havens), but there is a need to consider separation and disconnection from the ordinary: internationalisation through travel and multiple homes; globalisation through exchange relationships across national boundaries; and cosmopolitanism through how attitudes, orientations and possibilities are understood and embodied (Windle and Nogueira, 2015). Such dispositions are structured and developed through practice, but importantly through access to educational products that separate them and their children physically in regard to going to school and/or accessing educational products, and separating them in terms of their location and entitlements within capital accummulation (Spring, 2012; van Zanten, 2015; Kenway and Fahey, 2015).

Hence corporate elites tend to be outside public service education, but are directly within it in a range of ways. For example, Spring (2012) provides an account of the public school system in New York, where he maps how the interrelationship between Bloomberg,[1] Klein[2] and Murdoch[3] is illuminative of how billionaire ICT and media empires define and control the purposes and means of education as data in order to install their products. The focus on testing and the high stakes nature of it – where performance is linked to aspirations and security – has a long history (see, for example, Au, 2009). But focusing on testing and data in particular enables us to see how the current corporatising of education is visible in other ways. For example, Koyama (2010) talks about Supplemental Educational Services (SES) that are sourced to provide after-school tutoring for children in schools that are identified as failing under No Child Left Behind (NCLB): 'SES legitimizes tutoring by promoting the packaging, marketing, and selling of tutoring programs as commodities (complete with curricula and practices) that are then inserted into a dynamic network of relations, processes, and exchanges that traverse public organizations and private agencies' (p 6). The anxieties and fears around public education – getting the right test results, getting into the right school – that are generated by the choice agenda is handled through corporate solutions.

The autonomous independent school is promoted as being causally linked to the standards of public education. For example, Macrine (2003) outlines how Edison Schools was awarded a contract to run schools in Philadelphia, with funds for evaluation and the provision of schools. Burch (2009) provides some background on Edison Schools:

> Edison Schools, the brainchild of entrepreneur Chris Whittle, is perhaps the best known of the EMOs. Whittle had built a media empire around businesses such as television marketing broadcast in the waiting rooms of doctors' offices. Through Channel One, Whittle entered the public school market. Channel One provides schools with free television equipment and in return guarantees advertisers a captive audience of students. Whittle's next project, EMOs, gained traction, in part because it coincided with a push for public school vouchers by Republicans, under the administration of George H.W. Bush. Chris Whittle was part of what one political insider called the education privatization brain trust. This group included Lamar Alexander, former Governor of Tennessee and Secretary of Education under President Bush, David Kearns, the Chief Executive Officer of IBM, and William Sanders, Professor at the University of Tennessee among others. (pp 4-5)

Accounts of how people in different organisational locations are networked through shared ideologies and dispositions regarding the privatisation of public service education has been mapped by Ball (2007,

2012a; Ball and Junemann, 2012), with examples of companies and individuals who carry, communicate and commercialise knowledge about and for the privatisation of education, and how this integrates through public institutions at national, state and city government levels.

The creation of schools outside democratic processes is based on the promotion of school principals as leaders who do leading and leadership. This tends to be more corporate than educational, and is based on an espoused causal link between 'school leadership' and 'improvement' and 'effectiveness'. Saltman (2010) examines 'venture philanthropy' through identifying activist givers – such as the Bill and Melinda Gates Foundation, the Broad Foundation, and the Walton Family – and the impact this has had on reform of teacher education, schools and higher education (p 1). Saltman (2010) focuses on the Eli and Edythe Broad Education Foundation, with a remit for recruiting 'noneducator corporate, military, and nonprofit leaders' (p 79). Having made his fortune in real estate and finance, Broad is investing his retirement into public school leadership, particularly with an aim 'to shift administrator preparation away from universities and state certification to the control of outside organisations that embrace corporate and military styles of management' (p 80).

What is significant about such forms of philanthropy, in terms of finance, role models, time and intellectual work, is that while the proportion of giving in relation to the whole cost of public education is small, the impact is profound in at least two main ways:

- the way in which the entrepreneur's success is key to the curriculum, where those who work as educators and students learn about how 'inequality is not about money, but an idea of wealth-engineered eugenics ... (where) ... in their minds, they are not only richer than the rest of us, but also "better"' (Peretti, 2015, unpaged);
- the way in which the entrepreneur uses this separate (but connected) status to spread personalised ideas, thinking and practices about what matters to them, and where the advice to would-be philanthropists is that: 'you need to know what you are personnally passionate about' (Shah, 2015, p 30).

Giving as a gift, rather than paying public taxation, is a form of 'social investment' where the return is through the economising of education: 'public schooling is principally a matter of producing workers and consumers for the economy and for global economic competition' (Saltman, 2010, p 3). When giving is linked to advocacy, then the economic purposes of education are both normalised and promoted as a reform imperative, where the use of research evidence and the legitimacy of selected professors can enable reforms (see Gunter, 2012).

For example, Lubienski and Lubienski (2014) not only report on their data that show how public education delivers at a higher standard than charter and private schools, but they also demonstrate how the evidence used to denigrate public education was produced through philanthropic funding. They identify the Walton Family Foundation (of Wal-Mart) as being integral to getting reforms legitimised and enacted: 'not only do they fund pilot programs and individual researchers, but they also underwrite efforts to create institutional alternatives to advance their agenda' (p 135). The actions taken by corporations such as Wal-Mart are not a new phenomenon – and indeed have a long history (see, for example, Apple, 2013) – but they have intensified and have entered even more robustly into influencing the academic world as well. Lubienski and Lubienski (2014) help us to understand this, by also examining how many academics position themselves, where: 'having quite often declined or failed to pass their promarket research findings through established, peer-reviewed academic journals, [they] instead create alternative venues for publishing and promoting their work – a strategy not unlike what is employed by corporate-funded deniers of climate change' (p 136).

This brief overview of networked connections and power relationships demonstrates the complexities involved in the identification and charting of what is going on and unfolding in public service education. Explanations of this require a shift from elites studies – that focus directly on formal roles in a place – to an appreciation of activities within spaces, and how voice operates within (and external to) the bureaucracy of public service decision-making. In other words, the claim by Marx and Engels (1888) that 'the executive of the modern State is but a committee for managing the common affairs of the whole bourgeoise' (p 9), needs to be challenged in a range of ways.

Initially, we would say this because the fusion of stable organisational arrangements that are occupied by collective private interests has been questioned through the emerging heterogeneity of corporate elites. In addition, we would also want to note how the bourgeoisie is in an increasingly contradictory location regarding the relationship between the nation state and global mobility, particularly in regard to business and occupational locations, tax liabilities and school choice for their own families (Ball and Nikita, 2014). What we are saying here is that while research shows that those who dominate the economy also tend to dominate politics, culture, the military and faith, the 1% – as Dorling (2014a) identifies – are themselves differentiated, and this needs to be taken in to account. For example, while philanthropic people and families can be identified, they do not do corporate work on their own, so those with whom they associate nationally and globally also need to be engaged with.

Historically located analyses (for example Michels, 1958; Pareto, 1935; Mills, 1956; Mosca, 1939) and contemporary analyses (for example Jones, 2014) show as shared concern with how what is actually a small community are interconnected and seek to protect and enhance their interests. Research shows how elite schools are integral to this (van Zanten and Maxwell, 2015) and how, in a global marketplace, elite schools have a cultural identity product which is saleable to both national and international customers (Dorling, 2014b; Brooks and Waters, 2015). The elite school is a site for the structuring of dispositions as 'assured optimism' that is reproduced through social practices at school: 'this habitus is about living the future in the present and being confidently assured about navigating futures, now stretched to take in global labour markets' (Forbes and Lingard, 2015, p 134).

The retention of this position-taking at a time of social democracy is a key question – particularly how and why elites 'have managed to continue successfully hoarding educational opportunities despite increasing competition from other groups' (van Zanten, 2015, p 5). This tends to be explained through the handling of major ruptures and threats, or by giving concessions such as the funding of public service education (Miliband, 1973), but mainly it is through 'gifting' and being seen as giving something back (Saltman, 2010; Kenway and Fahey, 2015) as a means of disguising their prime focus 'to manage democracy, to make sure it does not threaten their own interests' (Jones, 2014, p 4). So elites are partly defensive through insulation from the world as it unfolds, such as in the structuring of gender relations through schooling (Forbes and Lingard, 2015; Goh, 2015), but mainly on the offensive particularly through how their world may be one that is out of reach for the majority but can be admired and aspired to through temptation, imagination and mimicry (Gunter, 2015).

The education system is thus integral to reality of segregation veiled by the possibility of at least co-option, where the fabrication of failed public education means that 'other people's children can be greatly denigrated', mainly by being denied a full and rounded education (Dorling, 2014a, p 26). Indeed, the parents of other people's children can be, in Ravitch's (2014) words, 'hoaxed' into a simulated private education – through vouchers, lotteries, scholarships (see Anderson and Donchik, 2016) and the benefaction of philanthropy and charity – as being the best for their children. When this fails, the state can provide residual services. However, it is more complex than this, because (as Savage and Williams (2008a) and Maxwell (2015) have shown) there has been a shift in how power is understood and examined within elite studies: from 'sovereign' power of entitlement, position and normality of tradition (family, inheritence, political leadership) towards understandings that are more about 'capillary and distributed power' (Savage and Williams, 2008b, p 12). Corporate elites are therefore not only developing and protecting the business through family, marriage and schools, but have moved towards breaking up, buying up, selling on, and benefiting from windfalls, so we need to focus on a 'distributional coalition which forms and reforms around the money-making deals and innovations in financial markets that change with each conjuncture' (Savage and Williams, 2008b, p 13).

Such analysis not only gives recognition to the stabilising force of those who own and/or control place-based structures, but also to those who create spatially located structures that form and reform around tasks and capital accumulation. Research shows that corporate elites do this through the construction and deployment of the working rich – those who earn large salaries, contractual fees and/or bonuses – and how this means they are in the 1% but are not at the top of the 1% (Dorling, 2014a). In the conditions in which 'everything is for sale' (Savage and Williams, 2008b, p 16), there are managers within organisations, and intermediaries who work at the edges and in between organisations. This needs to be linked to the important role played by particular factions of the professional and managerial new middle class, whose own positioning, mobility and ideological formation create the technologies and conditions for the growth of commitments to audit cultures and the constant need to provide evidence that one is acting 'correctly' (see Bernstein, 1977; Apple, 2006a; see also the relation between 'new managerialism', audit cultures and gendered specificities of paid and unpaid labour in Lynch et al, 2012).

Connell (2010) takes up this point, by focusing on the importance of managers, and with a need to shift away from the 'metropole' of Europe and North America and to relocate thinking about ideas and actions that give recognition to the south (Connell, 2007). Therefore there is a need to understand not only how different forms of capitalism work, but also how privatisation does not have to be done through major national policy changes (for example by selling off schools), but is done through how managers think and do their jobs (for example by bidding for projects). ICT, for example, is important, because 'the computer systems of the global firm become the intellectual environment for any individual manager' (Connell, 2007, p 783), where software owns their work, links their work to others, and enables surveillance and ongoing calculation. For such managers: 'globalisation … is seen as a pervasive and unstoppable process but not a catastophe. It is a field of opportunities for smart, modern players' (Connell, 2010, p 785). There are consequences to this, because 'the possibility of *reflective* intellectual work is constantly undermined by the conditions of managerial labor' (Connell, 2010, p 789, emphasis in original). Therefore, a school principal as a manager may not consider the way in which advantage and disadvantage operates when leading the conversion of a successful high school into an academy. But such a manager may present the self as intellectual through how fast and relevant thinking is done and admired, where speedy work with instant private gratification through deal clinching is core to understanding the payback on doing privatisation.

Paying more attention to the relatively autonomous positions of, and the work done by, the new middle classes is crucial, but it should not be used as an excuse to neglect the prime focus of this volume – corporate elites and dominant economic actors. Elites think and live globally: 'social class becomes more dynamic and mutable – not just aligned with cultural or geographical context, but having a sort of dynamic ebb and flow quality where some markers count in some ways at one time, and in different ways at a different time' (Greenhalgh-Spencer et al, 2015, p 161). Consequently, Savage and Williams (2008b) have identified the importance of 'intermediaries' who do not manage '"men and things" within corporate hierarchies', but who are focused on 'the switching or servicing of the flows of money through market trading and corporate deals' (p 9), and who are 'usually incentivized on the basis of sharing fees or profits' (Savage and Williams, 2008b, p 9). What this means is that 'those who control money are establishing themselves as central social and political agents, who can also embed themselves in wider circuits of power' (Savage and Williams, 2008b, p 9). They therefore locate in practice, which is 'conjunctural, contradictory and non-totalising' (Savage and Williams, 2008b, p 9). So economic power is more than the control of taxation through having people you are related to or went to school with in state bureaucracy; it is a shift to financialisation.

There are serious consequences of the disconnection of such elites from the everydayness of those who cannot exit: 'an overwhelming sense that our globalised elites have broken free from national loyalties, leaving the middle classes struggling to make ends meet in nation states they no longer control' (Leonard, 2014, p 27). Those within the nation state have indicators of how this works through investigative journalism, where banks such as HSBC are reported as having services that enable the concealment of undeclared wealth at a time of austerity (Garside et al, 2015). Sometimes this is more than a glimpse, where the financial crash of 2007–08 has affected public debate:

> with millions of US homeowners facing foreclosure, stock markets plummeting and major British insitutions such as Northern Rock and RBS teetering on the edge, many felt that a total collapse of our economic system was coming. It didn't but the hangover, which has been with us now for seven or eight years, has completely dominated politics, both here and around the western world. (Marr, 2015, p 28)

So far, we have directed our attention to larger politics and their accompanying ideological and educational transformation. But there are new directions that corporate elites are taking. Historically they have focused largely on international, national and regional politics and policies. But in the United States – and not only there – dominant groups have understood something that the great Italian political theorist and activist Antonio Gramsci noted. He reminded us that we are facing a 'war of position' not a 'war of manoeuvre' (Gramsci, 1971). That is, tactically *everything counts* – not only larger-scale but also small-scale struggles, cultural as well as economic struggles, local politics and actions, all of these are crucial.

Let us give one example from the United States. As Chapter 3 in this book documents, as of January 2015, the conservative billionaire Koch brothers planned to spend close to $900 million on the presidential elections. Although most of this money will benefit Republican candidates, the amount that these two individuals plan to contribute will be more than either the Republican or Democratic parties (Confessore, 2016). In some instances, these investments go to private organisations, such as Americans for Prosperity, a conservative political advocacy group. In other instances, they have invested in positions within public institutions, such as the University of Kansas's Center for Applied Economics, with the Koch brothers' using their extreme wealth to finance a public research centre that espouses their particular vision of economic conservatism (Pilkington, 2014). Yet the Koch brothers, Americans for Prosperity, and the very influential American Legislative Exchange Council, supported by the Koch brothers, do not merely invest in politically prestigious or powerful spaces at the national or state level; they are increasingly interested in small-scale political issues, like local school board races, in small cities and towns like Kenosha, Wisconsin. Why do these groups care about small-town school politics?

Understanding why multi-billionaire individuals and the political organisations they fund are interested in small-scale micropolitics helps us to decipher the larger ideological processes at stake in building corporate influence. In order to fully appreciate the growing political influence of major corporate actors, we must develop a forensic perspective on *where* these investments occur, looking closely at national political spheres, at public institutions like universities and at small-scale, municipal elections. We must also develop a nuanced understanding of *how* these powers build their influence (see, for example, Reckhow and Snyder, 2014). While the sheer volume of their economic capital gives them considerable power to determine political outcomes and processes, these powers form at least in partial response to particular situations, and require an explanation beyond their very evident economic determinism – that more money necessarily buys more political power. It also requires studying how these groups actively build new ideological networks, which not only justify their influence but also advance it (for example Ball, 2009a). Therefore, critical investigations of conservative movements must take into account how politically conservative forces assemble and gather power at the local level, and how they build coalitions and develop ideological strongholds. Such studies offer important resources for those who want to better grasp the current political climate surrounding public education (see, for example, Schirmer and Apple, 2016).

The contribution of this book

The research reported in this collection is concerned with locating the reform of education within the interplay between the state, public policy and the corporate world. We frame our contribution through a conceptualisation of *corporatised governance*, where we give particular attention to illuminating cases of interventions into the structures, cultures and practices *within* and *outside* public schools and higher education.

Based on claims for a vital reform imperative, discourses and reform packages are concerned not only to redesign organisations, work and identities but also to shift ownership from public to private, supported by the idea that educational purposes serve private interests in ways that are claimed to benefit all. Following Robertson and Dale's (2013, p 431) governance framework, we intend giving attention to corporate elites who:

- locate with 'distinct forms of education activity', whereby corporate elites are actively involved in funding, provision, ownership and the regulation of education;
- work independently with and alongside 'particular kinds of entities or agents with different interests' within the state, as well as for-profit and not-for-profit organisations;
- operate within 'different platforms or scales of rule' at local, regional, national and supranational levels.

Such forms of corporatised governance are evident in three main forms of entry into, within, against and outside public service education:

- The first is through influence, where corporate elite role models, lifestyles, aspirations and success indicators are combined with common sense, enabling discourses about ideas, identities, opportunities and practices.
- The second is through how corporatised influence is codified into meaningful, achievable and necessary changes within public service education, through the reworking of cultures and structures with new freedoms of risk, investment, competition and winning.
- The third is through how corporatised influence is deployed to replace public service education with private service products in the form of home schooling/tutoring, fees for schools/universities, with possible subsidies, gifts and/or co-payments for parents to choose, demand, enter and exit.

Our argument is that what we are witnessing is increased dominance by dynamic corporate elites in exchange relationships in ways that are economising civil society. Revealing what is taking place in regard to the macro ideological and political activities within and external to government systems, and what it means for those located in the complexities of change at a micro level of families, schools and universities is at the core of our task.

The essays in this volume have been commissioned to give insights into what is unfolding in a range of sites primarily in England and the US, but also with cases from Argentina, Indonesia and Singapore, and are based on primary research combined with conceptual analysis. We present the chapters in two interconnected sections: Part 1 has eight accounts on products and markets (Burch et al; Saltman); politics and the locality (Schirmer and Apple); identities and knowledge production (Gaus and Hall; Fitzgerald); and the impact of elite education (Lim; Prosser; Sinclair and Swalwell). Part 2 has seven accounts, with six focused on England: new forms of training (Duggan); schools (Higham; McGinity); school governance (Wilkins); and corporate work (Courtney; Gunter). Our final chapter examines the impact on learners in the school system (Smyth).

Part 1 is concerned with insights and evidence about corporatised governance by providing data and analysis that uses a macro or system perspective from the *outside in*; Part 2 is concerned with provision, where our authors take the micro as the starting point for analysis, whereby changes *inside out* enable analysis that begins *within* the realities of children, families and professionals. We do not present a binary of 'out' or 'in', as both interplay through all of the accounts. We are concerned to enable our authors to focus strategically and to drill down to the local – to examine the local and to interconnect with the global. Threads running through all the accounts are concerned with what is happening, where it is happening, how and why, and what outcomes and trends are emerging. Taken together, these analyses provide a richly detailed critical understanding of truly radical shifts in what education is for, who benefits from it, and what needs to be interrupted if we are to have an education that is more critically democratic.

Notes

[1] Spring (2012) identifies Michael Bloomberg as a billionaire ICT 'mogel' who was elected as Mayor of New York in 2001 (p 5).

[2] Spring (2012) identifies Joel Klein as 'school Chancellor' for New York. Klein was appointed by Bloomberg, and is a lawyer (p 5).

[3] Spring (2012) identifies Rupert Murdoch as the 'founder and head of News Corporation', who hired Klein as 'senior advisor' on matters that included '"business strategies for the emerging educational marketplace' (pp 6-7).

Part 1
Corporatised governance: system perspectives

ONE

Corporate elites and the student identity market

Patricia Burch, Andrew L. LaFave and Jahni M.A. Smith

Introduction

Some of the major ways by which private corporations attempt to exert their influence on government – including the funding of political activities, congressional lobbies and mass information campaigns – have, in recent years, manifested themselves in new ways. This chapter focuses on the relationships between corporate elites in the United States and two distinct aspects of that emerging landscape: a large not-for-profit firm called inBloom that stored and analysed student data; and a smaller not-for-profit firm called Geo Listening that monitors students' public social media profiles for negative behavioural indicators. We argue that the fortunes of these organisations rose (in the case of Geo Listening) and fell (in the case of inBloom) based largely on the ability of elite managers to manage the political environment in which the firms operate. As political elites learn how to be more responsive to organisations like these, the student identity market is gradually evolving from a less-regulated environment to one which is becoming more tightly regulated. As with any political reform initiative that intends to rein in unregulated markets, the firms operating in this space – and the elites who manage them – are presented with a central tension of organisations operating in free markets: embrace forward-thinking dynamism to respond to changes in the market, or remain static and, by so doing, ultimately fail.

In an era of unprecedented technological growth and the globalisation of information and trade, new markets are emerging that do not conform to the lightly regulated status quo in public education. These emerging markets challenge the existing framework, by continuing to outstrip changes in the political process. The changes wrought by increased private involvement in American public education have caught many policy makers by surprise, but the evolution of educational provision should have been easily anticipated. Much of the new education privatisation in the United States and elsewhere has been driven by accountability reforms that envelope a strong need to understand the implications of accountability frameworks on students with lower socioeconomic status, underserved English language learners and other underrepresented groups.

It has become essential to look closely at the processes of public response and legislation creation in order to understand the current pace of change that propels new laws. In the absence of good theory, we must draw on specific cases to guide inquiry in this vital area for two key reasons. First, they provide polarising views on how size and responsiveness to the market have no impact on sustainability. In the case of inBloom, we find a company that grew with significant funding and backing, rose to public attention, and then subsequently failed. By contrast, Geo Listening is a much smaller company without major investors and backers that grew its market share by responding to public scrutiny with a contribution to the dialogue around the necessity of its service. Second, these cases show us that, in the context of globalisation and privatisation, the nature of the firm is changing and that a demand from the public for responsibility, relevance and corporate responsiveness is increasing.

Who are the elites?

Broadly speaking in the context of this chapter, corporate elites are the managers and executives of the private organisations – either for-profit or not-for-profit – which enter into contracts with public education organisations. Although there is often an overlap between members of the board of directors and executives in the 'C-suite' (Chief Executive Officer, Chief Financial Officer, Chief Purchasing Officer, Chief Technology Officer and so on), these groups are not often grouped together, but we consider them both to fall under the umbrella of 'elites'. For example, this includes high-ranking members of the business world (corporate America), namely the directors, executives and board members. These elites leverage a potent combination of political and economic capital during the policy-making process through lobbying. It also includes educational leaders at the executive level (superintendents of public school districts in large cities like the Chicago Public Schools, the New York City Department of Education, and the Clark County School District in Las Vegas), and the people on either side of the divide who negotiate and/or write contracts that bring corporations into the public education system. The literal corporate elites are essential, of course, but without their counterparts in the public sector, their influence is largely meaningless. As more and more large school districts adopt the language and practices of the private sector, the line between what it means to be a member of a corporate board of directors versus a member of a school board has become increasingly blurred.

The cases in this chapter single out two segments of corporate elite operating in the student identity market, and the conclusions we reach here are the result of empirical research conducted between the autumn of 2015 and the spring of 2016. These qualitative studies drew on data from interviews, primary and secondary documents, and analysis of accounts in various forms of the media. Even though this research was undertaken in the United States, it has implications for scholars working to understand the influence of corporate elites all over the world. The elites who managed inBloom represented a cross-section of private involvement in public education. While what one might consider 'traditional' corporate elites (people from the world of for-profit business and not-for-profit foundations) were represented on inBloom's board, there were also education experts and representatives from the education technology markets. Although inBloom was in a very important sense entrepreneurial, its outsized financial backing and the prominence of its contracts meant that inBloom was unlike many of its small-scale for-profit competitors. This difference made inBloom unique in the student identity market. Geo Listening is a form of social media monitoring to prevent antisocial behaviour on school campuses.

It is useful to examine more closely the activities of these corporate elites in public education for two compelling reasons. First, as elites manage more and more of the functions of schooling, the research community needs to ask whether or not these private organisations are keeping the best interests of students in mind. In effect, the question becomes or who will monitor the actions of persons in positions of power. On the surface, and certainly in most firms' public-facing image, the notion of protecting students from a variety of social ills is at the forefront of their respective business models. The two cases we present here are no different in this regard. The motivation behind the development of inBloom's data management products was the idea that by effectively aggregating and managing the achievement data that students produce, education agencies can create individually tailored instruction for every student in every school – a situation which could result in improved student outcomes across a range of dimensions. Likewise, Geo Listening's platform monitors the social media presence of students for signs of antisocial behaviour. Here, the focus is not on improving academic outcomes, but rather on improving the climate of schools, helping them to become safer places for students to learn. These goals are laudable, but we must ask whether or not these are the sole motivators for investing in the market, or if some other motivation exists.

Second, academic inquiry into elite involvement in education is predicated on the idea that multiple parties can be simultaneously (dis)advantaged by the creation and operation of these private firms. If the firms are for-profit, who are the shareholders, and why are they invested in education? If the firms are not-for-profit, who are the underwriters, and what does it mean for a not-for-profit firm with a traditional corporate organisational form to be involved in providing services to public schools? This concern goes hand in hand with the protection of student interests: whose interests are being served by these firms, and for what purpose? As entrepreneurs continue to innovate and create new markets where none has previously existed, what regulatory structures are in place to safeguard the public good? Our primary argument in this chapter is that while regulatory structures always lag behind private sector innovation, bringing more regulation into a market does not always lead to adverse conditions for players in that market. This argument begins to address the larger question of how regulatory structures keep pace with corporate innovation.

To understand how these new markets are allowed to exist, we must first step back through the historical and political precedents that led to the creation of a market driven by student data and information. America's No Child Left Behind Act, signed into public law in 2002 'to close the achievement gap [in public education] with accountability, flexibility, and choice', is perhaps the best example to date of federal education policy that is aimed at enticing the private sector into education markets. In a White House report, President George W. Bush articulated the priorities of the act, stating that they 'are based on the fundamental notion that an enterprise works best when responsibility is placed closest to the most important activity of the enterprise, when those responsible are given greatest latitude and support, and when those responsible are held accountable for producing results' (Bush, 2001). The law attached high stakes to testing in reading and mathematics, spurring in the first years alone a multi-billion-dollar industry in test preparation, school remediation, data analysis and reporting, and curriculum aligned to standardised tests.

In this chapter, we use two cases as exemplars of emerging businesses in this new student identity market space. We begin with a brief discussion on the avenues of influence in the current market conditions and conclude with descriptive narratives of the two corporate cases.

Avenues of influence

Along with the more commonplace ways that corporations influence the political process such as lobbying and campaign contributions, corporate managers in higher-stakes situations find creative ways to bring their influence to bear. We argue that influencers exist in one of three categories:

- those who advocate for change;
- those who are opposed to change;
- those who exist in the space between the two extremes.

That is, there are those who push for legislation (presenting an image of corporate cooperation), and there are those who are vocally against legislation, demonstrating power to influence by withholding cooperation. In between, a new type of influence is taking shape. Here, corporations and the elites who manage them appear to be neither for nor against a given legislative initiative, instead waiting out the process as it plays out with other firms, entering into contracts only once the environment has stabilised. The cases we present here involve examples from all three categories.

The failure of inBloom

From its place as a prominent member of the student identity vanguard, inBloom's initial posture towards policy makers was vocal support of technological innovation in education. Before developing its data analysis platform, the organisation that became inBloom was chiefly involved with finding ways to integrate technology more effectively into classroom instruction. This involvement took a variety of forms, with the most influential being strong advocacy for tracking student data as a way to promote individualised instruction. InBloom offered education agencies the ability to track student data across a range of dimensions, all with an eye towards making it possible for educators to provide interventions for students in principle exactly when they need it and in the form best suited to each individual's learning style (inBloom, n.d.).

This model seemed promising, and school systems across the United States signed on to pilot inBloom's data management platform. The largest of these systems was the public schools in the state of New York, a contract which inBloom's managers pursued aggressively as a way to highlight the effectiveness of their services. By being the largest player in student data, inBloom enjoyed significant advantages as a first-mover. In the context of this chapter, the most important of these advantages was the ability of inBloom's management to effectively create both the business market and the policy environment in New York that allowed them to enter into contracts with education providers.

Under the best of circumstances, new markets are lightly regulated; in the case of the student data management subset of the larger identity market, the segment was not regulated at all. This type of expansion has both advantages and disadvantages. On the one hand, elites can exert massive influence over how the markets develop, virtually guaranteeing short-term success for their firms. On the other hand, long-term viability of first-movers is largely dependent on the ability of their management to adapt to inevitable changes in the market (Lieberman and Montgomery, 1998). InBloom's management failed to consider the ways that their dominance would be seen by community stakeholders, and this failure of imagination led ultimately to the firm's collapse.

Political backlash and organisational collapse

As inBloom's platform came online in New York, student privacy advocates and parent activists became concerned about the kinds of data that inBloom was tracking on behalf of the schools with which they contracted (Strauss, 2013). They saw inBloom's involvement in student data as being an invasion of privacy, with prominent education reform critic Diane Ravitch (2013b) likening inBloom's business model to identity theft. Over time, a group of parent activists and privacy advocates worked successfully to influence New York's policy makers enough to turn the tide against inBloom. Ultimately, New York's public schools cancelled their contract with inBloom, and in the wake of that cancellation, education agencies across the United States cancelled their contracts as well. Eighteen months after its founding, inBloom ceased operations, and the elites who managed the firm found employment elsewhere.

InBloom's story provides an opportunity to examine both ends of the influence spectrum. In its early stages, inBloom's management was able to use its vocal support of technological innovation to create a market for the firm's services. Likewise, the communities who had concerns about inBloom's involvement in student data were able to use their vocal opposition to the firm to put inBloom out of business.

This was a high-profile victory for these communities, but the lasting influence of inBloom's involvement in student data has made that victory largely moot. InBloom has been swept away, but smaller firms, themselves managed by corporate elites, have moved into the vacuum left by inBloom's demise. The student identity market – which inBloom helped to create – still exists, with smaller firms representing the middle of the influence spectrum. Many of the these firms were actively involved in other aspects of the student identity market while inBloom was operating, but were 'waiting out' inBloom's pilot phase to see how stakeholders would react to a private firm like inBloom warehousing student data (Herold, 2014). InBloom's story has provided valuable lessons for these other players, helping them to avoid the mistakes made by inBloom's managers.

Emerging lessons for corporate elites

As we have argued, part of why inBloom folded was due to mismanagement in two key areas:

- management failure to control effectively the political environment that made inBloom's business model possible;
- the inability to see the potential of social media as a technology that was used to influence policy makers and turn the political tide against them.

Unregulated markets offer firms the promise of rapid expansion and virtually guaranteed profitability. Even though inBloom was a not-for-profit organisation, the revenue that it was able to generate during its relatively short lifespan allowed inBloom to transform its income into technologically dynamic products that evolved as clients provided software developers with feedback. This rapid response to market forces on the product side of the organisation is a common feature of technology firms, and one which consumers expect.

But the rapid evolution of inBloom's products was not matched by evolving management strategies. While inBloom's data management platform was being refined by its software engineers, management expended valuable time and energy trying to secure future contracts as inBloom's products emerged from the pilot phase. The relationship between inBloom and the American state of Louisiana provides an instructive example of this dynamic. InBloom relied on each student in a school system having a unique identifier tied to all of the student's data points, allowing all of the data to be centrally tracked and recorded. The state of Louisiana chose to use students' social security numbers as this unique identifier when it released student data to inBloom for analysis. InBloom's official position on the use of social security numbers to identify students was that, while it was legally permissible, they did not recommend students being identified in that way. Nevertheless, inBloom fulfilled its end of the contract with Louisiana, and accepted Louisiana's social-security-identified student data. Shortly thereafter, parent groups discovered that their students' social security numbers had been passed from public to private hands. The resulting outcry led Louisiana to cancel its contract with inBloom, citing the sharing of social security numbers as its prime reason for seeking another data management provider (Ujifusa, 2013).

There is some disagreement as to whether the move to sever the relationship between Louisiana and inBloom came from state education officials or from inBloom's management. If the decision came from within inBloom, it represents a significant lost opportunity to manage inBloom's brand in the public imagination. That any doubt exists as to whether inBloom cancelled its own contract over the concerns of stakeholders is a key indicator of inBloom's mismanagement; inBloom lost the chance to control its firm's story and effectively allowed it itself to be seen as the villain in a narrative that fitted squarely into the public's pre-existing concerns over private engagement in American public education.

The second managerial failure at inBloom was the inability to see the potential of social media as a technology that was used to influence policy makers and turn the political tide against them. The story of Louisiana's withdrawal from inBloom, which likely would have been only of significant concern to local stakeholders just ten years ago, spread quickly to activists across the United States through posts on Facebook and messages on Twitter. Following the contract cancellation in Louisiana, JeffCo Schools – inBloom's pilot site in Colorado – cancelled their own contract. Over the course of the following 12 months, activists persuaded policy makers in the state of New York to pass legislation prohibiting the state department of education from sharing any personal information generated by students with private firms, a move which effectively ended inBloom's ability to stay in business (Haimson, 2014). In his public statement announcing inBloom's closure, CEO Iwan Streichenberger suggested that inBloom had been 'the subject of mischaracterizations and a lightning rod for misdirected criticism' (Bogle, 2014). Many of the 'mischaracterizations' and criticism to which Streichenberger was referring came to light through social media.

Social media tools are a mature technology and a dominant feature of personal communication in the developed (and developing) world. American politicians discovered the power of social media to influence policy conversations during the 2008 presidential election cycle, but corporate elites beyond the innovative hub of Silicon Valley have been slower to recognise the degree to which social media can be harnessed by activist groups. Streichenberger's remarks reveal that inBloom's management chose not to respond to these criticisms, because it believed that the utility of its products was self-evident. Activists coming together via social media had the opposite view, and that perspective ultimately won the day.

Not every firm ignores these avenues of influence, however. InBloom's role as a first-mover was central to its eventual downfall. Other players in the student identity market closely followed inBloom's story and drew their own conclusions about the correct way to expand into a market that was becoming increasingly regulated. Social media and political willpower can easily be leveraged by corporate elites who have chosen to collaborate with stakeholder communities. Geo Listening is one example of a firm that has been able to successfully navigate these increasing regulations and has become a significant player in its own segment of the student identity market.

The counter-narrative of Geo Listening

Geo Listening offers another perspective for exploring influence. Geo Listening's business model involves contracting with local schools to monitor the publicly available social media profiles of students, in an effort to capture signs that students are in crisis. The company offers a service that transitions social media profile posts into actionable evidence, to form individual interventions and to prevent negative behaviours and unsafe school conditions. Geo Listening represents a critical contribution to the dialogue on corporate elites, because it is a counter-indicator about size and influence. Unlike inBloom, Geo Listening did not begin as a nationally known corporation with notable political influencers on the board. Rather, it began as a smaller, organic provider of a critical service. Geo Listening catapulted to national attention because the service it provides happens to overlap with the present national concern over student data privacy generated by the highly scrutinised inBloom case and the National Security Agency leaks of Edward Snowden (Greenwald et al, 2013).

Geo Listening's rise to public awareness began in 2013, when it contracted with the Glendale school district (Caesar, 2013). District officials enlisted Geo Listening to help deal with issues that are not readily presented in the classroom, but which are expressed over social media and which deeply impact students' wellbeing. The district entered into the contract with Geo Listening at a time when there were no direct policies in place to guide these forms of contracting relationships, but the overall sensitivity of the public about the level of access that private companies have to students' information was ignited when news of the monitoring surfaced.

The general discourse around the services provided by Geo Listening involved much of the same rhetoric that applied to inBloom, specifically that parents wanted greater control and authority over who had access to their children's personal information. Of particular concern in Geo Listening's case was how the firm would use student information over the course of its contract with the Glendale public schools. Despite the owner, Chris Frydrych's, explanation of how the service interacted with only publicly available information, there was swift movement to get political action on this issue. Parents wanted to ensure that the conditions that allowed companies like Geo Listening to operate in school districts would be regulated and controlled in some way by the government (Smith, 2016).

Political response and organisational adaptation

In quick response to the scrutiny of Geo Listening, the California legislature crafted and enacted a bill designed to regulate the behaviour of vendors around contracting for social media monitoring. Although Geo Listening was not specifically named in the bill's text, the specificity of the legislation makes it clear that Geo Listening's form of contract was the target. The bill specifically addressed social media contracting, and mandated that these types of contracts would be held to a standard of accountability similar to all other contractors. Specifically, it echoed the general phrasing and outcry around student data privacy, by specifying that vendors are not allowed to use the data for any other purposes than those specifically stated in the contract and for the contracted period.

The responsiveness of Geo Listening during the legislative proceedings, and its willingness to engage with the political system, demonstrates a new way to frame the operation of corporations. This framing positions vendors and external contracting corporations in a position where they are neither proactively seeking regulation nor actively opposing them, but simply existing in the grey area of permissiveness until a policy is created. In a political system heavily influenced by lobbyists and activist groups, vendors continue to exist outside this space in the way that they engage with policy-making. This works to disadvantage policy makers, as they are always responding to a new market technology, and legislation continues to fall behind the pace of technological advancements.

California Assembly Member Gatto introduced Assembly Bill 1442 in January 2014, just a few months after the story of Geo Listening reached the public awareness. The conditions under which the bill was introduced and passed through Congress are still being analysed, but the timeline alone provides a clear data point about a systematic reactive response to an issue that meets with powerful political actors. Typically, lobbyists, action groups and other interested parties converge on the proceedings, all with the intent of staking out their position and protecting their vested interests. This bill was no different. However, once a basic language was crafted, this bill moved swiftly through the House and into law.

Parallel lessons for corporate elites

As we have argued, Geo Listening's management of a crisis and public scrutiny resulted in favourable outcomes where inBloom failed – and with striking parallelism. First, Geo Listening fully understood the unregulated market that it was occupying and its capacity within that market. The company was founded with a core focus of saving student lives and improving student safety by closing the loophole of lack of supervision and monitoring in cyberspace. Geo Listening entered the market space as one of very few service providers in this space. With the media outcry, the methods of acquiring information about students' wellbeing and state of mind were under fire, but there was absolutely zero pushback on the necessity for gathering the information. When questioned, parents and district officials expressed a desire to protect their students through early interventions, but were concerned that corporations could so easily be given contracting access without their knowledge. Following the legislation, Geo Listening maintained existing contracts and continued to acquire new ones. In some ways, the media exposure, scrutiny and responsiveness of the organisation acted as a means of legitimising the product.

Another factor contributing to the favourable outcome for Geo Listening is largely attributed to a combination of its size, business specificity and a corporate ethos dedicated to being engaged in the process of ensuring sustainability. This area of success is not uncommon in other businesses outside education, but in every emerging market there are risks to sustainability. The corporate leaders became responsive and efficient in dealing with media requests; they maintained a simplistic, accessible and honest business mission statement; and all of their actions were largely derived from their mission statement:

> Everything we do empowers more effective engagement with children. We illuminate the social and emotional needs of children, so they can be provided timely attention and guidance when facing challenging situations for which they lack the necessary coping skills or life experience. We believe that enabling a deeper connection to students will keep them more positively engaged in their education and with their peers. Addressing the social and emotional needs of students improves school climate, provides safer learning environments and disrupts negative foundational pathways that can limit opportunities for them. (Geo Listening, n.d.)

Much of Geo Listening's ability to continue as an organisation after such heavy scrutiny can be attributed to managerial decisions during the media crisis. Preliminary analysis of this case suggests that Geo Listening's persistence and clarity of mission allowed it to maintain a balanced approach to scrutiny, thereby preserving business relationships. This is exemplified by Glendale maintaining its contracting relationship with Geo Listening following the initial concerns and legislative changes. The merger of a mission statement dedicated to managing the core wellbeing of students, as opposed to the seemingly opportunistic data-mongering of inBloom, positioned Geo Listening on the successful end of a vast, and largely undefined, student identity market spectrum. Additionally, Geo Listening steers clear of some of the other more sensitive student data debate hotspots, by not offering a service dedicated to student outcomes but one dedicated to student safety instead.

Finally, one of Geo Listening's greatest assets, which for many corporations is largely out of their control, is the fact that the company was started and funded by the then CEO and Founder, and has grown organically without a board of investors. The symmetry between the vision creator and the way the company engaged with the public is one of the advantages of small businesses. The company now operates under a new CEO, but still with the same core vision as the original founding principle. The founder credits to this business model structure the company's ability to respond to the crisis so well.

The changing landscape of corporate elites

As we position inBloom and Geo Listening on these spectrums of influence and highlight their respective failure and success, we find that the current corporate structure is being challenged by local political advocates. Parents and local advocacy groups are leveraging social media to push back on the level of interactions that vendors have with their students and their data. As the regulatory environment evolves to take into account innovative uses of student data by private firms, regulators and policy makers are beginning to craft guidelines that will either cripple businesses, as in the case of inBloom, or sustain conditions that are viable to a firm's product, as in the case of Geo Listening.

It would be premature to say that a line is being drawn in the sand between products and services, but in the cases we have presented here, that is exactly how it has begun to play out. As with any change in corporate regulation, there will be winners and losers; some firms will be able to take advantage of the new regulatory context, while others will not. But regardless of how the student identity market comes to be regulated at the national level in the United States, it should be clear that while corporations come and go, the elites who manage them will remain a powerful political force whose influence will be increasingly important to examine as time goes on. Technology will not stop changing; corporate innovation cannot and should not be curtailed. Nevertheless, we must continue to ask ourselves in whose best interests these firms are acting, and who benefits most from their involvement in public education. Finding ongoing answers to these questions represents a good starting place for further investigation of the influence of corporate elites on public education.

TWO

The corporate false promise of techno-utopia: the case of *Amplify!*

Kenneth J. Saltman

Introduction

In 2013, Bill Gates predicted that in the next decade, educational technology spending would be about a US$9 billion market (Kamenetz, 2013, p 43). The *Silicon Valley Business Journal* predicts educational technology spending in publicly funded schools in the United States to double to $13.7 billion by 2017 (as cited in Malkin, 2014). News Corp's Rupert Murdoch has openly discussed education in the United States as a $500 billion market (Kamenetz, 2013, p 43).

Tablets represent a rapidly growing segment of educational technology and publishing contracting. Yet, some of the largest early adoptions of tablet technology have made news headlines as stunning disasters. In North Carolina, which received $30 million in Race to the Top funds,[1] 'The Guilford County public school district withdrew 15,000 *Amplify!* tablets last fall. Pre-loaded with Common Core apps … the devices peddled by News Corp. and Wireless Generation were rendered useless because of defective cases, broken screens and malfunctioning power supplies' (Malkin, 2014, unpaged). Similarly, the Los Angeles Unified School District (LAUSD) spent $1.3 billion for overpriced Apple e-books that came with Pearson's Common Core branded apps. Students 'breached the LAUSD's ipad firewalls and made a mockery of their adult guardians. Despite hefty investment in training and development, many teachers couldn't figure out how to sync up the tablets in the classroom' (Malkin, 2014, unpaged). However, there is much more at stake than questionable product quality, no-bid contract accusations, or even school commercialism. The expansion of tablet technology is part of a much larger trend in for-profit education.

Educational publishing corporations and media corporations in the United States have been aggressively pursuing public tax money and they have been converging, especially through the promotion of standardisation, testing and for-profit educational technologies. Educational publishing corporations produce, for example, textbooks, tests, curricula, lesson plans, apps, tablet content, evaluation software and data-tracking products, student teaching online platforms, and online education products. Media and technology companies – including News Corp, Apple and Microsoft – have significantly expanded their presence in public schools to sell hardware and curriculum products, such as tablets and learning software aligned with the Common Core State Standards. Media/technology corporations partner with education corporations, as in the partnerships between Microsoft and Pearson, and Apple and Pearson, to produce Common Core products. Media and education companies seek to profit not just from digital and traditional texts and testing, digital and traditional test preparation, and related digital and analogue curriculum products and hardware, but also from database tracking, administrator software products and web applications, teacher evaluations, professional development products and student teaching evaluations.

The Bill and Melinda Gates Foundation (funded with profits from Microsoft) promoted financially and politically more than any other force the Common Core State Standards that sought to advance the testing and standardisation agenda (Layton, 2014). As well, the four largest educational test and textbook publishers – Pearson, McGraw-Hill, Houghton-Mifflin and ETS (Educational Testing Service) – lobbied legislatures to promote the Common Core State Standards and other testing products, and they have commercially promoted their own products that respond to the changes for which they have lobbied. These four massive educational publishing corporations have spent more than $20 million to influence states and the federal government to pass legislation supporting standardised testing, the standardisation of curricula, and other 'reforms' for which these companies produce digital and traditional materials (Strauss, 2015a; Persson, 2015). The money invested in influencing politicians is a pittance compared to the $2 billion that these companies annually earn (Strauss, 2015a). In the United States, educational textbook, testing and media/technology corporations have contributed to, and profited from, a radical remaking of public education, in which constant testing, teaching to tests, and efforts to standardise and align testable curricula came to dominate the school day (Hursh, 2008).

Some commentators in the popular press have pointed out that these contracting scandals need to be seen in relation to scarce public money for public schools and the gutting of entire areas of study (such as the humanities) in favour of test-prep-oriented forms of pedagogy and vocationally oriented curricula (Malkin, 2014). Yet, both the mass media and policy discussions of educational technology equate the expansion of educational technology with capitalist growth, assume that technology is a prerequisite for the proper formation of future potential workers and consumers, assume that good teaching must utilise technology to be effective, and assume that even bad teaching can be made effective with technology. Technology is thoroughly wrapped up with a broader set of neoliberal educational assumptions and values, including vocationalism, instrumentalism, school to work, privatisation, growth and deregulation.

In what follows, I provide primary research and analysis to detail the tendencies of for-profit companies to standardise, homogenise and automate knowledge, curricula and pedagogy (see also Saltman, 2010, 2016). The first section examines the economic interests driving the expansion of media and education companies, with a particular look at the expansion of News Corp's *Amplify!* tablet products. The second section considers political and cultural implications of these trends.

Economic interests

The growing intersection of the media and education sectors is exemplified by a revolving door of prominent individuals between for profit media and education institutions. Joel Klein (CEO of Amplify), for example, began as an attorney for the media conglomerate Bertelsman, became a prosecutor and reached notoriety for antitrust prosecution of Microsoft, then became Chancellor of the New York City Public Schools and aggressively promoted the Gates Foundation's neoliberal agenda for school reform, only to leave and become education chief for Rupert Murdoch's News Corp's Amplify. Numerous former elected public officials from both parties – including former Massachusetts Governors William Weld and Deval Patrick, former New York City Mayor Rudolph Giuliani, Senator Lamar Alexander and former Pennsylvania Governor and first Secretary of Homeland Security Tom Ridge – have cashed in by going into for-profit education in the private sector. The contacts and influence of departing public officials is, of course, extremely valuable to private companies dependent on contracts with the public sector that will capture public tax money. Yet, it would be a mistake to understand the convergence of media and education corporations as a consequence of the actions of individual beneficiaries of the public–private revolving door. The growing role of for-profit media in public education is structural and systematic – the consequence of both the logic of capital applied to the public sector and the actions of elite policy actors and networks.

The convergence of the education and media sectors must be understood in part as the consequence of corporate consolidation and monopolistic tendencies that are endemic to contemporary capitalism (Harvey, 2014). As David Harvey writes, 'monopoly power is foundational rather than aberrational to the functioning of capital and ... it exists in a contradictory unity with competition' (Harvey, 2014, p 134). The convergence must also be comprehended as a consequence of a neoliberal regulatory atmosphere that allows for media and knowledge-producing companies to consolidate (McChesney, 2004) under the guise of 'free markets', as well as the expansion of technology-based educational products made possible by new technologies such as tablet hardware, web resources, big data applications, online testing, textbooks, database evaluation and tracking software. Despite the incessant rhetoric of 'competition and choice' that has been used to justify public school privatisation in all of its guises, the expansion of profit-seeking activities into the public sphere brings with it the monopolistic tendencies of markets. For example, as Gary Miron and Alex Molnar's tracking of the educational management organisation sector illustrates, large educational management organisations have consolidated over time (Molnar et al, 2010). Chris Whittle, pioneer of school commercialism (as creator of Channel One, Edison Learning, and Avenues), told the American Enterprise Institute in 2009 that he expects the for-profit education sector globally to consolidate into a handful of massive companies. Media corporations tend towards consolidated ownership and monopoly, as studies by Bagdikian (1997), Herman and Chomsky (2002), McChesney (2004) and others demonstrate. Indeed, as public education increasingly integrates media corporations, the media monopoly and its private sector knowledge-making tendencies become increasingly central to the future of public education.

The media education nexus and the case of Amplify discussed here needs to be understood as part of a broader neoliberal restructuring of public education by economic and political elites. Neoliberalism aims to demolish the public sphere in forms that do not directly provide commercial potential for capitalists nor control of the growing number of people it has rendered disposable. Neoliberalism has produced radical inequality and social precariousness, by disinvesting in and selling off the caregiving roles of the state, including public education. The expansion of corporate culture, curricular standardisation, testing, and the homogenisation and numerically quantifiable forms of teaching and learning have all been central to the neoliberal agenda. The Rightist project of making public education into a private industry involves privatising school management in the form of charters, vouchers and scholarship tax credits, and de-unionising teachers and replacing teacher and administrator labour with low-paid, low-skill workers and machines. The project also involves transforming the culture of education, by re-educating the public to accept education as a private consumable service – the teacher as a de-skilled deliverer of knowledge rather than as an intellectual, and knowledge as a commodity to be consumed rather than as the result of pedagogical exchange that centrally involves dialogue, curiosity and dissent. That is, the forms of teaching, learning and administration in the corporate project foster hierarchical and authoritarian social relations that model the values and imperatives of the corporation rather than those of a thoughtful and participatory democratic society. The expanded role of for-profit technology in schools plays a crucial part in furthering these trends.

There are two principal profit advantages to technology-based products for those who sell them, and Amplify tablets illustrate both of them:

- Corporate media/education products can be standardised, homogenised and hence mass-produced and distributed.
- Technology-based products replace the largest cost to any enterprise – labour costs – with cheap machines such as tablets. The largest players in the effort to hawk tablets and corporate curricula to schools include Apple, Microsoft and News Corp's Amplify.

The potential for enormous sums of money is inspiring these monopolistic media firms to rush into classrooms. Amplify's tablet technology, for example, is meant to capture scarce educational dollars that could be used to pay for more teachers and decrease class sizes. The tablets and the corporate curriculum are intended to become the basis for learning throughout the school day. As Anya Kamenetz writes, 'Amplify presents a vision of an integrated, 21st century classroom – though it's also very much a corporate minded dream, in which one company provides every need' (Kamenetz, 2013, p 43). In this corporate dream, the role of teachers and school administrators, parents and communities in deliberating about curriculum and pedagogy is replaced by corporate control of all aspects of the school. Standardisation and pedagogies of control figure prominently in the project, to decrease the single biggest expense in education: human labour. Technological automation in the form of learning analytics and mass-produced curriculum programs stand to displace not only teachers but administrators as well. This is a corporate dream that its promoters falsely present as being outside politics.

The politics and ideology of techno-utopianism in education

The trends to replace paper books, tests and record keeping with electronic formats are justified by proponents on the bases of:

- efficiency;
- technophilia – technological innovation and there being inherent pedagogical value in technological formats;
- the promises to economic growth discursively linked to technophilia;
- ecology – not killing trees.

The largest experiment in online K12 charter schooling resulted in test scores equivalent to students not going to school at all for a year (Strauss 2015b). While there are serious questions as to any inherent value of technological formats for teaching and learning, there is no question as to the ways that different technological formats are being used to consolidate corporate control as opposed to other technological formats that foster teacher autonomy and democratic educational practices. For example, companies such as Microsoft, Apple, News Corp, Pearson and others produce 'closed source' technology products that result in the adoption of hardware that assures a market for the software. Apple sells iPad tablets that set up the sale of software through iBooks and iTunes and also set up the use of curriculum produced by partner Pearson. Once a school has gone with one company's hardware, the software decisions for the future have already been made.

Neoliberal education leader Joel Klein is explicit in denying the politics of knowledge and curriculum in Amplify's products: 'Instead of relitigating the same fights about the workforce, accountability, and school choice, we're beginning to see a growing coalescence about the potential power of technology to empower teachers and engage kids' (Kamenetz, 2013, p 43). On the surface, Klein's technophilic doctrine of apolitical efficacy is hard to take seriously, coming from a company, News Corp, that is the single largest global promoter of right-wing politics in mass media through *Fox News* and *The Wall Street Journal*. However, the suggestion that technology in schools has nothing to do with privatisation (choice) and struggles over disciplining the teacher labour force is ludicrous. This is precisely what Amplify's technology products are about. They capture public money to be used in place of teacher work, and displace the dialogue between teachers and students with prepackaged curricula to be consumed by students. They come loaded with curriculum products that have distinct ideologies, narratives and ideas that represent particular points of view and group interests.

Neither the technology nor the knowledge loaded onto News Corp's products is apolitical. As Istvan Meszaros explains, technology and science, despite being incessantly framed as the solution to environmental destruction, cannot solve the problems they create (Meszaros, 2015, p 29). Public schools and the public sector more generally are targets for the class of people who own and control capital for accumulating profit. As public schools are framed by investors, corporations and tech companies as businesses, so those organisational forms (like the hierarchical and anti-democratic control structure of the corporation) take greater prominence in public schools. Expansion of these technologies as 'delivery systems' promotes both a transmissional model of pedagogy and the image of schooling as private business rather than as public good.

Public schools do not exist to accumulate profit (although increasingly they are being privatised and commodified to do just that); they exist ostensibly to serve the public interest. However, that has been successfully redefined in neoliberal terms of opportunity for students to compete in the national and global capitalist economy towards the goals of work and consumerism ('college and career readiness'). In this individualised economic promise, technology plays an important symbolic role, by being linked to capitalist growth, progress and the technologised workplace of the imagined future. Technology education (such as the trend in science, technology, engineering and mathematics – the so-called 'STEM' subjects) is interwoven with neoliberal false promises for individual upward mobility, and the false promise that educational reform on its own can mitigate poverty, economic inequality and a hierarchical class structure (Means, 2015). If more education on its own is alleged to result in more income, opportunity and consumption, then more technology education is alleged to result in even more market benefits.

Governments and corporations aggressively promote STEM education in line with their assumptions of human capital theory. In the fantasy, every student will become an app developer or video game entrepreneur, or do some other tech work that requires little more than knowledge of how to code. Such economic promises that are alleged to result from STEM education disregard crucial aspects of what determines economic mobility for most, such as capital investment. The ideology of STEM for economic mobility has nothing to say about how, in neoliberal globalisation, locally developed technologies have no reason to stay local in terms of their translation into commercial products and work opportunities. The rhetoric of STEM is used to justify K12[2] reform and to frame policy issues, especially through a neoliberal lens that equates tech industry with educational and labour opportunity. The point is not to suggest that there is no value in science, mathematics and engineering education; the point is that these educational disciplines cannot be relied on to save a locale from capital flight and the resulting unemployment, poverty and social precariousness. Social movements, political action, struggles to democratise institutions and to expand the commons, and popular educative efforts to link local public problems to global justice aspirations stand a much better chance (DeLissovoy et al, 2014).

Technologies of knowledge production in schools play a crucial social reproductive role in that they 'preserve and promote the necessary mental conceptions of the world that facilitate productive activity, guide consumer choices and stimulate the creation of new technologies' (Harvey, 2014, p100). Indeed, aside from amassing wealth for the owners of media corporations such as News Corp, the social reproductive role of the ideologies conveyed by and through technologies such as tablets and corporate curricula software programs are of primary importance in terms of their service to people from the ruling class. For example, there are ideological boundaries with regard to what can be taught and whose perspective can be taught in corporate-produced curriculum products. Corporations, like other institutions, do not commit suicide. Corporations, whether they are media or educational corporations, are largely not going to produce knowledge and curricula that call into question undemocratic social arrangements from which corporations and their owners benefit. Corporate curricula tends to make narratives, histories and perspectives that affirm, rather than contest, elite power. They promote values for consumerism, 'progress' understood through corporate stewardship, the corporate media monopoly, money-driven elections, capitalism as the only imaginable economic system as opposed to economic democracy, and representative forms of republican democracy rather than direct and participatory democracy. Corporate knowledge production also fosters rarified views of culture, rather than culture as contested, produced from below, and capable of transforming civil society, consciousness and structures of power. In short, corporations favour knowledge that represents the interests and perspectives of economic, political and cultural elites at the expense of the interests and perspectives of workers, the poor, immigrants, women and other historically oppressed people.

What kinds of social relations are fostered when teachers are replaced by tablets or other machines that are corporate products loaded with corporate curricula? What kinds of social relations are produced by replacing dialogue between students and teachers with students using touch-screen apps that are standardised in terms of their content and unrelated to particular contexts and subjectivities of the student or the teacher? The rise of adaptive curriculum software is far from apolitical (Roberts-Mahoney et al, 2016; Means, in press). Adaptive learning software is like the movie-streaming service Netflix. Netflix utilises a program to predict the consumer's likely interest in particular films, and consequently it tailors what is readily available based on past selections. This builds a consumer identity profile based on the programmed assumptions of the software engineers as to what are the intelligible categories of film viewership. Of course, such categories are based on marketing and the interest in delivering inexpensively obtained content while retaining viewer subscriptions. Very different categories and suggestions would be developed if the aims were, for example, to promote viewership of films valued by and discussed by film scholars. Different aims and assumptions would result in a very different adaptive model.

Adaptive learning software changes the curriculum based on the test performance of the student. Consequently, it forms a case or identity profile of the student that is then used for sorting and sifting the student, determining capacities, interpreting intelligence and potential, and providing particular future curricula. As Zygmunt Bauman and David Lyon argue, what is at stake in the rise of surveillance technologies such as these is not only the loss of privacy and the expansion of secrecy for the wielding of unaccountable power, but also the tendency towards *social sorting* and the making of 'cumulative disadvantage' (Bauman and Lyon, 2013, pp 13-14). What is particularly insidious about this new form of tracking is that it is wrapped in the ostensibly disinterested and objective guise of techno-science that naturalises the outcomes of sorting as being beyond human evaluation and judgement, free of assumptions and values, separated from the vagaries of all-too-human subjective error. Of course, these software curricula are made by people with particular values and ideologies, and the content of the curricula expresses ideologies, values and assumptions of particular classes and cultural groups.

One of the most significant political and pedagogical dimensions of the expansion of corporate tablet technology is the usurping of the role of the teacher by the corporation in making decisions about what and how to teach. This is not just a matter of the displacement of labour through technology, but the replacement of teacher control over cultural production – signifying practices that affirm or contest broader public constellations of meaning. The makers of tablet hardware and software curriculum claim not only that are they *not* usurping the roles of teachers, but also that they are actually expanding teacher autonomy and control in the classroom. Joel Klein, CEO of Amplify, claims that the tablet is not taking control away from teachers, but rather is simply responding to teachers' demands (Bloomberg LP, 2014). Anya Kamenetz describes the Amplify software curriculum design that is alleged to give teachers control:

> … many educators are still skeptical of tablets in the classroom – and Amplify seems designed to put them at ease. Its operating system gives teachers and schools an unprecedented level of control over the devices in students' hands. There is no HOME button, for example: Students can't just exit out of a math program the way they can close Angry Birds on an iPad. Instead, if a teacher hits her EYES ON TEACHER button, any or every student's tablet in her classroom suspends; a message tells the student to look up. Or the teacher can call on a student randomly, and a message pops up on her screen. Or with just one click, a teacher can pose a multiple-choice pop quiz and see instant results, set a five-minute timer for an activity, or divide students into discussion groups. Or she can automatically give individualized homework assignments based on the day's performance. (Kamenetz, 2013, p 43)

What the teacher does not control in these examples is the making, selecting and administering of the curriculum itself nor the testing of that curriculum. The teacher does not put that maths lesson up on the board, write that pop quiz, or engage in dialogue with the students about the object of knowledge. Instead, the teacher becomes a facilitator of prepackaged and standardised curricula and assessments made by the company. In this case, technology takes the practice of scripted lessons a step further away from teacher control. Those individualised homework assignments are not the result of the teacher's decision-making and thought. Nor do they allow the student to comprehend knowledge and subjective experience critically, that is, in terms of the broader forces, structure and material and symbolic contests informing their production. Rather, these assignments are the result of the learning analytic program that sorts students and makes the student into a case for future sorting.

Furthermore, as students use the prepackaged software, their scores are recorded and the data are managed by those in a position of authority over the teacher for evaluation of the teacher's 'performance'. The teacher is caught in a data surveillance web, in which control over the making of the knowledge with the student is replaced by automated measures of learning determined by the accounting practices installed in the machine.

Anya Kamenetz (2013) frames the problem of technology as a battle between total corporate control over, on the one hand, knowledge and the school, versus, on the other hand, the use of technology for 'open access' to freely accessible knowledge and curriculum. She asks education investor Matt Greenfield whether the Amplify model of total integrated corporate control of the classroom will win out over the 'open source' model. In the integrated 'closed source' model, a company such as News Corp seeks monopoly control over the integrated hardware product and proprietary software product. In the open source model, computer hardware such as laptops and tablets can accommodate a variety of web-based applications, such as Wikipedia or the curriculum software that a school or district develops itself (assuming that it has the time and resources to develop it). This, however, is a false dichotomy between future technology models. Once the technology is in the classroom, the public is beholden to it. That is, educational spending gets channelled towards acquiring, maintaining and upgrading the hardware – if not also the software. Such spending comes at the expense of decidedly low-maintenance resources, such as books, that also rely more centrally on the teacher.

Kamenetz (2013) in conversation with Greenfield frame the debate over the future of educational technology as being between the Amplify model of total corporate monopoly versus open source technology. This framing misses the crucial issue of the different capacities that different schools have for implementation. A monopolistic model such as Amplify that controls hardware and curriculum means that not only do working class and poor schools get targeted for highly standardised and scripted forms of pedagogy and prepackaged curricula, but also that these cash-strapped schools are beholden to high-technology spending on the most integrated models, in place of such proven beneficial reforms as smaller class sizes. Classroom technologies that tend towards standardisation foreclose the possibility of critical pedagogies that relate learning to power, ethics and politics.

Some technologists position 'open source' technology as a hopeful alternative, in that technology allows schools to access Wikipedia or other information sources. Bill Gates, for example, celebrates the open source charter school Summit Public Schools for 'building its own learning platform that is student driven' (Kamenetz, 2013, p 43). It is easy to see the allure of open access technology, especially for leapfrogging over an historical failure to invest in books, libraries and pre-digital information forms. Hundreds of schools in Chicago have no libraries. Why invest in print books? Schools in many African nations have no material resources and yet the population has wide access to cell phone technology. Open access technology projects paired with hardware seem to offer a promise of instantly creating access.

However, unless governments provide public schools with access to a network of all public libraries, such 'openness' is a false promise from the start. It will replicate the market-driven, tiered access model of the subscription-based, for-profit publishing industry. For example, there is a radical difference in the access to library information and databases between elite universities and third-tier universities. Worse, if the subscription model is abandoned in favour of a commercial advertising-driven model of 'open source', public schooling collapses into the commercial culture of advertising-saturated television and internet. Furthermore, a pattern of targeting working class and poor urban and rural schools for repressive pedagogical approaches and standardised curricula appears to be continuing in the ways that these two approaches – vertical integration and open access – are being discussed. High degrees of bodily control, discipline and standardisation have a historical legacy intertwined with efforts to make poor students and non-White students docile and compliant for exploitative work and for assent to political marginalisation. Students have also become increasingly valuable for short-term profit, as they are commodities in for-profit schooling contracting and privatisation schemes. As Alex Molnar and Faith Boninger have shown, technological forms of school commercialism are on the rise (Molnar and Boninger, 2015).

Perhaps most pertinent here is the question of how different schools and students have different capacities to make curricula within the open access model. It is crucial for students and teachers not simply to default to using whatever pre-existing curricula are readily available. Instead, to be involved in making knowledge, teachers and students need both the material resources and the critical intellectual tools to do so.

If Amplify's monopolistic design is about more tightly controlling and replacing teacher labour, it is also deeply in line with the trend to more tightly controlling student bodies, as expressed by the repressive pedagogies found in the Knowledge is Power Program,[3] the discourse of Grit,[4] biometric pedagogy and the use of smart drugs (Saltman, 2016). Amplify sells its hardware by promoting teacher control in the form of its One Click feature that freezes the computer screens of the students. It also sells tablets with the promise of technological relevancy: 'Among the features of *Amplify!*'s digital curriculum is the ability for teachers to see if students really understand vocabulary words when they use them in Twitter-like hashtags and other social media contexts' (Rich, 2014, pA13). Aside from the dubious pedagogical benefits of such innovations, a basic question arises as to why anyone would want to teach comprehension of vocabulary through the most limiting of social media formats like Twitter, rather than through intellectual traditions, interpretation of texts, literature and essays that convey ideas while teaching dispositions of interpretation and judgement. Amplify's approach seems to suggest that allegedly catchy media formatting is the basis for learning. Amplify aims to be stylistically and technologically relevant, rather than meaningful to students in ways that would help them to understand themselves, to understand how social forces make them as selves, and to develop a sense of the capacity to act with others to control and transform their life conditions. In other words, the basic limitation of these technology products is that their degree of standardisation, homogenisation and displacement of the role of the teacher actively prohibits forms of engagement aimed at reconstructing experience and fostering political – rather than merely consumer – agency.

Conclusion

The corporate commitment to education appears to be limited to its profit possibilities, as exemplified by News Corp's 2015 announcement that it intended to sell its education division Amplify because it is not profitable enough. The sale of Amplify, which began as a purchase by News Corp of Wireless Generation, provides a reminder of the difference of commitment to education represented by public and private institutions. While public institutions ideally represent service to the public over the imperative for profit, private institutions maintain their commitment to the public only as long as it appears to its investors as maximally profitable relative to other opportunities. Private institutions oriented around maximising short-term financial gain bring the vicissitudes of markets into the public sector, raising questions as to their reliability and stability over the long term.

The educational possibilities and even critical pedagogical possibilities of technology should not be discounted for their potential to contribute to genuinely democratic social movement. However, the question of education cannot be comprehended in neoliberal terms favoured by economic and political elites of the technical efficiencies of delivery of knowledge nor the liberal terms of the development of critical thinking as problem-solving skills. Rather, public schools ought to create the conditions for a thinking society capable of democratic self-governance, humane and collective forms of control, and the reduction of arbitrary and authoritarian forms of control. The development of technological tools for education ought to be considered for how they can foster critical identifications and dispositions for social and self-interpretation that can form the basis for democratic social transformation throughout all institutions.

Notes

[1] Race to the Top initiated a competition among US states for a pool of money. It incentivised states to compete to fulfil federal mandates including especially for privatisation.

[2] STEM [Science Technology Engineering Mathematics] is a widespread trend in elementary and secondary education that largely promotes a vocational and instrumental approach to science and mathematics education.

[3] KIPP [Knowledge is Power Program] is a charter management organisation that privately manages public schools.

[4] Grit is a pedagogy of control that aims to make students obedience to authority and persistent in task completion. I have explained it as a new form of neoliberal character education in Saltman (2016) *Scripted Bodies*.

THREE

Fighting for the local: Americans for Prosperity and the struggle for school boards

Eleni Schirmer and Michael W. Apple

Introduction

The United States is witnessing the growing power of neoliberal and neoconservative agendas. One of the major sites of the increased influence of such political forces has been Wisconsin. In 2011, the conservative Wisconsin Governor Scott Walker historically cut the state's public education budget and curtailed the collective bargaining rights of the state's public sector employees. These changes spurred a mobilisation by progressive and grassroots groups around the state. In response, national corporate actors and organisations, especially those funded by the billionaire fossil fuel magnates the Koch brothers, used their money and organisational power to support neoliberal and neoconservative policies. After swathes of voters petitioned for a new election to remove ('recall') the governor, the Koch-funded political advocacy organisation Americans for Prosperity spent millions in advertising, bus tours and phone banks during the campaign for Walker's recall election (Lavender, 2011). Backed by such extensive corporate support, Walker won the recall election, emboldening the corporate sector to further engage in social and educational policy reform. This extension of influence is part of the story we wish to tell in this chapter.

The Koch brothers' influence extends beyond high-profile state-level elections. These billionaires' dollars have begun moving into municipal affairs in small cities and towns, such as school board elections like Kenosha, Wisconsin (Smith, 2014a) and Jefferson County, Colorado. This raises a crucial question. Why do groups like Americans for Prosperity care about small-town school board elections?

Understanding why multibillionaire individuals and the political organisations they fund are interested in small-scale micropolitics helps us to decipher the larger ideological processes at stake in building corporate influence. While the sheer volume of this economic capital reveals a new form of political economic determinism – that more money necessarily buys more political power – other dynamics are also at play (see, for example, Ball, 2009a; Reckhow and Snyder, 2014). Critical investigations of conservative movements must consider how politically conservative forces assemble and gather power at the local level in order to develop ideological strongholds.

This chapter highlights two particularly significant local examples in the United States: school board elections in Kenosha, Wisconsin in 2014 and in Jefferson County, Colorado in 2015. Through documentary analysis of school board records, news reports and district evaluations, in both Wisconsin and Colorado, we chronicle the political contest for control of each school board. Using a process tracing model, we note key sequences of events, outcomes and alliances (Collier, 2011). Our findings illustrate the ideological and political project of corporate, conservative influence in public education in the United States.

Understanding the Right

In previous work, such as *Educating the 'Right' Way* (Apple, 2006a), one of us has given significant attention to diagnosing and explaining the elements of various Rightist movements that have formed an influential alliance of what might best be called 'conservative modernization' that has taken hold in the United States and elsewhere (for example Hall, 1988; Apple, 2010). *Educating the 'Right' Way* shows how that conservative alliance in the United States has effectively changed the domains of common sense, especially around education, shifting the focus of education from equity to efficiency.

The idea of a complex alliance is important to take seriously:

> the right is not a unitary movement. It is a coalition of forces with many different emphases; some overlap and others conflict with each other. Thus, one of the goals of [critical work] is to examine the contradictions within this movement, demonstrating how these tensions are creatively solved so that this society *does* in fact change—but in particular directions. (Apple, 2006a, p 7)

Through an analysis of different agendas and groups that gathered in Kenosha and Jefferson County, we show how the Right is neither monolithic nor predetermined, but continuously fashioned.

Conservative forces became attracted to both Kenosha and Jefferson County because of these cities' attempts to challenge components of mounting conservative agendas. In the next sections, we will review the sociopolitical context of Kenosha, the recent political and economic history of its school district, and how these factors affected the 2014 school board election. We will then turn our attention to the school board in Jefferson County, to compare how it tried to push through a conservative agenda, and how the community responded. We conclude by highlighting key lessons from both Kenosha and Jefferson County about the ideological struggles over schools.

When the global collapses the local: Kenosha, Wisconsin

Kenosha, Wisconsin is a small mid-west city, whose economy has long depended on its automobile industry. Its relative prosperity and its respect for the economic and cultural rights of workers disintegrated due to the repeated economic crises that 'rust-belt' cities have experienced. A bad situation became worse in the past decade. Global political-economic changes had major effects in Kenosha following the 2008 financial collapse. A crisis in school funding – and the politics surrounding it – became centre stage. It was a situation ripe with possibilities for a successful neoliberal intervention at the local level. Understanding how this happened requires that we look more closely at the politics of local corporate involvement.

Declining state aid to public education, coupled with rising healthcare costs, ushered school districts such as Kenosha into unstable financial markets of private investment. Like many others prior to the 2008 collapse, the Kenosha school district hastily took financial advice to invest millions of dollars in a complex system of corporate bonds. However, this advice proved poor and untrustworthy. Within a few months, the district had not only lost all of the $200 million it had invested, but also more than $150 million it had borrowed, crushing its credit ratings (Duhigg and Dougherty, 2008). This loss of both capital and credit alongside the massive shortfalls in state aid of 2011 painted a bleak financial picture for the Kenosha Unified School District (KUSD). The financial crisis also provided extremely fertile ground for more conservative policy changes in the district. As the school district scrambled for financial restitution, it became more willing to embrace further funding cuts and programme streamlining. It searched for a new superintendent of schools who could handle this crisis.

Economic crisis meets education reformer

When Michele Hancock, the new superintendent, arrived at Kenosha in 2010, the district was still financially wobbling from its 2008 collapse. Hancock, a former 'human capital officer' from the Rochester, New York school district, was immersed in the corporate management of education (see, for example, Ravitch, 2013c). Within a few months of the start of her tenure as superintendent, Hancock issued 'The Transformation Plan' to KUSD. This several-hundred-page document offered an analysis and roadmap for Hancock's education vision, largely centered around education reform buzzwords such as building 'life and career skills', deploying 'relevant global knowledge' and increasing the use of technology in the classroom (Clegg et al, 2013, p 40).

Yet the gap between Hancock's rhetoric and the actual practices in schools felt jolting to many teachers and community members in Kenosha. "It was simply too much at one time," proclaimed an incumbent school board member (Flores, 2013). Though the school district was still struggling from the disastrous financial investments it had been advised to make, the Transformation Plan proposed investing in increased technology for the school district, such as laptops, tablets and online textbooks (Hallow, 2011). Meanwhile, Hancock called for massive staff lay-offs. Although Hancock herself earned a salary over $320,000, near the end of the 2010/11 school year Hancock issued lay-off notices to more than 300 teachers in the district (Flores, 2011b; Smith, 2014b). In addition to providing devastating job losses to the town's largest employer and unionised workforce, the reduction in staff changed the education provided across the district. Class sizes rose. Foreign language teachers were replaced by the online instruction programme Rosetta Stone (Flores, 2012; McDarrison, 2013). In a school district with a very quickly growing Spanish-speaking population, the decision to eliminate foreign language instructors and replace them with computer programs signalled a sharp divestment from some of the community's key resources. The loss of jobs, increased class sizes and changes to curriculum priorities frustrated parents and teachers alike.

Furthermore, Hancock's Transformation Plan had few positive effects on educational outcomes. An independent curriculum audit conducted in 2013 (Clegg et al, 2013) revealed very little progress in the actual adoption of technology by students or in pursuit of the district's educational goals. More seriously, the curriculum audit suggested that the Transformation Plan did very little to address the significant race and class inequalities in the school district (Clegg et al, 2013, p 205). The audit of the Transformation Plan revealed that teachers and administrators disproportionately suspended Black and Latino students, while under-enrolling them in special curricular offerings or advanced programmes. Programmes specifically designed for English language learners – largely Latino students – were grossly under-resourced (Clegg et al, 2013, p 213).

What is more, students of colour and low-income students had less access to the district's school choice programme. KUSD had developed a well-respected, district-sponsored school choice programme, offering several public charter schools, an open-enrolment policy and an in-district transfer policy (Flores, 2013). However, the school choice programmes were not equally accessible to all Kenosha families. First, many of the public charter schools were not served by the district's school bus system. Second, selection into choice programmes was determined by an elective lottery, which imposed a language and education barrier on under-represented families who did not have sufficient background information necessary to participate (Clegg et al, 2013; Brighouse and Schouten, 2014).

Kenosha's education reformer and the neoliberal state

The KUSD administration's adoption of an austerity regime – laying off staff, while simultaneously increasing investments in technology and administration, while using the economic downturn to justify the rollback of public services – had other very significant effects. Rather than defending schools as vital social institutions, public education became defined in terms of efficiencies, returns on investment and profit margins (Saltman, 2007, 2009a; Lipman, 2011a).

Between 2010 and 2013, the KUSD followed the classic neoliberal roadmap: financial collapse provided justification to reorganise elements of the state, altering both the content of the social services and their organisation. This reorganisation placed new premiums on efficiency, market nimbleness and choice as the central mechanisms of social provision. Meanwhile, racial and class inequalities in the school district got no better, or even worsened. While Hancock and her administration did not independently cause any of the economic preconditions for this reorganisation – in either the economic collapse or the district's financial response – they responded with the inflection of what one of us has called the 'new managerial' class (Apple, 2006a), prioritising efficiency over equity.

In the meantime, the dissatisfaction with Hancock's leadership dovetailed with rising discontent about Walker's cuts to public sector institutions and workers' rights noted earlier (Hallow, 2011). Mobilised labour and public education supporters took action themselves in the Kenosha school board in 2011. Alarmed by the direction of both Walker and Hancock, the Kenosha school board stepped forward to protect the rights of teachers.

Yet the mobilisation against Walker also galvanised conservative forces in Kenosha. One of the chief ways this occurred was through the organised efforts to recall Kenosha's Democratic state senator, Bob Wirch, a lifelong Kenosha resident who had served as a public official in the district for the past 20 years (Olson, 2011). Wirch had been an outspoken opponent of Walker's school voucher plan, which had targeted Kenosha as a site for expansion. "By proposing to expand the school voucher plan," Wirch stated, "the Governor is ignoring the voices of people of Kenosha" (Steinkraus, 2011). When it became clear that Walker and his administration were unwilling to negotiate the extreme budget cuts and legal changes to public employees' rights proposed in the bill first called the Budget Repair bill, now known as WI Act 10, Wirch and 12 other Democratic state senators left the state for nearly two weeks (Nichols, 2012).

Unsurprisingly, this tactic enraged conservatives around the state. As a response, a group of conservative citizens in Kenosha, dubbed 'Taxpayers to Recall Robert Wirch', began a recall campaign of their own (Steinkraus, 2011). The campaign to recall Wirch attracted the first out-of-state groups to Kenosha. More than half of the campaign donations came from out-of-state organisations (Olson, 2011). Though Wirch survived his attempted recall election, the campaign itself made conservatives even more active in the area and stimulated national interest in Kenosha politics.

Meanwhile, members of the Kenosha school board took careful note of the unfolding state-level political drama. After the failed attempts to recall both the governor and enough Republican senators to reclaim Democratic control of the state legislature, liberal political elites shifted their strategy to the legal overturn of Act 10, the law that curtailed collective bargaining. In September 2012, municipal judge Juan Colas ruled that portions of Act 10 were indeed unconstitutional. This meant that municipal employers, such as school boards, were no longer legally prohibited from bargaining with teachers' unions, as Act 10 mandated. This fact is crucial to understanding conservative national groups' focus on Kenosha.

Members of the Kenosha school board seized this opportunity to restore bargaining with their district teachers' union. In October 2012, they approved employment contracts, rather than mandating teachers' adherence to the employee handbooks, which had become the common replacement. Whereas handbooks unilaterally dictated teachers' employment conditions, contracts were produced through mutual negotiations between teachers and the school board. In a climate of increasing conservative legal hostility to public education and labour unions, the Kenosha school board's willingness to bargain contracts with the teachers' union went against the political current and challenged the 'new commonsense' (Gramsci, 1971) that conservative modernisers were seeking to create as the dominant forms of social and educational understanding.

In addition to preserving teachers' rights to a union, the school board also opposed Walker's plans to expand school voucher programmes across the state. This too was crucial. Kenosha was one of nine school districts in the state that Walker targeted for a voucher expansion plan in February 2013 (Flores, 2013). Despite the governor's proposal, the board unanimously passed a resolution opposing any expansion of vouchers to the district, declaring that voucher programmes circumvented important mechanisms of public accountability, such as school boards. Expanding vouchers, school leaders declared, would take money away from public schools and siphon these funds to private schools. These schools, they continued, were not subject to the same curricular standards, regulation or accessibility requirements as were public schools (Kenosha Unified School Board, 2013).

Ideological clash in school board elections

School choice supporters and anti-collective-bargaining forces coalesced in Kenosha. Both programmes attracted the Koch-funded organisation Americans for Prosperity to Kenosha. In the winter of 2013, Americans for Prosperity held a panel discussion promoting school choice in Kenosha. Though their previous activity in Wisconsin largely related to the 2011 state senate recall elections, now the group turned their attention to shifting the agenda around public schools. In essence, Americans for Prosperity argued that both the 'public' and teachers unions were jointly threatening 'democracy', and school boards were key participants in this threat (Board Opposed to Private School Voucher Proposal, 2013). Americans for Prosperity turned to Kenosha to form new 'common-sense' links between school choice politics and reduced union rights for public sector employees.

At the same time, the Right also pursued legal sanctions against the resistant school board. Within a few months of the school board's approval of teachers' collective bargaining agreements, the board came under fire. The school district's legal standing for bargaining with the teachers' union was shaken in September 2013, when the Wisconsin Supreme Court overturned Judge Colas's ruling against the constitutionality of Act 10. Immediately, two anti-union teachers in the district sued the school board and Kenosha's teachers' union, the Kenosha Education Association, for violating Act 10. The conservative, libertarian public-interest law firm, Wisconsin Institute for Law and Liberty (WILL), funded by the conservative Bradley Foundation, backed the anti-union teachers' lawsuit (Murphy, 2011). The teachers, one of whom had recently left her job teaching in the school district, sued the school board and the union for collecting union dues through automatic dues withdrawal. Overlooking the fact that teachers' unions have been among the strongest supporters of teachers in their historical struggle to be treated as professionals, one of the anti-union teachers, Kristi Lacroix, wrote in an op-ed to the *Milwaukee Journal Sentinel* that 'teachers are not blue-collar labourers; they are academic professionals like lawyers, scientists and engineers. Industrial-style union representation does not advance the respect that educators deserve in Wisconsin or nationwide' (Lacroix, 2013, para 7). In addition to deeming the class associations of labour unions irrelevant, Lacroix disputed the political direction of the union, particularly its opposition to Act 10 and Governor Walker (WisPolitics.com, 2015).

In their case against the school district, these teachers claimed legal standing as 'taxpayers'. Interestingly, this legal standing positioned the plaintiffs as pseudo-employers of the district teachers, authorised to audit and direct salary funds. As 'taxpayers', the teachers positioned themselves as customers, entitled to public benefits in a fee-for-service model. This positions an individual as sole proprietor of his or her skills and resources, with the unfettered right to market these skills. The individual owes nothing to society, but rather is entitled to dictate the terms of their social participation based on responsibilities as a taxpayer. Furthermore, the possessive individual seeks freedom from state-enforced regulations. Kenosha displays the ways that neoliberal ideology does not simply follow the interests of corporate actors and their commitment to profit; it also restructures the common-sense notions of teachers about their rights as workers.

Yet, in spite of the plaintiffs' extensive backing from outside conservative organisations, the courts initially denied WILL and Lacroix's attempt to void the union contract (*Lacroix v. Kenosha Unified School District*, 2013). Having failed to legally overturn the school board's decision to continue to extend teachers' contracts, right-wing groups looked to take over the school board itself. After a court-ordered injunction stalled WILL's lawsuit, Lacroix's father, Dan Wade, former Kenosha chief of police, decided to run for a seat on the district's school board. In the February 2014 primary, Jo Ann Taube, the incumbent board president and union-supported candidate, earned the most votes. Yet, the tide turned between the February primary and the April election. During those weeks, Wade and fellow conservative candidate Gary Kunich received support from the Koch-funded conservative organisations American Majority and Americans for Prosperity (Smith, 2014a). Almost overnight, glossy flyers and yard signs for Wade and Kunich appeared on the streets of Kenosha. In addition to providing campaign contributions directly to the candidates, these groups also brought in outside staff to telephone Kenosha voters and knock on doors.

Despite the dissent among some Kenosha voters, the conservatives defeated Taube and the other union-supporting candidate in the April 2014 elections. The increase in advertising, 'phonebanking' and outside field organisers changed the nature of the district's elections, from a neighbours-voting-for-neighbours brand of politics to one in which major corporate and philanthropic money continually transformed the politics. This not only affected the 2014 school board race, but also generated a far more conservative common sense within the community. The school board's willingness to take a politically oppositional stance threatened conservative organisations, triggering their interest and persistence in the district's political affairs. What started out as a local issue became a national testing ground for conservative mobilisations (see Apple, 1996, for other examples), and the conservative mobilisations won. But as we shall now see, such victories are not always guaranteed.

Curriculum control in Jefferson County, Colorado

For Americans for Prosperity, their victory in Kenosha only marked the beginning of their interest in school board elections. In late summer 2015, field organisers for Americans for Prosperity marched through the streets of Jefferson County, Colorado (known as Jeffco), knocking on doors and leafleting voters about the upcoming school board recall election. Like Kenosha, Jeffco had become deeply tangled in political battles, and the school board became a key site for these struggles. Indeed, the similarities between Kenosha and Jeffco were notable. Like Kenosha, Jeffco had a mix of conservative and liberal tendencies. This mix was important outside as well as inside the town. In such a political context, skirmishes between conservative and progressive forces were considered predictive for the rest of the state. As one political analyst told news reporters:

> 'As Jefferson County goes so goes the state of Colorado, that's why the stakes are so high here because it is a leading indicator or a bellwether … it is ground zero for all kinds of political wars but at the moment that political war is over the public education system.' (CBS Denver, 2015, unpaged).

In 2013, three conservative school board members gained control of the Jeffco school board, and immediately pushed forward a series of controversial educational policies:

1. The school board recruited and hired a new superintendent, whose starting salary of $280,000 a year – one of the highest paid education employees in the state – provoked public consternation (Garcia, 2015b).
2. The conservative school board and superintendent expanded school choice models, by increasing funding for additional charter schools and requiring that private and public charter schools receive equal per-pupil funding as public schools (Garcia, 2015a).
3. The school board disbanded the union-approved teacher pay salary scale and instead implemented a highly controversial performance-based pay compensation model.
4. The final straw in the school district, however, was when the newly conservative board ordered changes to the school district's Advanced Placement US History curriculum, to promote more 'positive' aspects of national heritage by eliminating histories of US social movements. The curriculum changes were designed to 'promote citizenship, patriotism, essentials and benefits of the free-market system, respect for authority and respect for individual rights', while minimising and discouraging the role of 'civil disorder, social strife or disregard of the law' (CBS News, 2014).

In response to the curriculum changes, hundreds of students walked out of six high schools in the district in protest, marching and carrying signs that read slogans such as: 'There is nothing more patriotic than protest'; 'People didn't die so we could erase them'; 'My education is not your political agenda'; 'I got 99 problems and the [Board of Education] is all of them'. The students' demonstrations caught national attention.

What is more, the students' willingness to mobilise inspired teachers to conduct a two-day 'sick-out' in protest at the changes to their pay scales, which would now implement performance pay for teachers based on students' standardised test performance. This change frustrated many teachers, who believed such compensation models were not only disproved by research, but also damaged the collaboration and mentorship necessary for effective teaching (Robles, 2015). Parents also began to organise, creating an online petition, which garnered tens of thousands of signatures from around the country (Standup!, 2014).

Fed up not only with the curricular changes but also with a lack of investment in important school programmes – for example, the school withdrew funds from an all-day kindergarten for at-risk students – a group of parents, teachers and community members organised a recall election of the three conservative school board members (Garcia, 2015. This grassroots recall election triggered the interest of Americans for Prosperity, the same corporate-backed group that took an interest in Kenosha. Determined to support the conservative candidates and defeat the community recall effort, Americans for Prosperity spent more than $180,000 on their opposition campaign, paying for flyers, door knocking and a $70,000 television ad (Moreno, 2015). As the Colorado state director of Americans for Prosperity candidly declared: "We advocate competition. Education shouldn't be different ... Competition really raises the quality of education ... Where you get the best solutions is through free market principles" (Robles, 2015). Despite their heavily financed campaign to protect the conservative school board, Americans for Prosperity were not successful. In November 2015, the people of Jeffco voted to recall all three of the conservative candidates

Conclusion

At first glance, the similarities between Kenosha and Jeffco are striking. Both school districts faced neoliberal education reform agendas: high-paid administrators, expanding school choice policies at the expense of educational equity, changes to teachers' employment rights, and diminished community morale. In both districts, progressives mounted opposition campaigns to the conservative policy regime of the school board. In response to organised progressive activism, Americans for Prosperity poured funds into the conservative campaigns in both districts. Yet, progressives in Jeffco successfully defeated the conservatives, whereas progressives in Kenosha suffered losses. Given the similarities, why did conservatives win control of the school board in Kenosha, yet lose in Jeffco?

Three key differences exist in the struggles in Kenosha and Jeffco. First, conservative forces in Jeffco expanded their vision to key *educational policy forms,* such as teachers' contracts and school choice proposals, as well as *educational content* itself – the knowledge, values and stories that get taught in schools. This recognition of the cultural struggles at stake in educational policy signalled their engagement in a deeper level of ideological reformation. By overtly restricting the curriculum to supposed 'patriotic' narratives and by excluding histories of protest and injustice, the conservative school board majority attempted to exercise their power to create ideological dominance (see Apple, 2014). Yet, despite the school board's attempt to control the social narratives of meaning, they missed a key component of ideological formation: meaning is neither objective nor intrinsic, and therefore cannot simply be delivered by a school board or other power, no matter the amount of campaign financings. Rather, meaning is constantly constructed and co-constructed, determined by its social surroundings.

Second, in the case of Jeffco, this meant that students' response to the curricular changes became quite significant. Students' organised resistance encouraged teachers to mobilise against the school board. In Jeffco, *both* students and teachers alike engaged in direct actions of protest and, importantly, of exit: students walked out of school and teachers withheld their labour in coordinated sick-outs. As social movement scholars inform us, the most significant impacts of social movements are often not changes to social policy or programmes, but rather the personal consequences of participating in activism. Once engaged with networks of other activists, participants have both attitudinal willingness and structural resources and skills to again participate in other activist efforts (for example McAdam, 1989). Organising and participating in a series of effective walk-outs created activist identities for Jeffco high school students. Cultural struggles over what should be taught, struggles that were close to home for students and parents, galvanised action. This has important implications for how we think about what kinds of struggles can generate progressive transformations. As Nancy Fraser reminds us, a politics of recognition as well as a politics of redistribution is crucial (Fraser, 1997; see also Apple, 2013, 2015). In Kenosha, on the other hand, the struggle foregrounded redistributive rights – especially teachers' rights to unions – and positioned questions of recognition, such as racial justice, as secondary. Furthermore, neither students, nor parents nor teachers engaged in direct action. Rather, the struggle between conservative and progressive visions of education occurred either through electoral organising, or through skirmishes among institutional elites, staged in board meetings and legal courts. This restricted the capacity for participation, engagement and deliberation among Kenosha teachers, students and community members. As a result, public school supporters in Kenosha failed to develop the dialogic power necessary for democratic transformation (Offe and Wiesenthal, 1980).

Third, supporters of public education in Jeffco were able to develop a coalition around multiple issues: curriculum, teachers' compensation models and school choice. This mobilised coalition had sufficient popular support and power to successfully recall the conservative candidates. In Kenosha, however, progressives were not able to mobilise a broad-based coalition to defend against the changes to public education. Instead, conservatives in Kenosha managed to suture together seemingly disparate programmes into a unified political programme. Whereas progressives in Jeffco were able to form a powerful alliance that addressed multiple registers of the impending conservative reforms, in Kenosha it was conservatives who formed such alliances. The Kenosha school board became a site for the Right to closely connect school choice arguments with anti-union arguments. Because of the school board's capacity to articulate policy priorities, it became attractive to both school choice proponents and those opposed to teachers' unions.

The triumph of conservative actors in Kenosha, as well as their failure in Jeffco, reveals three key lessons in the strategies of Rightist movements:

1. These cases highlight the Right's growing commitment to small political spaces, and the political persistence necessary to take control of them. As these cases show, the Right successfully occupied micro political spaces, by waging lawsuits against the liberal school board, running political candidates to take over the school board, and providing large amounts of financial support for these candidates.
2. Conservative movements offer identities that provide attractive forms of agency to many. For example, as 'taxpayers', individuals are able to position themselves as being entitled to public benefits *and* authorised to dictate the terms of these benefits.
3. Effective movements combine multiple ideological elements to form a more unified movement. In Kenosha, this meant connecting momentum from anti-collective bargaining mobilisation and pro-vouchers programmes. In Jeffco, this meant uniting students with parents and teachers around curricular changes and anti-school choice plans, and against merit pay for teachers.

Struggles against conservative alliances in Jefferson County, Colorado and Kenosha, Wisconsin provide important lessons for those of us committed to a critically democratic education for all of our children. Public schools increasingly become a site of convergence and interest for corporate elites and conservative actors, as evident in both Kenosha, Wisconsin and Jefferson County, Colorado. As in Kenosha, these forces can form powerful alliances, capable of hollowing out democratic institutions. Yet, when teachers, students and community members find broad-based solidarity, as in Jefferson County, Colorado, these alliances are more powerful than corporate interests. Corporate and conservative logics weaken in the face of widespread commitments to democratic processes, institutions and outcomes. We hope that these lessons are indeed learned.

FOUR

Axis of advantage: elites in higher education

Tanya Fitzgerald

Introduction

Since the 1980s, schools and universities have been reconfigured in the interests of a broader neoliberal project that is driven by economic reform, the privatisation of public services, the marketisation and commodification of public goods and the acquisitive demands of consumers (Nixon, 2011; Giroux, 2014). These market-driven educational reforms that have permeated public higher education have repositioned students as consumers; degrees and diplomas are commonly referred to as products; curriculum has been commodified and standardised to ensure that outcomes are delivered; websites such as 'My University' seek comment on product and provision; and research is subject to audit for quality and impact (Deem et al, 2007; Hazelkorn, 2011). Accordingly, discourses of commercialisation, privatisation and regulation are used to justify and defend market-driven policies and practices that promote individualism, competition and consumption. The neoconservative values at work here emphasise the transmission of relevant skills and appropriate knowledge to meet the demands of the global economy. Consequently, what is valued is what can be translated into individual financial benefit. Success and worth are aligned with market logics and further used to drive the educational reform agenda.

It is not so much what has been adopted – educational reform driven by economic rationale – but what has been lost: public education as a public good. Accordingly, there has been an incremental, yet persistent, shift from the notion of the public institution with a mandate to contribute to the public good, to the corporate institution reoriented towards the demands of commerce, regulation and the market (Giroux, 2002, 2014). The relentless processes of modernisation have led to the corporatisation of universities (Aronowitz, 2000). What is rapidly being lost in the adoption of ideological and economic reforms is the idea of the university as an autonomous space for debate and dissent and its role in educating students as engaged citizens (Fitzgerald, 2014). Higher education has become a private good to be consumed by those who possess social, economic and cultural capital and who have the choice as to which degree to take and which university to attend.

Universities have uncritically adopted a corporate culture that values production, distribution, exchange, accountability, strategy, investment and entrepreneurialism. The structures and processes that drive this reform are, in turn, influenced by corporate elites. For example, over the past two decades, consultants and consultancy firms have increasingly been contracted by universities to provide advice on restructuring the workforce, asset and human resource management, strategic planning, product development and marketing, as well as delivering leadership training for senior academics. These corporate elites now directly intervene and provide market-driven solutions that further assist universities to be competitive in the educational marketplace.

There are multiple examples of ways in which corporate elites have influenced and reconfigured university governance and management. For example, the global firm PricewaterhouseCoopers (PwC) cites education as one of the 'industries' that it serves. Similarly, the Huron Consulting Group based in North America advertises that its clients are public universities and it promotes services that include university performance improvement. In Australia, the business of the Higher Education Consulting Group is to assist universities with student recruitment. Even more overtly, the Hobsons Group broadcasts its abilities to 'enable institutions to reach and connect with students that are the right fit' (www.hobsons.com). In addition, corporate firms specialise in the recruitment of 'global talent', that is, academic and managerial staff. Academic practices such as teaching, research and leadership have been reconfigured to ensure that commercial priorities are managed and delivered (Altbach, 2004; Blackmore et al, 2010).

The buying in of these services as part of the corporate makeover of higher education is no less than the selling out of a public institution. The corporate university (Aronowitz, 2000) has become the new global business. Corporate elites have expanded their own range of services and expertise to meet these new demands and to take advantage of new opportunities to generate profit. But not all universities have benefited equally from this corporate makeover. In the global educational marketplace, a premium has been established whereby entry to – as well as graduation from – elite institutions secures an individual advantage.

The corporatisation of higher education has increased the visibility and desirability of elite institutions.

Mills (1956) has cogently argued that understanding elites is critical to understanding how power and privilege operate. My intention in this chapter is to invite serious consideration of how the axis of advantage intentionally and actively works to reproduce and preserve elites in the corporate university (Aronowitz, 2000). I suggest that the educational marketplace works to the advantage of universities that use their histories and traditions, image and reputation, to further reinforce their privilege, position and power. Furthermore, it is these elite institutions that are deeply attractive to already advantaged individuals, who are able to use their purchasing power as consumers to secure places in desirable degrees (Khan, 2012). Elite institutions are well recognised and they accrue esteem based on those who work (or have worked) there, those who study there or who have studied there, and the philanthropic bequests received. Much like corporate elites such as PwC or Microsoft, elite institutions have become brands in the global educational marketplace.

Elite institutions are not new. These institutions have consistently shaped public visions of and for higher education

Visions for higher education

Visions for higher education in Australia and New Zealand in the mid to late 19th century were deeply influenced by British academic traditions that stressed a meritocratic rhetoric infused with discourses of class and family status, gender and religious affiliation (Pickles, 2001; Pietsch, 2013; Forsyth, 2014). University administrators and professors primarily viewed their role as protecting scholarly standards by regulating merit. As such, university examinations, structures of knowledge, personal and family connections, and observed accomplishments were used to ensure that those deemed to have the requisite skills, knowledge and cultural capital were afforded access to university (Dyhouse, 1995; Batson, 2008). Thus, merit worked to shape privilege for the constituent group that defined it, as well as to create a barrier around elite individuals who were able to access a university education (Teese, 2000; Reay et al, 2005).

The architects of higher education in the new colonies of Australia and New Zealand never asked the indigenous communities, the First Peoples, for their vision of what a university should look like, what knowledge to impart, or who might participate and on what terms (Forsyth, 2014). From the outset, the scholarly traditions that were imagined were exclusive and exclusionary. These new universities drew on expertise from the white imperial North to establish institutional structures, devise entry examinations and degree curricula, and regulate disciplinary knowledge.

Indigenous peoples were not alone in their exclusion from these visions for higher education. By their very nature, meritocratic dreams protected those who considered themselves born to rule and excluded all others from participation. Or at least, participation was made more difficult for those who were not white, middle class and wealthy (Fitzgerald, 2010, 2014; Fitzgerald and Collins, 2011). Curriculum and degree programmes that were limited to the sciences, medicine, dentistry, mathematics, classics, philosophy and languages such as Latin and Greek were overt signals that there was no space for those who did not belong. Higher education was a hegemonic space, in which meritocratic rhetoric and ideologies were gendered, raced and classed, and access and entry were protected through the production and reproduction of advantage.

These first universities, relatively small and located in metropolitan areas, were elite institutions. Visions for these first universities in the colonial South were predicated on the image and traditions of the elite British university. It was these images and traditions that favoured a specific group of individuals: those who were white, male and middle or upper class. These were the original benefactors of the first universities established in Dunedin (New Zealand) or Sydney (Australia), and they did not envisage a university that was open to all (Fitzgerald and Collins, 2011). From their inception, universities were to be elite places for the socially privileged and economically advantaged, and their central mission was to educate young middle-class men for elite professions such as law and medicine. In order to maintain this remit, these universities were highly selective, with the majority of students coming from private middle-class schools (Fitzgerald and Collins, 2011). In effect, elitism and privilege were in circulation from family to school, to university and to the professions.

Historically, universities have been places of exclusion and privilege. The massification of higher education in the mid-20th century shattered class and race stratification in elite institutions (Stevens, 2007). Indeed, the marketisation of higher education over the past two decades has intensified the production and maintenance of social and economic inequalities. Highly selective admission processes, high student fees, as well as merit-based scholarships to attract and support high-achieving students have made it less possible for low-income and first-generation students to attend university. Although higher education has been opened up to previously underrepresented groups (Marginson, 2008; Donnelly, 2014; Gale and Hodge, 2014), free market mechanisms have ensured that the most advantaged can afford to attend high-priced prestigious institutions (Brown with Carasso, 2013). Participation in elite universities is available for those already privileged (Khan, 2011) and who can purchase admission through their educational and social privilege (Walford, 1990).

Access to power is one of the markers of an elite (Griffiths, 2010). This can evolve from connections through being at the same school, links with professional and social organisations, and mutual acquaintances. These connections and links assist in the creation of a network of elite institutions and individuals that further accrue benefit. In the global marketplace, elite institutions offer a distinctive product that is attractive and saleable.

It is this consistent and uncontested intersection of entitlement, privilege, position and power that I refer to as the 'axis of advantage'. This axis of advantage ensures that elite individuals are less than ordinary and are able to take their place in elite institutions.

Less than ordinary

The hallmarks of being an elite individual, or belonging to an elite group, include recognition, public prominence, visibility, power and status. Historically, monarchs, warriors, athletes and great thinkers have captured the public imagination. Fame, prestige, recognition and honours were bestowed on these influential individuals, and their achievements, conquests and virtues were widely discussed and extolled (Mills, 1956; Gamson, 1994; Hellmueller and Aeschbacher, 2010). These individuals were depicted as being less than ordinary and were, in effect, well known precisely because of being extraordinary. Being extraordinary further suggests a disconnection with the ordinary, the everyday. Being extraordinary is out of the reach of the majority. Being part of an elite is not for those individuals and institutions that are ordinary.

The notion of the extraordinary can be extended to thinking about higher education. Universities, predominantly those in the northern hemisphere, are well known for:

- the prestigious achievements of staff – for example Ernest Rutherford at the University of Manchester, Marie Curie at the Sorbonne and University of Paris, Stephen Hawking at the University of Cambridge;

- the careers of past students – for example Mark Zuckerberg, internet entrepreneur who dropped out of Harvard University;
- their notable alumni – for example Barack Obama, a graduate of Columbia University and Harvard Law School;
- generous benefactors, legacies and bequests – for example Dr James Martin, who provided a £60 million endowment fund to the University of Oxford;
- links with elite and aristocratic families – for example the Duke and Duchess of Cambridge, who met at (and graduated from) St Andrews University in Scotland.

Histories of elite institutions are decorated with the names of elite individuals and their cumulative and distinct contributions (Rothblatt, 2006), many of whom have buildings or facilities that bear their name (for example, Alan Gilbert (1944-2010) has two buildings named after him at Melbourne and Manchester universities, where he served as Vice-Chancellor). Prestigious awards named after key statesmen or prestigious individuals offer opportunity for individuals to attend elite institutions, as well as providing access to elite networks of current and former recipients. These awards include, for example, the Rhodes Scholarship for non-British students to attend the University of Oxford. Similarly the Winston Churchill Scholarship gives US students the opportunity to attend the University of Cambridge. The Kennedy Scholarship is open to British students to study at Harvard University or Massachusetts Institute of Technology. More recently, philanthropists such as Bill and Melinda Gates have sponsored the Gates Scholarship to the University of Cambridge, and Stephen Schwarzman, CEO of a multinational private equity firm, has sponsored the Schwarzman Scholarship to Tsinghua University (Beijing). These are scholarships linked with elite universities and increasingly with corporate individuals. This is a network of privilege, in which status and distinction work to identify those who are less than ordinary

A more visible sign of links between elite individuals, privilege, and elite institutions is evident in the roll-call of chancellors. Individuals such as Prince Edward, Duke of Kent (University of Surrey), the Earl of Wessex (University of Bath), the Archbishop of Canterbury (Canterbury Christ Church University) and HRH Princess Anne (University of Edinburgh) add a significant level of prestige to these institutions. Dawn French (actor and comedienne, Falmouth University) and Alan Titchmarsh (television presenter, University of Winchester) offer a level of celebrity to their role. Baron Waheed Alli, a media entrepreneur and multimillionaire, is Chancellor of De Montfort

University, and Tim Waterstone, founder of a retail chain of bookstores, is Chancellor of Edinburgh Napier University. What I am suggesting here is that elite individuals are not necessarily denoted by title or family privilege, but might also include celebrities as well as those from the global economic elite. These are less than ordinary people, whose links with universities offer an additional level of privilege, prestige and esteem and a more saleable product in the marketplace.

The competitive performance logic of New Public Management has permeated the university sector. International league tables now assess institutional performance, and more managerial regimes stress competition for students and research resources (Deem at al, 2007; Hazelkorn, 2011). The net effect of these numerical rankings has been a heightened gap between elite and non-elite universities. There is a relentless commodification of higher education, whereby products (degrees) are available for purchase for those with the necessary income; demand for that product over other options available in the educational marketplace have increased; pressure on staff to ensure that the outputs of their labour (teaching and research) continue to 'count' in league table exercises is accelerated; and performance demands and performance measures trend upwards (Fitzgerald et al, 2012).

A hidden aspect of league tables and ranking exercises is that elite universities are viewed as less than ordinary. That is, they are extraordinary as a direct result of their standing, global reputation, market attractiveness and desirability. These elite institutions employ carefully constructed narratives and imageries that reinforce and normalise their histories, traditions, scholarly ideals and intellectual heritage. The cumulative emphasis on reputation, distinctiveness, ambitions and connections creates a strong and unequivocal public impression of these institutions as exceptional and less than ordinary. Accordingly, these universities accrue an unequal power base, based on their global appeal and status. Elite universities have disproportionate financial resources, have significant connections to individuals with high social status and privilege, possess an impressive list of alumni, benefactors and sponsors, and confer conspicuous prestige on their students, academics and administrators (Zimdars et al, 2009). Less than ordinary universities have unambiguous claims to academic distinction, and graduates have almost monopoly access to elite careers and elite positions. Elite universities, the less than ordinary institutions, are 'well known for their well-knownness' (Boorstin, 1961, p 57). The power of these institutions lies in their domination of the production and distribution of knowledge, their significant resources and their world-class status. As top-tier global institutions they are at the academic centre, and their lesser-known, or ordinary, cousins are located at the academic periphery (Altbach, 2004).

Networks and clusters such as the Russell Group in the United Kingdom, the Group of Eight in Australia, the Ivy League in the United States, the Grandes Écoles in France, the National Seven in Japan (previously known as the Imperial Universities), and the Universities of Excellence in Germany work to reinforce both difference and distinctiveness. Within these universities, patterns of class stratification remain, primarily because students from low socioeconomic backgrounds are less likely to apply for entrance than their privileged peers (Mullen, 2009; Boliver, 2011). It is the Oxbridge (collective term for Oxford and Cambridge universities) or Ivy League seal that offers a distinctive pathway for graduates to elite professions. Through a tangled and mutually reinforcing web of public and private (as well as national and international) networks and connections, elite universities are able to define success and to act as sponsor for the successful.

Elite universities are well known in the public imagination. Books are written about them, biographies of notable students and staff are produced, films and television are set in their grounds and buildings (for example the 'Inspector Morse' television series in Oxford, or the film 'Good Will Hunting' (1997), based at Massachusetts Institute of Technology), and literature is written (for example 'The Prelude' (Wordsworth, 1805) is set at the University of Cambridge). Elite universities are glamourised and celebrated in popular culture. For example, the ancient academic traditions depicted in the 'Harry Potter' films have added to the mystique and glamour of ancient universities; Christ's College at the University of Oxford inspired the set design for Hogwarts School, and the University of Durham, among others, now offers courses on the Harry Potter novels.

This leverage in popular culture adds to the 'well-knownness' of these elite universities. In addition, institutional lineage, historical longevity, geographical location, architecture and influential alumni serve as markers of these elite institutions. From their prospectus and website, to their iconography of symbols and mottos, as well as monuments and gardens, elite institutions promote themselves as desirable and exclusive (Rothblatt, 2007; Howard and Gaztambide-Fernández, 2010).

The global status of these institutions is reinforced by rankings such as the Times Higher Education World Rankings, Quacquarelli Symonds (QS) World University Rankings, or the Academic Ranking of World Universities released from Shanghai Jiao Tong University (Marginson, 2014). These ranking exercises and the league tables produced are high-stakes games that confer and reinforce reputation, status, prestige and advantage. A high level of visibility in the global educational marketplace is one of the immediate intrinsic rewards for those institutions at the top. Being a world-class university that is globally recognised accrues a number of significant advantages (Marginson, 2008; Halffman and Leydesdorff, 2010; Hazelkorn, 2011). These include, and are not limited to: attractiveness to an expansive international fee-paying student population; capacity to secure the best academic staff, increased research funding and philanthropic bequests; ability to accrue significant financial and physical resources; as well as global recognition. In addition, elite universities have expanded their internationalisation activities and global outreach, by establishing satellite campuses in other nations (Pusser et al, 2012). Further evident from these ranking exercises are the widening disparities between elite universities and those that fall outside the UK, US, Asian and European nexus.

Predominantly located in the English-speaking world, elite universities are more likely to be situated in North America, Europe, the UK and more recently in Singapore, China and Japan (Altbach, 2004). English has become the global language of scholarship and academic exchange, and the global 'pull' of these universities has diminished capacity in developing nations as students and academic staff evacuate 'home' in the eternal quest for prestige, status, resources and recognition (Altbach, 2013). These are the students of the new economic and cultural global elite, who are able to purchase higher education in a privatised market. They are mobile, have access to financial resources to pay high tuition fees and accommodation costs, their passports show they are well travelled, they have been educated in elite, usually Western or Westernised, high schools, and they may speak more than one language. Living and studying away from home requires financial, physical and emotional resources, and their exposure to their own country and culture as well as their host country further advantages these students in their career prospects (Howard and Gaztambide-Fernández, 2010).

A cursory glance at websites and online materials of universities such as Harvard, Oxford, Yale, Stanford and Cambridge reveals confident assertions that theirs is a unique global institution. Yet these marketing discourses then proceed to describe this uniqueness in exactly the same way. Terms such as 'excellence', 'world class', 'distinctive' and 'transformative' litter the webpages. Ostensibly designed to differentiate the institution, these conspicuous terms work to inspire and reassure past, current and future students, staff and community that they are in the 'right' place (Rothblatt, 2006). Furthermore, the insistent rendition of their histories solidifies the axis of advantage, whereby the 'old' represents privilege, prestige and distinction. The danger that then emerges is that 'new' universities (such as the post-1992 group in England and the Innovative Research Universities in Australia) are deemed to be outsiders.

My proposition at this point is that the axis of advantage for elite universities is distinguished by a number of characteristics. These are:

- reputation and permanence;
- visibility and prominence;
- recognisability;
- global networks and connections;
- distinction and desirability;
- accumulated prestige.

It is in the corporate university that inequality and elitism can simultaneously flourish. What marks the corporate elites – distinguishing the less than ordinary from the ordinary – is their separation and disconnection from the ordinary, their histories and traditions, their status and prestige, wealth accumulation, and networks and links with other influential and elite institutions and individuals. In turn, these networks and elites extend beyond the universities, and these connections work to secure prestigious positions within corporate elites. As pointed out earlier in this chapter, notable alumni from elite institutions dominate political, economic, social and educational systems. That is, there is an abiding web of connection between elite individuals and families, elite schools, elite institutions, elite professions or occupations and the corporate elite (such as Bill Gates and Microsoft, PwC), who in turn influence their alma mater through donations and scholarships as well as their products and corporate services. It is therefore no coincidence that elite universities are populated with elite individuals who, through their current and future connections, continue to advantage 'people like us' (Ferris, 2010).

Taking one's place

A number of studies have shown that students from low socioeconomic backgrounds are underrepresented in elite institutions (Mullen, 2009; Boliver, 2011; Gale and Hodge, 2014; Wakeling and Savage, 2015). These debates have shown that social class and race are significant factors that work to limit students' choices. There are complex and multiple reasons why barriers exist at each stage – from application to entry to access.

An immediate difficulty is that students from non-traditional backgrounds predominantly perceive elite universities to be the preserve of their privately educated white middle-class or upper-middle-class student peers (Reay et al, 2005; Boliver, 2013; Donnelly, 2014). In the globalised economy, privileged parents and families work to maximise advantage via a neoliberal market that offers choice and access to highly valued secondary schooling (Brennan and Naidoo, 2008; Weis and Cipollone, 2013). Nothing is left to chance. First, as Mullen (2009) has shown, parents with knowledge of elite institutions are able to communicate this information to their children. Second, seldom is an alternative presented, and parents convey to their children the importance of attending an elite institution, and more likely the institution that they themselves attended. Third, privileged families send their children to prestigious schools, which in turn familiarises children with the elite places, introduces them to 'people like us' (Ferris, 2010) and fosters aspirations. The cumulative advantage is that these students feel 'at home' when they 'take their [rightful] place'. These are the invisible 'rules of the game', which are well known by those already with privilege and who feel comfortable about these rules (Archer et al, 2003; Ball, 2003a; Stevens, 2007; Boliver, 2011; Khan, 2011; Donnelly, 2014).

It is not surprising that less-advantaged students are disinclined to apply for and to attend elite universities. Numerous studies have reported students feeling that they do not fit in and experience elite universities as alienating places (Archer et al, 2003; Mullen, 2009; Weis and Cipollone, 2013; Gale and Hodge, 2014). Students from less-advantaged backgrounds may not have families who have actively shaped the choices available to make, or experienced the same levels of cultural socialisation, such as holidays abroad, visits to museums and art galleries, attendance at the theatre, and so on. These are the cultural markers that their privileged peers carry with them, and which offer an elevated level of educational advantage (Donnelly, 2014). It is no coincidence that elite universities are replete with 'people like us' (Ferris, 2010).

Revelations such as $36.4 billion in endowments in 2014 (Harvard University), or that 84% of graduates are debt-free (Yale), or that some of the rooms at the University of Oxford have a grand piano as part of the furniture, are used to entice and seduce 'people like us' (Ferris, 2010). These webpages are full of confident and persuasive assertions that appeal to 'people like us' (Ferris, 2010). 'People like us' who have attended Oxford University include world-leading scientists and inventors, acclaimed novelists and writers, A-List Hollywood actors, modern world leaders, Olympic athletes and Nobel Prize winners (www.ox.ac.uk). In bold terms on their website these individuals are uniformly referred to as 'Oxford people'. There is a powerful message here that signals to the wider community the sense of who is admitted, who succeeds and what makes an elite education distinctive. The implicit message here is that elite universities are out of reach for the ordinary and an impossible dream.

'Oxford people' as well as those described as 'Oxbridge material' (Donnelly, 2014) possess and exhibit their cultural knowledge, cultural attributes, cultural resources and cultural capital. 'Oxford people' are not ordinary; they are distinguished by their less than ordinariness and although there might be a desire to be like us (Ferris, 2010), the reality is that breaking down the exclusionary walls of privilege and advantage is almost impossible. If individuals cannot immediately connect with the roll-call of 'Oxford people', this acts as an exclusionary mechanism. It is 'Oxford people' who continue to play a dominant role in the social, cultural, economic, intellectual and political reproduction of society (Zimdars et al, 2009).

The term 'Oxford people' might conceivably be designed as a broad expression; as a term, it actually works to further cement the elite status, accomplishments and dispositions of a particular community. Elites exist *within* prestigious institutions. For example, a named chair such as 'The Regius Professor of History' at the University of Oxford or the 'Lucasian Professor of Natural Philosophy' at the University of Cambridge, are elite titles that are connected with academic knowledge, prestige and esteem. The possession of a prestigious title assists with becoming and being well known. These super-elite academics can act as a magnet for doctoral students and ambitious academics, who strive to mimic their achievements or to be part of their scholarly network. Thus, 'being one of us' is a preliminary step towards 'being like us', and 'being at the right place'. This is nothing less than a smokescreen of meritocracy.

Educational reform, driven by an economic rationale that emphasises choice and competition, further cements the existence of elite institutions. The argument can be forwarded that elite institutions exist precisely because the market and consumers wish to purchase their goods and services. Global corporate firms have made higher education their business. That is, these corporate elites have assisted with the neoliberal makeover of public higher education. The commercialisation, commodification, marketisation and modernisation of higher education have been secured through the reform agenda, and assisted through the buying-in of corporate services. Universities now resemble corporate entities, and their institutional language, culture and governance reflect this changed environment. Furthermore, their clients or customers (students) seek to purchase products (degrees) that will, in turn, secure their own advantage in the marketplace.

Prestige, status, hierarchy, tradition, wealth and reputation have created the desirable institution. Desirable institutions are inextricably linked with elite individuals, elite communities and elite scholarships. Membership further offers access to influential networks and advantageous opportunities. Consumers with the necessary social, cultural and economic capital have 'choice' as to which university they might select and which degree course in which to enrol. The educational marketplace has worked precisely to their advantage; the choice is theirs to make. As I have shown in this chapter, the reform and makeover of higher education has disproportionately advantaged elite institutions, as the educational marketplace has confirmed the desirability of these institutions as a highly sought-after commodity and product, to be purchased in order to further solidify and accrue advantage.

Conclusion

Trow (1976, p 376) comments that elite higher education is: 'sustained by powerful and continuing functions for society, for government, for industry, science and culture, and for the growth and satisfaction of individuals'. Elite universities are an appealing proposition. They enjoy world-class status, are able to attract outstanding academic staff and wealthy benefactors, have excellent resources and facilities as well as spacious grounds and gracious architecture. Their graduates take up positions in elite professions and occupations. The popularity of such institutions remains precisely because of their global ratings, or celebrity prestige, and the entitlements that admission and attendance accrue.

Ranking exercises serve to further differentiate 'old' and 'new' universities. These reputational data simultaneously impose difference and hierarchy. These data stir the public and policy imagination that elite and ordinary (or mass higher education) institutions make choice possible.

However, in their quest to name and label their achievements, distinctions, status and prestige, differences between universities appear to have collapsed as they have become more like one another; more like each other and, arguably, more ordinary. Elite universities both produce and reproduce themselves and, increasingly, replicate each other. There is, I would suggest, an unanticipated and high degree of homogeneity between elite institutions.

Students (and their parents) mobilise their social, economic and cultural advantages in order to take their place at elite institutions. Students from elite secondary schools gain admission and access to elite universities, because they can draw on the social, cultural and symbolic resources they develop within one elite institution in order to gain access to another. It is both simple and complex; *people like us take their place*. In other words, making the right choices, being in the right place, procures a rightful place in the right university. These are the normative beliefs and practices that contribute to, and solidify, the axis of advantage.

'People like us' (Ferris, 2010) is a ubiquitous term that serves to normalise as well as standardise privilege. Standardisation is important, as it provides a level of certainty about achievement, connections and privilege, and assurance that their children are exposed to 'people like us' in order to become more 'like us' and 'fit in'.

The picture that emerges of elite higher education is not one that we ought to continue to dream about. The picture is of a socially differentiated higher education sector, with the elite universities dominated by middle-class, white and privileged students, many of whom move seamlessly from elite private schools to prestigious universities. This is the cycle of educational advantage; the axis of advantage that accrues intrinsic and positional advantages.

Historically, higher education has been an important environment that has fostered critical thinking, democratic practices, and moral and political agency. As public intellectuals charged with responsibility to act as the critic and conscience of society, academics vigorously defend critical dialogue, democratic freedoms, justice and equality (Fitzgerald et al, 2012). This is what we ought to preserve. Importantly, we are at a critical moment, in which we can reject what are presented as commonsense assumptions that higher education is synonymous with economic demands of the global marketplace and that an engaged citizen is no more than a literate consumer. We should not rule out the possibility that a new dream is possible.

FIVE

Corporate elites and higher education reform: the corporatisation of academic life in Indonesia

Nurdiana Gaus and David Hall

Introduction

The past few decades have witnessed a rapid growth in the power and influence of corporate elites in higher education linked to a notion of education in general that foregrounds its economic importance (Giroux, 2003) and, as such, is intimately associated with a human capital theory of education. The influence of corporate elites and a concomitant heightened economic role for higher education is nowhere more apparent than in attempts made by affluent Western countries to transform the legal structures of world trade through the World Trade Organization (WTO) and its associated General Agreement on Trade in Services (GATS).

Under the WTO/GATS, higher education is constructed as a tradeable commodity on the global market, whereby member states take on obligations to reduce barriers to their higher educational services and policies (Robertson et al, 2002), opening up commercial markets for private sector investors and traders. This is viewed as being linked to the immediate interests of corporate elites including, in particular, wealthy investors and large corporations, who stand to benefit directly from a marked expansion of profit-making opportunities in higher education. Indeed, the influence of corprorate elites on the WTO and other international agencies promoting neoliberal change is well documented. Research has revealed how key networks, such as the Bilderberg Conference and the World Economic Forum, have played important roles in promoting the interests of corporate elites and in enabling their integration with, and influence on, political elites (Gill, 1990; Stone, 2001; Carroll, 2009; van Apeldoorn and de Graaf, 2012).

Indonesia, as a developing country and a member of the WTO, has become strongly enmeshed in this particular version of global reform since 1995 via its ratification of the 'Agreement Establishing the World Trade Organization' through [Indonesian] Act no. 7 1994 (Effendi, 2005). According to the terms of this agreement, Indonesia is legally bound to implement relevant measures via higher education reform policies. As a consequence, it has become exposed to the dangers of homogenised corporate cultures (Lipman, 2011b), as elites seek to impose neoliberal change on institutions and organisations far removed from the matrix of global capitalism. Within higher education in Indonesia, such exposure for institutions and academics became heightened with the Higher Education Act 2012, which became the prime legal statute in the provision of higher education in Indonesia. As can be seen later in this chapter, the influence of economic interests of international corporate elites is evident in this Act, by the opening up of higher education to the market and the instigation of a significantly enhanced audit culture (Gaus, 2015).

Strongly allied to this, and central to the focus of this chapter, the reform process in Indonesia – and in particular, the reform of higher education under the Higher Education Act 2012 – has elevated within this context a corporate discourse closely associated with international corporate elites as represented by the WTO/GATS. This has emphasised the application of commercial practices that foreground a rationalistic and competitive ethos underpinned by market principles (Olssen and Peters, 2005; Roberts, 2007). This application of market principles to higher education has resulted in the gradual displacement of the traditional roles and functions of higher education as a social institution into corporate roles and functions as a business (Deem, 1998; Gumport, 2000; Ball, 2003b; Harris, 2005; Billot, 2010). International literature has highlighted this issue. Research conducted by Billot (2010) in New Zealand, Kolsaker (2008) in the UK, and Ylijoki and Ursin (2013) in Finland has reported the changing public roles of academics into corporate roles.

This chapter explores the phenomenon of corporatised academic life within the context of Indonesian higher education. While the corporatisation of academic life has been examined in a range of different national contexts, significantly less attention has been paid to the particular ways in which these changes have impacted on academics working in the global South, and the manner in which the actions and interests of corporate elites have percolated through to academics working in such contexts. By examining these processes in the context of Indonesia, new insights are afforded into how the interests of international corporate elites have been translated into Indonesian higher education management reform and how academics have responded to these changes. As such, this is an example not of corporate elites directly operating within higher education, but of how their power and influence have led to dramatic changes in the working lives and practices of academics in one setting geographically at some distance from the global centres of corporate elites.

This chapter is divided into several sections. The first section examines those corporate elites and corporate reforms that have contributed to changes in the public roles and functions of universities more generally. The next section addresses the impetus for Indonesian higher education reform framed by the influence of the external environment, including multinational corporations and multilateral agreements directly linked to corporate elites that have shaped the formulation and content of higher education policy in this context. The final section examines research data (Gaus, 2015) that illustrate the extent to which reform has shifted Indonesian higher education into corporate modes. The data were part of the principal author's PhD research project on Indonesian higher education reforms, undertaken during 2013–15.

Corporate elites, corporate reforms and the corporatisation of universities

Prior to discussing higher education in Indonesia specifically, it is important to remind ourselves of the reach and influence of corporate elites in universities more generally. Corporate reforms of public higher education can be viewed as an attempt to adapt and respond to a neoliberal external environment (Slaughter and Leslie, 1997; Winter and Sarros, 2002). Central to this is the heightened and expanded use of corporate or entrepreneurial activities that are profit focused, and which seek to generate revenue frequently linked to declining funding from central governments (Slaughter and Leslie, 1997; Rhoades and Slaughter, 2004). In this new academic context, scholarly activities are conceptualised in a commercial narrative that decouples scholarly activities from their social, public and civic responsibilities, and marries them instead to corporate values, which stress accountabilities as defining tools to measure productivity, cost-efficiency and quality of academic work. While such practices have been perceived as undermining the autonomy and academic freedom of those working in higher education, they continue to be regarded as the appropriate guiding aspect of organisational life (Giroux, 2003), shaping corporate identities, values and the activities of academics.

This situation has been viewed as encouraging academics to reorient their intrinsic values as scholars to ones more focused on their role as corporate actors seeking to gain profit (Deem, 1998). As such, the involvement of corporations in determining those research proposals to be sponsored has caused academic research to be compromised to the commercial interest of corporations (Giroux, 2003; Rhoades and Slaughter, 2004), for example through the marginalisation and/or underfunding of academic research that does not demonstrate substantial economic or commercial benefit for corporations.

Corporate elites and values have also increasingly influenced teaching courses and curricula (Rhoades and Slaughter, 2004). Accordingly, the vocationalisation of higher education curricula can be viewed in terms of its contribution to the subordination of teaching and learning activities to the interests of market, whereby teaching activities become focused less on critical teaching for the public good and more on market values for the corporate good (Giroux, 2003). In this context it is perhaps unsurprising that higher education institutions have been described as having transformed themselves into corporate or 'McDonaldised' institutions (Altbach, 2004; Lorenz, 2012). In line with this, corporate reform has come to be seen to have reoriented the moral values, collective practices, relationships and bases of educational practices towards corporate dogmas and individualism (Ball, 2012b; Lorenz, 2012).

The influence of corporate elites and corporate reforms of higher education are worldwide in reach. In Indonesia they have taken a distinctive form, where the government acts in the interests of international corporate elites, adapted to the patrimonial[1] system of Indonesian society (Gaus and Hall, 2015; Gaus, 2015). It is, therefore, interesting to explore how these are intertwined and are recontextualised in Indonesia – and how far this impacts on the corporatisation of academic life in Indonesian universities.

Corporatised higher education reform in Indonesia

For the most part, the impetus of higher education reform in Indonesia has been affected by its membership of the WTO, more specifically its legally bound ratification via Act no. 7 1994, and the desire of the government to elevate the economic competitiveness of Indonesia in global markets (Effendi, 2005). In parallel with this, higher education reform in Indonesia poses a marriage of interests between international corporate elites and the Indonesian government itself. The enactment of the Higher Education Act 2012 has become a manifestation of these groups' interest to marketise higher education in the trade languages of the WTO and GATS of *deregulation, privatisation, liberalisation, competition and accountability* (Higher Education Act 2012*)*. This Act then becomes a milestone towards the implementation of corporate reforms in Indonesian higher education, intended to transform Indonesian academics with corporate values, identities, culture and practices.

While the main purpose of the WTO/GATS is to reduce barriers in the trade of higher education services through deregulation and privatisation, the Indonesian government continues to play an active role in steering higher education institutions in Indonesia at a distance (Gaus, 2015). This is achieved via the Directorate General of Higher Education (DGHE), whose audit culture of monitoring and surveillance has led to the establishment of both internal and external boards of quality assurance in each university. This has been a significant manifestation of a provisional and partial autonomy endowed by the government to academic communities in Indonesia, and has been accompanied by significant attrition in the collegial and professional work relations of academics (Gaus, 2015). In this case, the reaffirmation of the state is visible amid the endeavour of minimising, or even diminishing, the roles of government. Such developments in Indonesia fit a wider picture of 'steering at a distance' (Kickert, 1997) and the use of political technologies (Shore and Wright, 1999). Thus despite claims regarding the growth of government as enabler and with the granting of 'autonomy' to Indonesian universities, the implementation of this process has been characterised by a strongly interventionist government, as reflected in the rationalisation of universities' management.

The application of auditing, accounting, reporting, recording, punishing and rewarding mechanisms in Indonesian universities reflects an adoption of corporate technologies and techniques into Indonesian higher education institutions to extract compliance, spur performance and hold institutions accountable. This is reflected in the Higher Education Act 2012, which provides 'autonomy' to universities to develop academic culture, which will be based on: accountability; transparency; non-profit; quality assurance; effectiveness and efficiency (Higher Education Act 2012).

However, universities can have their full autonomy by changing their status from public service to state-owned legal institutions endowed via a government-led assessment of eligibility. With the award of this status, government funding is completely eliminated, and universities will have a greater freedom to manage and finance themselves (Gaus,

2015). Here, a complete deregulation, privatisation and liberalisation process, as promoted by the WTO, has the potential to take hold in Indonesian universities.

The other form of international corporate elites' interest in Indonesian higher education is the establishment of partnership and cooperation with industry in research, curriculum programmes tailored to industry needs, licensing and patenting agreements, and vocationalisation of study programmes. In the case of Indonesia, the government becomes the main sponsor of funding in all of these market activities, as there is still little funding by large corporations for research in universities. It is, therefore, the government that has provided many incentives to motivate lecturers to produce patenting and licensing agreements, to strengthen research collaboration with industry and to open more vocational study programmes (DGHE, 2013).

The rise of corporate academics

In our effort to analyse the extent to which corporate reforms of higher education have impacted on Indonesian academics, we make extensive use of empirical data taken from research conducted in three universities (research-intensive and teaching-intensive universities) from three different regions in Indonesia (western, central and eastern) (Gaus, 2015). The universities are identified using pseudonyms as the University of Mawar, the University of Melati and the University of Anggrek (Gaus, 2015). Semi-structured interviews were used as the main instrument to collect data. The interviews were conducted with over 30 academics (from lecturers to deans), investigating the principal changes being experienced by academics in their working lives.

Data from interviews indicate that corporate values or identities have been influential in changing the culture of academic life, and that this change process has given way to the corporatisation of academic work. In particular, there was found to have been a substitution of faculty governance for management linked to the regulatory mechanisms of auditing and monitoring imposed on teaching and research activity:

> 'All our scholarly activities relating to the three functions of
> higher education, such as teaching, research and publication,
> and community services are controlled by the DGHE. We
> have a particular board in our university whose tasks are to
> monitor, evaluate, and assess our performance periodically
> – and the results of this Board's assessment are directly

reported to the central authority.' (Ali, Cultural lecturer, University of Mawar)

'The DGHE do not fully control and manage us, there is still an Internal Board of Assessors within our institutions.' (Hendra, Literature lecturer, University of Melati)

'Our teaching is monitored and evaluated. We have a Board of Quality Assurance at the faculty level which monitors lecturers' activities, for example what they teach, what the output of their teaching is and so on.' (Radi, Literature lecturer, University of Anggrek)

What is noteworthy from these data is the delegation of auditing and monitoring to the Internal Assessor Board and the associated establishment of *manager-academics* and *managed-academics* (Deem, 1998; Winter, 2009). The former are academics (internal assessor boards), who are responsible for organising, assessing and evaluating academic performance within individual universities, but directly in line with government directives. The latter are the managed academics who are the subjects of this process, thus creating the practice of *principal-agent* line management, in which the principal (the DGHE) delegates work to the agent (the internal assessor board). As a consequence, work relations between these two parties are played out from the top down to the bottom in a pyramid or line of hierarchy – a pattern of organisational form and work relations resembling business organisations.

It is not only the work relations between the government and academics that are affected by principal-agent line management, but also the work relations among academics themselves by the segmentation between manager-academics and managed-academics. Central to this change is a shift from flatter, collective and horizontal forms of relations (espoused in models of collegialism for assessing academics' work) to one dominated by the work of manager-academics:

'… the use of the threat to force compliance can increase the pressures by top officials in our institutions. I mean the top official can push us to comply with this regulation because they have to ensure that all assessments required by the DGHE can be promptly reported.' (Santoso, Engineering lecturer, University of Mawar)

'We are not children. Centralistic management and its arrogance have lost their acceptance and they are irrelevant implemented in this reformation era.' (Sucipto, Cultural lecturer, University of Mawar)

The corporatisation of academic life is further traced from the audit culture in forms of performative assessment and evaluation in teaching and research. Teaching and research productivities have come under the scrutiny of the government. Lecturers' teaching performance is increasingly assessed and evaluated in quantitative or calculable indicators. For example, performance indicators used to assess teaching are those relating to the amount of time spent in teaching in each semester and the number of students able to complete studies within a set length of time.

The purpose of the application of this performance assessment is to enhance the improvement of lecturers' professionalism through the introduction of incentives and disincentives. The incentives for career promotion, ascendancy to a higher ladder in academic rankings and fiscal benefits of certification will be given to lecturers who can meet all requirements defined in the guidance document. Some academics reported:

'These teaching workloads are one of the requirements to improve academic rankings, positions, and professional standing, and to get fringe benefits from the government.' (Santi, Cultural lecturer, University of Mawar)

'If we do not comply with this regulation, we will get our fiscal and academic benefits terminated.' (Nina, Literature lecturer, University of Melati)

What can be understood here is how moral values and emotional and social relations embodied in the teaching process have been subverted: 'experience is nothing and productivity is everything' (Ball, 2012b, p 19). As a consequence, academics may experience a sense of loss in relation to the meaning of their work and of what is important in their work, as the value of their work is based on quantifiable measures to assess qualities and outcomes:

'However, can all the life skills be measured in a scale in the explanation of figures? What about our endeavours to prepare learning materials, our sincere dedication of our time and energy to teach, and our patience to interact with students in classrooms?' (Santoso, Engineering lecturer, University of Mawar)

'Can the quality of education be measured by the proof of numbers or figures? Are these figures or numbers the form of loves and passions in the world of higher education?' (Sela, Culture lecturer, University of Anggrek)

This evidence has come to be seen as a characteristic of corporate principles. *Quality* and *outcome* have become the defining tool to determine the productivities of academic performance rather than experiences and emotional and moral values, as these elements evade quantification (Ball, 2012b).

However, many academics, particularly Muslim academics interviewed during the research, pursue their personal commitment and dedication to teach, with their religious values frequently guided by an aspiration to engage in good deeds by sharing knowledge with others:

'It was a soul summons. I like the teaching profession, because through teaching I can share and apply my knowledge to other people, and this according to my religion is considered and viewed as a good deed to help me to reach a happy afterlife.' (Santoso, Engineering lecturer, University of Mawar)

'My prime motivation to enter the teaching profession was driven by my willingness to practice [sic] my religion's teachings. We are taught to become most valuable creatures by being valuable to others. This can be achieved, among others by sharing our knowledge with other people.' (Hambali, Literature lecturer, University of Melati)

While, as previously discussed, corporate values continue to shape the identity and motivation of Indonesian academics, these academics still view their job as a sacred aspect of their life, which cannot be described instrumentally. Instead, their work as academics is viewed as a spiritual journey in which they are accountable to God. This notion of scholarly commitment might be usefully compared to monastic models of education prevalent in Western medieval universities (Currie et al, 2000). Accordingly, some Indonesian academics were found to establish their authenticity as lecturers within a principled autonomy, which acted to both legitimate and construct their identity (Archer, 2008). This corresponds closely to what Clegg (2008) called a 'principled personal project', with Indonesian academics found to have established their personal ways of being authentic and being successful by referring to religious and spiritual values in doing their work.

Yet within this context, academics were also increasingly managed and commodified, with both teaching and research being measured by performance indicators:

> 'We are asked to publish our research findings in accredited international journals. This imperative is also important for us if we want to gain professional benefits, to improve our rankings in academic ladders, and to get promotion.' (Sucipto, Cultural lecturer, University of Mawar)

> 'The number of publications is also used in the quantitative measurements, for instance to count cumulative points of a lecturer's performance.' (Ida, Engineering lecturer, University of Melati)

> 'We are encouraged to patent our research used by industries and establish partnership with industries.' (Indra, Engineering lecturer, University of Anggrek)

Here we can see performance indicators applied in teaching, research and publications, with the quantifiable aspects of academics' work being elevated as ideal types and the process of learning and teaching being relegated to a lower position.

In common with other national contexts, the amount of research grant allocated to universities in Indonesia is determined by the potential of the research to contribute to national strategic development priorities. The consequence of this is the potential inequality between different disciplines, frequently divided in terms of their location as 'soft' or 'hard' sciences:

> 'Besides, the schemes of this grant which is grounded on the basis of the "strategic research" has brought inequality for other scholars from social disciplines in particular, for example those from anthropology whose disciplines happened to have no direct contributions to the economic development of Indonesia. It is a pity you know, they

are marginalised and not being prioritised to obtain the fundings.' (Ali, Cultural lecturer, University of Mawar)

'It is not easy to get the research grant and to patent and licence [sic] it, it is highly competitive. Besides, the opportunity to get the grant will be measured by the extent to which this research will have direct links to Indonesian strategic development priorities.' (Hendra, Literature lecturer, University of Melati)

These comments reflect the increased practice of managed research (Deem, 2001), through the establishment of research selectivity embedded in a competitive ethos. Once again, moral values – in the form, for example, of curiosity-driven research – have been superseded by the instrumental. Consequently esoteric knowledge (Veblen, 2018) and what Beck and Young (2005) refer to as an 'inwardness notion' have been relegated in the pursuit of knowledge and scholarship in higher education. As Collini (2012) argues, a human capital approach to universities overlooks important aspects of university provision with certain subjects, particularly in the arts and humanities, which do not always have direct economic usefulness or the capacity to demonstrate a direct contribution to the economy (Gaus, 2015). This reflects a tendency to direct and transform lecturers' roles into a *utilitarian* perspective; one that requires lecturers to have direct economic utility to society. This change of roles is facilitated through the developments of vocational courses provided in Indonesian universities, notably in the three universities under study:

'We have transformed our institutions to become a research university … one of our goals is to produce entrepreneurial graduates who will be able to create jobs or to become skilled graduates who can work in [an] industrial-related workplace.' (Ali, Cultural lecturer, University of Mawar)

'In response with this, we have opened and run several new study programs, for example department of agriculture technology. So the point is the strengthening of vocational education to be utilised by vocational schools.' (Sanusi, Engineering lecturer, University of Melati)

There has been a tendency towards a shift in the production of knowledge too – from traditional purposes of the provision of higher education to providing theoretical-related knowledge mastery to practical-related knowledge production. To articulate it in the language of Gibbons et al (1994), this trend has been the shift from 'mode 1' knowledge production, where the goal is knowledge as an end in itself (Delanty, 1998; Bleiklie and Byrkjeflot, 2002), to 'mode 2' knowledge production, based in practical problem-solving (Delanty, 1998; Bleiklie and Byrkjeflot, 2002). Mode 2 knowledge production is closely associated with the Indonesian government's call for universities to become more vocationally oriented.

A further aspect of the corporatisation of academic life in Indonesia has been a shift from heterogeneity to homogeneity in terms of gender, ethnicity, race and class, regardless of whether people from different backgrounds are able or not to compete equally within rationalistic economic principles (Darder, 2012). From the data gathered, this indication is strong: women, married women in particular, report having to struggle with their dual roles and responsibilities to produce more research and more publications, all the while spending more time teaching:

'I myself find it difficult doing so. I am married and I have a little child. Every day, five days a week I have to start working from 7.30. Going back home almost at night, and at home I have to take care of my children, so can you imagine how much time is left for me to focus on research and writing?' (Bunga, Literature lecturer, University of Melati)

'I feel twenty four hours a day is not enough for me. I wish there would be an additional hour for one day [laughing]. Why? Twenty four hours is only enough for doing my academic job, what about my family?' (Tati, Engineering lecturer, University of Melati)

'When I was still unmarried, I could focus more on my work, but now I am married, I have two little children. My husband also works as a lecturer. Sometimes, this situation makes it hard for me to focus more on my work, particularly on doing more research and writing.' (Nisa, Engineering lecturer, University of Mawar)

Conclusion

This chapter has revealed the extent of corporate reforms in Indonesian higher education, and their relationship to corporate elites outside academic institutions and their co-option within them. Accordingly, the change process has been strongly influenced by technologies and techniques adopted from corporate elites and implanted in Indonesia via the WTO – and with the active participation of the Indonesian government – in interventionist ways that have contradicted and challenged aspects of university autonomy.

As such, these corporate reforms and their implementation are of particular interest, because they are conceptualised within interrelated relationships between the economic interests of international corporate elites as represented by Indonesian government higher education policy (Higher Education Act 2012) and academic communities. In this way, individuals and groups of academics in Indonesian universities can be said to have become embroiled and enmeshed in neocolonial corporatised change processes originating within networks of corporate and political elites in affluent Western nations.

These changes have not only reoriented the structure of universities, but have also challenged the values that once governed Indonesian academics in pursuing their teaching and research. Through the infusion of corporate-like principles, Indonesian academics are being directed towards an ethos most commonly found in corporate organisations. While this ethos contradicts the professionalism and autonomy of academic communities, a quasi-market contextual prerequisite continues to be perceived as a necessary condition to enable the implementation of corporate values. Accordingly, academics have been strongly encouraged to behave in a conformist and corporate manner in ways that directly conflict with pre-existing values and practices linked, in particular, to gender roles, religious values and more traditional academic values.

Note
[1] The patrimonial system in Indonesia is rooted in the practices of early Javanese kingdoms, in which the relationship between the rulers and the ruling elites was practised in personal and mutual relationships. The introduction of such a system in Indonesian universities has impacted on the lack of clear separation between the 'private' and 'official' sphere played out by the Indonesian government and the perception of universities as the government's private property. So, this can lead to the exploitation of power imposed on higher education by the Indonesian government.

SIX

Becoming a 'better' elite: the proliferation and discourses of educational travel programmes for elite youth

Kristin Sinclair and Katy Swalwell

Introduction[1]

In the US, elite elementary and secondary schooling has long contributed to the creation and maintenance of the ruling class, by cultivating students' privileged identities, easing access to highly competitive institutions of higher education, and nurturing networking ties that often translate to the corporate world (Cookson and Persell, 1985; Howard, 2008). Recent economic uncertainty and intensifying globalisation have shifted some of the complex forms of this school-based 'class work' to new domains (Weis et al, 2014). This chapter shares findings from a study that explores the recent proliferation of supplemental and substitutional educational travel programmes for elite high school students in the US. What types of programmes exist? What discourses circulate through these programmes' promotional websites? What elite identities do these discourses reflect and construct?

Before we address these questions, this chapter briefly summarises the literature on elite schools and class formation, looks at the role of educational travel and 'class work', and outlines our theoretical framework, methodology and data sources. We argue that these programmes reflect the corporate elite's influence on education in two ways. First, they provide educational experiences that are purposefully separate and disconnected from public schooling as a means to confer distinction and advantage on elite children. Second, they represent what the editors of this volume refer to in the Introduction as 'commodified, demanded, [and] supplied' education.

Attending elite schools is not 'enough' to compete in the new educational marketplace; instead, students must make the most of extracurricular opportunities – such as these programmes – in order to reproduce and maintain elite status. Notably, discourses on these programmes' websites show an attempt to construct a 'better' elite adolescent through claims of profound personal transformation and critiques of conventional elite schooling – all while reassuring families that participation will protect their elite status. While these programmes have never been intended for the general public, their existence represents the id of elite identity formation, rooted in a logic that embodies the 'spirit of capitalism' – the driving force behind many reforms of public education. For example, the personal transformation promised by these programmes embraces a meritocratic, personally responsible, entrepreneurial identity that is unlikely to disrupt efforts of corporate elites to transform public education.

Elite schools and class formation

Gaztambide-Fernández and Howard (2010) define elites as members of 'social groups who have attained a degree of financial influence and are able to mobilise economic, social, and cultural resources in order to secure access to particular kinds of educational experiences' (p 196).[2] The schools that elite children attend play an important role in the production and maintenance of ruling class power and include a range of public and private educational institutions. As enclaves of privilege and affluence that can largely control their student body and teaching force, elite schools (meaning those that serve elites' children) reinforce a sense of collective identity and enclosure through delineated economic boundaries and prescribed ways of feeling, experiencing and embodying privilege (Cookson and Persell, 1985; Howard, 2008; Gaztambide-Fernández, 2009a; Gaztambide-Fernández et al, 2013; Kenway and Koh, 2015). Boarding schools, for example, function largely as 'total institutions', through which students, isolated from their families, develop a strong identity as members of the ruling class and become 'soldiers for their class' (Cookson and Persell, 1985, p 124).

This class solidarity reflects a complex collection of ideas – what Gaztambide-Fernández (2009a) termed a 'discourse of distinction' (p15) – that rationalises schooling advantages, legitimates privilege, naturalises hierarchies and justifies inequalities (Peshkin, 2001; Howard, 2008, 2010; Gaztambide-Fernández et al, 2013). In addition to nurturing class solidarity, elite schools place a heavy focus on individualism and competition, largely in the service of capitalism and whiteness (Peshkin, 2001; Gaztambide-Fernández, 2009a; Howard, 2010).[3] Wrapped up in the legitimation of privilege and inequality are conceptions of the relationship between worthy elite students and unworthy others (Howard, 2008; Gaztambide-Fernández and Howard, 2013). Peshkin (2001) termed this conception 'permissible advantage', the justification of inequalities that makes elite students' advantage over others morally acceptable. Accompanying this moral acceptability is a distinction between good and bad elites – the former being those who engage in charity and philanthropy, albeit in ways that maintain or obscure forces reproducing inequality, the latter being those who do not (Swalwell, 2013, 2015).

A shifting global economic context, in which heightened competition and a worldwide recession destabilised the middle and upper-middle classes, has weakened the ability of corporate elites to maintain privilege via traditional mechanisms (Khan, 2010; Weis et al, 2014). Elite schools, parents and students have responded to this shifting context in novel ways that protect their status (Hill, 2009). For example, while they have always encouraged social and professional bonds (Cookson and Persell, 1985), elite schools now prepare students to become global citizens who succeed in national and international labour markets through a range of social, cultural and symbolic global capital with high international and national exchange rates, particularly in the corporate world (Kenway and Koh, 2013; Kenway and Fahey, 2014). Schools nurture these forms of capital, largely by exposing students to a broad range of course offerings and extracurricular opportunities that encourage students to engage in cross-national exchanges, so that they can create transnational class networks (Kenway and Fahey, 2014) 'as befits a global citizen or business person' (Cookson and Persell, 2010, p 22). These opportunities help students to pack their transcripts with unique experiences and indicators of a 'good or interesting character' (Khan, 2010, p 103), increasingly important ways for students to distinguish themselves during the college admissions process (Peshkin, 2001). Weis et al's (2014) study of competition for college admissions at elite schools called these efforts 'class work', through which elite parents and students create 'marked distinction' (p 203).

Educational travel and 'class work'

Elite 'class work' is not a new phenomenon. Middle- and upper-class people have often used travel to differentiate themselves and to gain valuable experiences and skills (Munt, 1994). Summer camps in the US, for example, have long played a role in cultivating class advantage and constructing elite identities. Van Slyck (2006) noted how the growth of 'sleep-away' wilderness camps intended for middle- and upper-class youth in the late 19th century was a response to demographic changes that elites interpreted as a threat to their class status.

More recently, Scarbrough (2013) described how upper-middle-class students used elite boarding schools' summer programmes to construct class advantage and to become what Gee (2004) calls 'shape-shifting portfolio people' (Gee, 2004, p 105). While a few studies have focused on short-term international travel for high school youth (for example Jones, 2011; Stone and Petrick, 2013; Angod, 2015), most research on study abroad programmes has been at the collegiate level (for example Stone and Petrick, 2013; Wakeford, 2013). The multiple discourses operating in collegiate-level study abroad programmes depict an experience that positions US students, culture and educational institutions in opposition to (and, in some cases, as consumers of) host families, citizens of other countries and host educational institutions (Zemach-Bersin, 2009; Doerr, 2012, 2013). Study abroad programmes are thus part of a 'globalist project' (Doerr, 2012, p 257) that both depends on and strives to overcome cultural difference and, in doing so, commercialises and commodifies host people and nations, and reifies the knowledge, power and ownership of US students and their culture (Zemach-Bersin, 2009; Jones, 2011).

Our findings on the types and proliferation of supplementary and substitutional educational travel programmes and our analysis of their websites suggest that these programmes employ discourses that respond to elites' shifting demands for distinction, and use several strategies to reassure students and parents that their elite status will be maintained and enhanced by their participation. Yet these programmes also offer an implicit critique of conventional elite schooling in ways that appeal to elite students' desire for distinction and, perhaps, their desire for a more humane existence. These websites stress particular forms of personal transformation that result from opportunities for personal risk, hard work and overcoming challenges as well as intimate, caring relationships with teachers. In sum, these programmes pull off the tricky feat of both critiquing elite class status and promising to protect it, by offering an alternative (that is, 'better') elite identity that will increase students' competitive edge in the collegiate and corporate marketplace.

Theoretical framework: ideology, discourse and identity

How elites maintain and expand class advantage rests upon a notion of social reproduction, by which social interactions maintain unequal social structures (Bourdieu and Passeron, 1990). These deeply political processes depend on hegemony – the manufacturing of consent to the logics that legitimate inequalities – in order to maintain an unequal social order and to ensure elite power (Apple, 1990); school is one space where hegemony operates (Chiapello and Fairclough, 2002). While they can and do serve as sites of disruption and interruption, schools also nurture the ideologies fuelling social class reproduction in obvious and subtle ways. Although people have agency, these structural forces shape their identities. Through a range of interactions and experiences, including schooling, students from dominant groups are often socialised to accept and to defend ways of knowing and ways of doing that protect, justify and naturalise advantage (Howard, 2010). Along the way, they also accumulate social, economic and cultural capital that can be converted to class distinction and advantage (Bourdieu, 1986).

These constructed identities are embodied and enacted discursively (Van Dijk, 2006). Through the 'textual world' (that is, discourse), people 'develop a new sense of self and collective identity and relate to each other' (Giroux, 1992, p 121). Because discourse is both part of the social activity within a practice and a representation of that practice, it is fundamental to the constitution of identities (Chiapello and Fairclough, 2002). While not always hegemonic or ideological, discourse is often the medium through which groups' ideologies are communicated within a nexus of cultural, racial and economic hierarchies (Van Dijk, 1993). In today's complex web of transnational corporate capitalism, hegemonic discourse glorifies neoliberal ideals that support the remaking of ruling class distinctions (Harvey, 2007). Arguments for gaining legitimacy and support for this system (even among the very communities it hurts most) make up what Chiapello and Fairclough (2002) call the 'spirit of capitalism': an emphasis on how capitalism stimulates people's enthusiasm, offers security to those who are involved in the system and invokes a sense of justice through its supposed contribution to the common good. Knowledge of this broader ideological landscape provides important context for understanding which discursive strategies are being used to encourage particular elite youth identities. For this study, we identified educational travel programmes as one 'site' in which to examine such discursive strategies.

Methodology and data sources[4]

To begin establishing the scope and nature of educational travel programmes for elite high school students, we conducted a comprehensive online search of programmes offered to students in the United States.[5] We included a programme in our data set if it provided educational travel programming that supplemented students' high school curriculum or could be substituted for a semester or year of high school.[6]

We divided the programmes into four categories as follows, based on duration, where and with whom students lived, the topical focus or content, and who delivered the programme:

- *educational travel* – short-term travel experiences that may or may not have associated coursework;
- *semester schools* – programmes that are similar to independent boarding schools, in that students live in dorms and participate in self-contained coursework;
- *study abroad* – programmes that mirror collegiate study abroad programmes, in that students live with host families while attending school;
- *volunteer/service* – programmes that engage students in community service or volunteer projects.[7]

We used Critical Discourse Analysis to explore what discourses may be circulating within seven programmes' websites and what those discourses suggest about current 'class work' in constructing elite identities. Using Gaztambide-Fernández's (2009b) list of 27 elite boarding schools as a guide, we identified which of the programmes these boarding schools advertised on their websites and which programmes listed any of the 27 schools as 'sending schools'. After cross-referencing both sets of data, we distilled a list of seven programmes that we know serve elite students:

- CITYterm;
- The Island School;
- Oxbow School;
- Maine Coast Semester at the Chewonki Foundation (Chewonki);
- The Mountain School;
- Rocky Mountain Semester at the High Mountain Institute (HMI);
- School Year Abroad (SYA).

These schools are also expensive, with modest financial aid available. They function as total institutions, in that they control the curriculum that students participate in and students' day-to-day lives, whether through 'carefully selected' host families or dorms and community living. Some programmes have no internet access and require students to 'leave their cell phones at the door'. Such isolating conditions often serve to reinforce a sense of collective identity among students

(Cookson and Persell, 1985). Thus, we see these programmes as fertile ground for examining the discourses that shape elite students' social identities.

Critical Discourse Analysis is one way to account for the complex relationship between discourse, cognition, social interaction and power relations (Fairclough, 2003). For each programme, we analysed multiple genres of discourse: blog posts, website text, promotional images, downloadable brochures, videos featuring student testimony; and quotes from students, alumni, parents, programme administrators and college admissions officers. We understand these genres as steps in a possible chain of events wherein a student (or parent) seeks out information and decides whether or not to apply to a programme. Advertisements and promotional materials are particularly important, in that they can influence students' programme selection and frame the stories that students develop to explain their choices (Zemach-Bersin, 2009). The various discourses on programme websites represent multiple styles, or ways of being, which we grouped into several themes (Fairclough, 2003).

Findings: scope and nature of programmes

Overall, we identified 47 programmes that provide supplementary or substitutional educational travel programming for high school students.[8] Several patterns emerged:

- All programmes experienced a notable uptick in the 1980s just as neoliberalism was taking root worldwide,[9] with semester schools increasing the most in recent years (see Figure 6.1).
- Semester schools are significantly more expensive than the other three categories of programme (see Figure 6.2). For example, the price of a semester averaged US$25,672, while the price of study abroad programmes averaged a low of $16,300 to a high of $19,587.
- Semester schools are primarily located in the US; volunteer and service programmes are primarily located in central Asia and South America; most study abroad programmes are in countries in western Europe, China, Japan and Brazil; and most educational travel programmes are located throughout North and South America, Europe, central Asia, and Australia.
- The majority of volunteer/service and educational travel programmes were operated by for-profit organisations, which suggests that they represent a relatively new industry operating in

the educational marketplace – one that can only be accessed by those with the necessary financial and cultural capital.

Figure 6.1: Proliferation of educational travel programmes

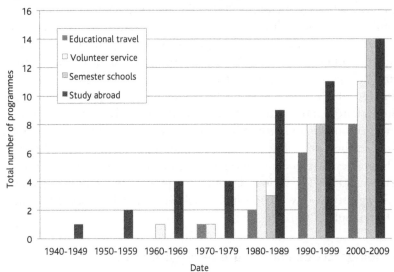

Figure 6.2: Average maximum and minimum price

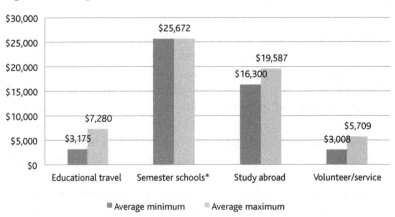

* Semester schools have only one price point

Note: Programmes that were free or missing price data were excluded from these calculations

Findings: discourse and elite identity

We found that the seven programmes' websites:

- emphasise their rigorous academics and ties to eliteness;
- claim to offer something 'different' – and better than conventional elite education;
- imply that through hard work, risk and challenge, students undergo personal transformation that makes them better people.

'The best preparation:' rigorous academics and elite ties

Discourse on all seven websites emphasises the programmes' ties to eliteness. By explicitly emphasising their connections to elite schools, they reassure parents, students and sending schools that students will receive a high-quality academic experience and will be surrounded by like-minded peers. For example, the 'history' and 'who we are' pages of these websites reveal deep roots in elite schools. Several were founded by, or with the support of, one or more of the elite 27 boarding schools (Gaztambide-Fernández, 2009b); and most list a small group of 'officially affiliated' 'member' or 'sponsoring' schools that typically send at least one or two students to their programme every semester. Many websites also include a long list of 'sending schools' that is dominated by elite boarding, private and public schools.

These programmes emphasise eliteness, by describing 'challenging' and 'rigorous' academic curricula consisting of honours and Advanced Placement-level courses that, as Oxbow's website puts it, are 'designed to fulfill the requirements of the nation's best public and private high schools'. Some programmes, such as CITYterm, HMI and SYA, explicitly align their courses with the 'rigor and content' of students' sending schools, to ensure that students 'keep in step' with their high school curriculum. Generally speaking, programmes work to reassure their audience that students will 'not lose ground' and will 'return home with the skills to ... remain on track' and 'equipped for continued academic success'.

Programme websites use a variety of tactics to show that their programme will prepare students for college and help them to stand out in the admissions process. Several websites include testimony from alumni that their experience was 'the best preparation I could have had for college'. SYA and CITYterm both argue explicitly that their programmes give students 'a competitive edge for college and employment' and provide experiences that allow students to "more effectively frame a college application'. Other programmes indicate which colleges and universities alumni have attended. The Mountain School, for example, lists prestigious colleges such as Brown, Middlebury, Yale, Oberlin, and Wesleyan as among the seven colleges most frequently attended by graduates in the last seven years. Some websites use laudatory quotes from college admissions counsellors to convey that these programmes will, to quote The Mountain school's website, 'help distinguish you from other college applicants'. Additionally, programmes work to reassure their audience that students will be surrounded by a 'selective' group of peers. All programmes emphasise that they attract students from a 'diverse range of beliefs and backgrounds' including 'private and public schools from across the US and internationally'. Programmes describe 'ideal candidates' as 'academically driven', 'adventurous', 'intellectually curious', and 'motivated' students, who have 'made the decision to do something different'. In the next section, we will describe how websites characterise programmes as 'something different'.

'A different form of education', more than just elite

Programmes' websites emphasise their connection to eliteness and simultaneously position themselves as offering something 'different' or 'more' than students' sending schools. Descriptions of rigorous academics are often followed by a conditional phrase starting: 'but', 'and' or 'with'. As one HMI student said: '[HMI] balances the rigorous courses that you would get at your standard high school experience *but* you get so much more than that' [italics added].

All seven programmes use students' voices to argue that the combination of rigorous academics with something 'totally different', 'new and exciting', 'more than [my home school]' makes that particular programme a worthwhile experience. Further emphasising this point, programmes aim to develop more than just a student's intellect, as they 'cultivate passions by teaching to the whole student' to 'illuminate connections between different parts of our lives' and to provide 'limitless opportunities to shape who you are as a person, learner, and thinker'.

Programmes promise to accomplish these goals in part through an interdisciplinary education 'where ideas are understood in context' – context being the physical places in which programmes are located. All seven programmes describe their curriculum as rooted in place, experience, and, in the case of SYA, the 'larger global community'. Programmes take 'full advantage' of their settings and 'unique local environment', and 'cultivate learning and discovery through relevant experiences' through 'real-world research and problem solving'. Chewonki, The Mountain School and The Island School organise their programmes around environmental sustainability and low-impact living, or, as The Island School's central question asks: 'How can we live better in a place?' Embedded in such approaches to teaching and learning is a belief that, in the words of the CITYterm vision, 'the most profound learning takes place when it is rooted in experience'. Current and former students featured on programmes' websites reinforce this vision, when they speak with enthusiasm about the positive impact of place-based, experiential learning: 'Being able to be in what you're learning … is really cool to me'; 'We get to look at the things we're learning about, to touch and feel them'; 'learning about the ground we're walking on, the water we're fishing from, is really neat'.

Another way in which programmes claim to realise their goals is through a supportive atmosphere characterised by close, caring relationships between teachers. Programmes' websites emphasise small class sizes, 'meaningful and lasting connection(s)' with 'compassionate adults' and 'working closely with caring, innovative teachers' with whom one can 'easily engage'. Nearly every website includes videos of students praising their teachers. Students describe 'mutual respect' among 'a family' of students and faculty who are 'more than teachers'. Instead, teachers are 'friends' who 'truly care', 'guides who were … enthusiastic about learning from us' and complete people whom students are able to see from multiple angles.

Websites claim that by participating in their programme, students will 'learn how to learn' and develop a unique set of skills. Some programmes advertise that students will learn hard skills: agricultural practices needed to run a farm, culinary skills, and language skills, as well as survival and navigation skills during expeditions. Most programmes also claim that students will develop soft skills, such as critical thinking, leadership skills, the ability to ask questions and to 'seek and scrutinize alternatives', and will engage in collaborative, creative problem-solving. For example, CITYterm 'challenges [students] to think, question, speak up, and grow', while Oxbow's mission is to 'strengthen students' abilities in creative and critical inquiry'. Along the way, programmes claim that students will 'take ownership over their education' and, as noted earlier, 'learn how to learn'.

'The most formative aspect of my academic career': transformed identities

Student and parent testimonials from all seven programmes reiterate that students return from time away with greater self-awareness and changed attitudes towards the planet and their futures. Websites also indicate that hard work, challenge, risk-taking, and personal discomfort play an important role in students' transformation. Alumni describe returning home more 'self-confident' and 'self-reliant', with greater 'self-knowledge' and a 'stronger sense of identity'. Students 'learn about' and 'come into' themselves, and 'know who they are' and 'what [they] want to do with [their lives]'. Additionally, students report '[enjoying] life more' and that their time in the programme has changed 'the way I think about the world'.

Alumni and their parents characterise this new perspective on the world as 'broader' and more 'optimistic'. Students who have attended programmes that focus on sustainability articulate a new awareness 'of their place in the natural world'. Similarly, some programmes explicitly aim to help students to 'think about ways they can make a difference'; whether by preparing students to 'reach beyond the self and focus on the common good' at The Mountain School, or by offering 'tools' to 'help [students] become a force for positive change in the world' at The Island School and to 'participate constructively in their community' at CITYterm. Exactly what counts as 'positive change' or 'the common good' is never clearly defined by programme websites or student testimonials.

These programmes promise that students' exposure to both a 'different' approach to teaching and learning and 'hard work', challenge, perseverance, and risk will result in personal transformation and development of a new outlook on life. At HMI, for example, 'hard work' preparing meals on 'cook crew' promises to 'give back to the community and take away some life-long skills in self-reliance'. For example, one student was 'challenged by the honesty of physical labor' through the 'formative experience' of The Mountain School. Several websites emphasise the prominence of 'hard work' in everyday life at their programmes, whether chopping firewood as part of the 'work programme', 'stoking the wood stove on a winter night' or completing athletic challenges. Finally, programmes also help students to grow by '[forcing them] out of [their] comfort zones' and '[allowing them] to take risks'.

Conclusions

Unlike the discourse of distinction found in some elite schools (Gaztambide-Fernández, 2009a), these supplemental and substitutional programmes demonstrate a more complicated discourse that reinforces conventional elite status and emphasises that students who attend their programme will be 'different' – perhaps better – people as a result. In doing so, these programmes both reassure students that they will maintain their distinction from the masses and distinguish themselves from other elite youth in the college admissions process and beyond.

Implicit in what we call 'elite plus discourse' or 'double distinction' is a critique of the means but not the ends of traditional elite schooling and identity. Programmes' strong emphasis on learning – as rooted in context and cultivated through a caring, collaborative atmosphere that supports the growth of the whole student – suggests that more conventional modes of elite schooling fall short of this ideal. While this double distinction has the potential to indicate a break from the values that elite schooling writ large may prioritise, programmes' efforts to 'reassure' parents also reveal how little elites are willing to risk.

The tension inherent in 'class work' that both maintains and critiques particular manifestations of elite status dissolves in light of Chiapello and Fairclough's (2002) spirit of capitalism. By celebrating experiential learning in caring environments with passionate teachers and students, these programmes tap into the ways that capitalism seeks to stimulate people's enthusiasm. The 'spirit of capitalism' invokes notions of the common good and of justice, albeit in ways that tend to reflect the 'trickle down view' of charity found in some elite schools (Peshkin, 2001, p 100; see also Howard, 2008; Gaztambide-Fernandez, 2009a; Swalwell, 2013). Similarly, these programmes refer to 'community' and 'sustainability' but offer fairly vague, circumscribed definitions of these ideas that fail to challenge the status quo. Lastly, through explicit connections to established elite schools, active networks of powerful alumni, and access to elite institutions of higher education, these programmes offer a promise of security to those who participate – a promise that their elite status is never in jeopardy despite doing something 'different'.

These programmes' discourses may encourage students to adopt social identities as self-aware, critical thinkers who take responsibility for their own learning, can 'make a difference' in the world and have known 'hard work' as defined by the programme. However, given the ways in which programmes emphasise their historical and contemporary roots in elite schools and alumni networks filled with 'better' elites, these new codes and capitals, however humanising they may appear, may be better understood as efforts to reproduce elite status, largely by equipping students to be stronger competitors for college admissions and positions in the corporate world.

We approach these conclusions with caution. Discourse analysis is most effective when conducted alongside ethnography, because the 'social effects of texts depend upon processes of meaning-making' (Fairclough, 2003, p 11); we need both 'intentions and interpretations' to more fully understand ideological communication (Van Dijk, 2006, p 128). While our analysis suggests that these programmes are likely an important site of 'class work', we cannot say how students are actually engaging with these programmes or what identities they might develop as a result over longer periods of time. While we have analysed student quotes and voices from videos on these websites, programme administrators and marketers chose these comments to cultivate a certain image. What our analysis here can highlight is the messages they are transmitting to their potential customers.

As a result, we hope that this study provides a point of departure for future research to better understand how – and to what extent – the discourses we have identified play out in daily life at these programmes, what short- and long-term impact these discourses have on students' identities, and how students and parents use these programmes to create distinction for themselves.

The programmes that we analysed promote opportunities for elite students, as 'shape shifting portfolio people' (Gee, 2004, p 105), to build 'kinder and gentler' elite identities and to reinforce elite distinction, network, and power. In doing so, these programmes and the 'double distinction' they promise – particularly considering that their proliferation parallels the rise of neoliberalism and globalisation – may function as a form of 'class work' rooted in the spirit of capitalism that is behind so many corporate educational reforms.

Notes

[1] We would like to thank Jennifer Gallagher and Sarah Pamperin for their assistance with data collection and Dr Betty Malen for her helpful feedback. All figures are of our own creation.

[2] Corporate elites are one subgroup within this category and refer to those senior executives whose wealth comes from income rather than inheritance.

[3] Students' experiences in elite schools are raced, classed and gendered in ways that not only complicate how elite identities are constructed and embodied, but also undercut the potential social benefits of elite schooling. Often functioning as 'outsiders within' (Cookson and Persell, 1991, p 225), students of colour and

working-class students often experience social isolation as well as interpersonal and institutional racism and classism (Gaztambide-Fernández and DiAquoi, 2010).

[4] We collected data from online searches and programme websites between July and October 2015.

[5] Of course, there are programmes with home bases in other nations that send students abroad. We think it useful, however, to bind our study to looking at a subset of students from one nation for focus and logistical reasons (for example, we encountered technical difficulties in translating promotional materials produced in a variety of languages). Future research should certainly expand the scope of this analysis to include programmes in other countries.

[6] We used the following search terms: 'high school study abroad', 'high school semester programmes', 'high school educational travel abroad', 'high school international travel programmes' and 'high school international volunteering'. We excluded programmes geared toward teachers (for example, EF Educational Tours), as we were interested in programmes that students and/or parents might seek out individually to gain advantage.

[7] These categories are fluid and overlapping; some programmes may fit into multiple categories. Gap year programmes are not included here, since we consider them postsecondary experiences.

[8] For more detailed information on these 47 programmes, please contact the authors.

[9] Thirty of the 47 programmes have been founded since 1990.

SEVEN

Double standards: everyday corporate strategies at an elite school in Argentina

Howard Prosser

In the executive elite school, work is developing one's analytical intellectual powers. Children are continually asked to reason through a problem, to produce intellectual products that are both logically sound and of top academic quality. A primary goal of thought is to conceptualize rules by which elements may fit together in systems and then to apply these rules in solving a problem. Schoolwork helps one to achieve, to excel, to prepare for life. (Anyon, 1980, p 83)

Introduction

The revival of interest in elites and elite education follows directly from the exposure of the market fantasies that led, yet again, to concentrated wealth among the few and expropriated means from many. That such revelations come as a surprise to some, especially those reaping benefits from financial speculation and corporate interests, is a function of capitalism's amnesia. After all, the global recession that has dogged many nations since 2008 was foreshadowed by the implosion of regional economies in south-east Asia, Russia and Latin America. Argentina's spectacular decline in late 2001, for example, saw almost half the population fall into poverty. Many beneficiaries of the neoliberal 1990s came undone. But others retained and expanded their wealth as the economy upturned after 2003 thanks largely to a boom in agricultural exports. Much like any primary-producing economy, Argentina's corporations' successes had roots in the provinces and, within a few years, corporate elites took full advantage of forgetful capital quickly reassembling.

This chapter outlines some of the ways that these corporate elites shore up their social position, by cultivating educational opportunities that maximise local and global currencies of knowledge. In the study of elite education there is a need to define the ways in which the elites being examined employ specific policies – formal and informal – to ensure success for their students and their social class. Much like Anyon's observations more than three decades ago, recent scholarship in the field consistently shows how corporate elites are reproduced with assistance from elite schools. Students learn a range of skills and behaviours that are well suited to success in tertiary education environments as well as in the halls of financial and governmental power.

What needs further elaboration, however, is how elite schools imitate corporate strategies to ensure high student results and thus fortify the schools' reputation and competitiveness in educational markets. Some of these points may seem prosaic, given the ubiquity of market logic, not just in schooling. But the nature of class reproduction through social relations demands consideration not just of class difference but also of class strategies in place (Ball, 2003a). In this sense, scholars working in the space must consider how economic elites derive status from processes of class exploitation (Prosser, 2016) that are 'dissimulated', as Thompson (1990) put it, to obscure social domination and its symbolic mechanisms. Consequently, even everyday policies and practices in elite schools should be read as being defensive class strategies.

Based on historical and ethnographic research, I show here how one elite school in greater Buenos Aires – what I pseudonymise as the Caledonian School – has been drawing upon its corporate culture and capital to transform itself into an innovative, globally oriented institution that is distinct from the sluggish Argentine public system.[1] First, I point to the educational landscape in Argentina and how the schools chosen by corporate elites are increasingly segregated from the other options available, mainly public (meaning state) or low-fee Catholic schools. Second, I position the Caledonian School within this educational landscape, which includes a state sector that has long been resistant to any neoliberal reform agenda. In so doing, it has arguably allowed elite private schools to become more exclusive and innovative. This contextualisation includes a discussion of how the school manages its relationship to the state curriculum through corporate techniques. Third, I signal some curriculum chicanery that allows the Caledonian School to offer such an array of subjects under the state curriculum as well as, more importantly, the International Baccalaureate (IB). The IB is used to target the trajectory of graduates to the relatively new private universities as well as offering a globally recognisable educational commodity. Finally, I conclude with some thoughts on how this situation of social detachment allows elite private schools like

Caledonian to retain a reputation for innovation in comparison with, and thanks to, the torpid state system.

Education and elite education in Argentina

Education in Argentina is increasingly separated between its private and public schools. The variegated nature of the system – with its mix of state, quasi-state and private schools – means that children's schooling experiences differ vastly across the nation. This same divergence is replicated in the capital, Buenos Aires, where the majority of the population lives. As a city divided into 'winners and losers' (Svampa, 2001), the areas that are home to corporate elites have become more and more isolated over the last few decades. Indeed, the shift of elites into private neighbourhoods to the city's north has become the leitmotif of discussions about Latin American inequality (Davis, 2006).

Where elite families live, elite schools propagate. The growth of private schools has certainly gone hand in hand with the expansion of these suburban regions. Key to these schools having a solid reputation for educational excellence is their emulation of the 'public' schools of Britain or the 'preparatory' schools in the United States – both in their appearance and curricula. At the top of these private schools are the high-fee 'English schools', many of which have migrated further north of the city throughout the last century or so.

Fitting this bill, the Caledonian School's eliteness stems from the standards of education it offers, the high cost of the school fees and the corporate class to which it caters.[2] It can be defined as a British-tradition school that is one of Argentina's most prestigious co-educational, independent, private schools catering to students from kindergarten to year 12. It has long been associated with the production of successful business people who go on to work in the local and global corporate sector. This reputation stands in contrast to the state-funded, select-entry elite secondary schools that are closely associated with the *Universidad de Buenos Aires* (UBA). These too are highly regarded, but are attended by students often associated with the governing and cultural elites of the nation (as well as some precocious students from around the city and the nation) (Mendéz, 2013).

Those who attend the Caledonian School tend to come from families headed by business people. The definition of such business is difficult to pinpoint. According to the school's research, as well as my conversations with the leadership team, most businesses are linked to agricultural production or manufacturing. There are exceptions to this rule; but high fees and few scholarships ensure that the school's profile is made up of business people or highly-paid professionals. This corporate expertise also extends to the running of the school, which has managed to navigate the, often vertiginous, circumstances of Argentina's economic past. Private schools there are not allowed to make a profit, but the business acumen of the school board and administration ensures that the school can meet its aspirations. Board members tend to work in the corporate sector, and others in the leadership staff had spent time working in the private sector before returning to their alma mater as teachers.

Such social homogeneity engenders insularity within and between the schools to which Argentine corporate elites send their children. As a result, these elites are further separated from the public system. To be sure, key connections remain, because students are taught the state curriculum as well as English-language ones.[3] But this link is one of only a few. Hence the school is relatively unknown to most *porteños* (locals) I spoke to, and those who did know it were often disparaging about its lack of 'Argentinian-ness'.

This public/private divide is not necessarily new or isolated to Argentina. But the divergence between the two systems has become more pronounced in the last two decades. Such divergence is a sign of the neoliberal times and runs counter to the historic egalitarianism, however mythological, of the Argentine system. Yet, if elsewhere around the world corporatisation is infiltrating the public sector, Argentina remains something of an exception to the rule. Indeed, Argentina's public education system has been regarded as a 'black swan' (Beech and Barrenechea, 2011), swimming against the neoliberal educational tides engulfing public education around the world.

The state continues to have a strong hold on education, and private educational enterprises have limited influence over public schools. Such limits are a direct result of recent social and political history – namely the swift arrival and departure of Argentina's monetarist heyday between 1989 and 2001 – as well as a long tradition of nationalised (and nationalist) schooling and unionised teacher activism (Narodowski and Nores, 2002). This continuing stance was assisted between 2003 and 2015 by the successive Peronist (or Kirchnerist) governments of Nestor Kirchner and Cristina Fernández de Kirchner. *Kirchnerismo's* continuity espoused a new form of populism – based on policies including protectionism, wealth redistribution and human rights – that was consciously anti-neoliberal and anti-elites (Cohen, 2012).

Neoliberal logic nonetheless continues to press against this public system in ways that inspire more innovative thinking on the part of capital (Beech and Barrenechea, 2011). Indeed, the post-2001

Kirchnerist governments, for all their anti-neoliberal rhetoric, instituted social and economic policies necessary to alleviate global market pressures placed on them by important trading partners (Cohen, 2012). Educationally this has seen some corporate partnerships – the exemplar being laptops distributed to every public school child (Martínez, 2012). But the public school system's ongoing resistance to marketisation has also meant that it remains resistant to change of any sort. This suspicion of reform actually reinforces the social divisions both within the public system and between the public and private schools.

This latter division, the classic public versus private trope, is especially pronounced when it comes to exploring the type of schooling on offer in those that cater to corporate elites. But it needs some nuance. Most Argentine private schools are very low-fee Catholic schools with state-subsidised wages. Such schools account for the high participation in private education, especially in Buenos Aires. The Caledonian School, by contrast, falls into a much different definition of private: that of the high-fee bilingual 'English' schools to the north of the city. Such schools have their own particular profiles, based on the expectations of the clientele who send their children there. For the most part, they can be said to offer their students three important attributes for success in life: sound English-language skills, solid social networks and sturdy liberal values.

Private/state interface

However, the school is not entirely free from state scrutiny thanks to its curricula offerings. Caledonian students can leave school having completed exams under the Cambridge IGCSE (at year 10 level), Buenos Aires Province's state curriculum (year 12) and the IB (year 12). Juggling compliance with all three takes some resources on the part of the school, to say nothing of the students themselves. The school must follow the strict standards set by the curriculum bodies and, in the case of the national curriculum, this means dealing with the state inspectors.

There is an important history here about the Caledonian School's relationship to the state. As one of Argentina's oldest private schools, Caledonian has had to negotiate the nation's variable social and political history. For much of the nineteenth century, the school was a parochial school for the children of British migrants, especially Scots, who worked in agriculture and, increasingly, the British-owned railways. The massive investment that the latter brought to the nation meant that a number of 'English schools' emerged to service the needs of the

British community, which was affluent, if not elite, in comparison to the local population (Rock, 2008).

By the early twentieth century, as Argentina was seized by the virulent enthusiasms of nationalism, the schools of these foreign business people came under increasing scrutiny following consolidation of the Argentine education system (Narodowski and Andrada, 2010). Educational inspectors visited the schools regularly, perhaps every three months, to keep an eye on what was being presented in class as well as the conditions of the school itself. These visits were usually a formality, but sometimes the inspector was more critical. In 1909, for example, the General Inspector of Private Schools expressed to the school a 'dissatisfaction with the scarcity of maps of the Argentina [sic] and the absolute want of pictures of the great Argentine patriots and intimated that these wants must be supplied immediately (School Logbook, 1896–1926). Within three days, a dozen framed portraits of the nation's founders arrived.

The state's nationalistic touch became even heavier between the 1940s and the 1960s, when all private schools were brought into the state system through a series of incremental policy changes favouring a state quasi-monopoly of all schooling. Some schools, like Caledonian, remained independent, but were made to offer the state curriculum alongside the other foreign-language curricula (Morduchowicz, 2005). This situation established the precedent for the current dual curriculum approach. The Argentine state component is still overseen by visits from inspectors. The state education department's more traditional approaches are tolerated by a private school with resources and nous that outstrip their public counterparts

Such elite schools' autonomy makes them quite different from their public counterparts, whether elite or not, in terms of the amount of capital available for everything: from infrastructure and materials to curriculum and pedagogy. On the one hand, an elite private school like Caledonian is at the forefront of educational innovation and prides itself for being so. On the other hand, the school benefits from remaining a part of the state system, with which it strongly identifies, and is no longer a British school in Argentina but an Argentine school with a British heritage and global outlook.

State inspection

A serendipitous fieldwork experience provides an instructive tale of the school's strategic engagement with the state. It occurred during an interview with the director of the agency that represents English-speaking schools in Argentina and rolls out the Cambridge IGCSE curriculum. The conversation turned to the issue of how the state's inspectors were dealt with by private schools. She said there was someone in the office who knew a lot about this from their experience in school leadership. Leaping up from her desk, she brought in her colleague, Rosario, who was more than happy to talk at length about the way inspections work.

The ministry of education assigns inspectors to visit specific schools unexpectedly two or three times a year. Rosario explained: "Some of them are nice and there to help you; others are there to see if all of the birth certificates are in order and IDs ... you know, very bureaucratic type of things." Any issues that arise tend to be based on the inspectors' personalities and the relationship between the inspector and the school. She suggested that the schools that had a familiarity with the inspector had fewer fault-finding experiences. This relationship was first and foremost strategic on the part of the schools.

As part of this strategy, elite private schools employed former inspectors to oversee state compliance. The recruitment of the state's inspectors, or other education department employees, in this way is strategically sound according to the ambitions of elite private schooling. The Caledonian School, for example, employed a lawyer with experience in the state education department to deal with its compliance. Accumulating symbolic knowledge and co-opting, or headhunting, staff are classic corporate moves, from which the education sector is not immune. The knowledge that comes with these employees, some of whom are not always former inspectors, is extremely useful to the schools when planning their curriculum. As Rosario, pointed out, they work with the other administrative staff to ensure that the school complies with the requirements. Today, this inspection is about bureaucratic adherence, rather than checking the number of portraits of Argentina's founding fathers. But they are very strict about schools meeting the state's curriculum requirements.

Managing state inspection is just one part of how the schools like Caledonian organise multiple curriculum demands. The other is how the array of subjects fit within a constrained timetable. The Caledonian School was particularly astute in this regard. A number of secondary teachers spoke to me about the curriculum chicanery that made timetables more manageable. This meant that certain subjects in the IGCSE and the IB curricula were taught as part of the state curriculum. These subject's titles were often broad enough to meet the state's requirements as well as the international stipulations. A subject could be called *chemica* (chemistry), for example, but then teach some form of science, not necessarily exclusively chemistry, so as to prepare students for the IGCSE and the IB. When it came to state inspections, however, these specific details of classroom learning were not disclosed.

This is not to say that this curricular overlap was an underhand arrangement. In fact, the Caledonian School complies with the state curriculum by choosing a specific route available almost exclusively to bilingual schools. Most schools choose to follow an arrangement that defines the subject requirements, but within the Province of Buenos Aires curriculum there is a possibility to follow particular guidelines (*orientaciones*) that allow for specialisations in particular subjects. I was told that the leadership team decided that the guideline approach gave the school the most latitude within curriculum requirements. There are no specific demands from each subject – except some prescriptions for History – so the international curricula are easily accommodated.

This decision shows a degree of innovative thinking within the school that is in keeping with a corporatised logic. That is, the administration had to think creatively to maximise the efficiency of the teachers' and students' time, given the volume of offerings at the school both within and outside the formal curricula. That the subjects met the requirements of both the local and international curricula – whatever the subjects may have been called – is a way for the students to complete the subject demands within what is a very long school day (usually 8am to 4pm excluding extracurricular activities).

In other words, the way that the school is arranged fits the corporate ideals with which it has long been associated. Demands on teachers' and students' time correspond with the corporate sector's overwork ethic and credentialism obsession. As such, the Caledonian School is regarded as leading educational innovation in Argentina. Its leadership team is in contact with other elite schools around the world, especially in the United States, and keeps its staff up to date with curriculum and pedagogic developments. The introduction of a service-learning curriculum followed suit from other elite schools in North America and Europe; so too has the whole school's migration to a new state-of-the-art campus, which was designed with a mind to information and communication technologies (ICT) and pedagogy beyond classrooms and disciplines.

The state system pales in comparison. The state system continues in what many educators would regard as an old-fashioned approach to teaching and learning with massive disparities between different parts of the capital and the nation (Gvirtz and Beech, 2008). When it comes to ICT, the post-2010 national roll-out of laptops for all state students did not come with the same degree of pedagogic support that is possible in a well-financed independent school. In this sense, the independent school's autonomy fits well with the entrepreneurial desire for innovation free from the complexity and inertia that come with demands for equity and access in state systems.

Corporate elites have the wherewithal and mindset to remove themselves from this system, which they believe, often with good reason, is stymied by lumbering populism – hence the success of schools like Caledonian in producing graduates for whom the world is truly their oyster. True to Marx and Engel's (1888) classic assessment of the bourgeoisie, today's corporate elites remain the most revolutionary class in the ways that they retain their dominance and reproduction through innovative entrepreneurship. This corporate outlook suffuses almost all ways of thinking about the world. Even if corporate or economic elites must ameliorate or disavow any claims to superiority or inhumanity through commitments to social responsibility (Schleef, 2006) – or, in the case of education, to service learning (Prosser, 2015) – they can still hone a niche for themselves in society via private schooling that manages the state education system to their advantage, as well as offering international qualifications to its students.

Why IB?

The Argentine education system is bound to the nation's liberal traditions. Universal education remains a pillar of Argentine society. Nowhere is this belief better illustrated than in the opportunity for all high-school graduates to attend university. Public universities, especially the largest and best-regarded UBA, permit anyone to enrol in the first year of studies, provided that they have a secondary certificate. This ideal makes for large undergraduate classes as well as a very high attrition rate early on (to say nothing of blindness to other factors – like socioeconomic status – influencing the likely success of students). A university system such as this is obviously out of step with the corporatisation of tertiary education around the globe. But the general point is that the successful completion of high school guarantees university entry for Argentine students.

Such assurance raises an obvious question: if university is open to all, then why does Caledonian School and its compeers bother teaching students the IB curriculum? When I raised the question of the IB's import with the staff at the school, there was certainly a consensus about the IB diploma's value. Most teachers spoke of its grounding the students in the discipline of studying for exams and the rigour of having to write on an extended essay topic. The IB curriculum, with its inclusion of a service component, also dovetailed neatly with the school's new emphasis on service-learning. One teacher agreed that the IB gave students a certain discipline for study that serves them well when it comes to university life: 'They need to be aware of what are the tools necessary for a particular exam and why it is necessary to know the nature of the exam'. With an IB in hand, Caledonian graduates emerged in good stead for tertiary success.

So the IB offers students something by way of grounding in content and skills. But its popularity among elite schools, as well as their imitators, means that its presence signifies something beyond mere pedagogy and as part of what I have elsewhere called an 'economy of eliteness' (Prosser, 2016). That is, the IB works as part of a symbolic and material value that improves the school's brand and thus its eliteness and appeal to elites. For elite schools in Argentina, offering international curricula is part of a consumer performance that is now part and parcel of elite private education.

When it comes to the IB, three such exchangeable values are patent. One is that the IB provides rigour and prestige. As Maxwell and Aggleton (2015) have pointed out in their discussion of elite education in England, the IB assists non-selective elite schools in distinguishing themselves from other local schools by offering a globally recognised curriculum. Such exclusivity was not, as Tarc (2010) has pointed out, the IB organisation's original, or even its continuing, liberal intention; but the reality to date is that the diploma is synonymous with eliteness. Having the IB in place means that the standard of education offered is already vetted as well as seen as a cut above merely the state-based curriculum. Such differentiation is certainly part of the Caledonian School's offerings. Its reputation as a school with connections to British academic standards in the past transitioned smoothly to the more globally ambitious IB system.

This change brings up the second point: namely that the IB's introduction in the late 1990s coincided with a stronger emphasis on global connections. Caledonian's British heritage remained important, but other changes were made to orient the school in multiple ways. These included forging links with more schools and organisations around the world, particularly with the United States. Then followed the expansion of the students' third language option, which was French, to include Portuguese and Mandarin. All of these moves were signs of global economic times.[4]

Finally, and more practically, Argentina's private universities recognise the IB as an indicator of tertiary potential. Such recognition is certainly due to the IB establishing itself as an international marker of student achievement. It should be said, the IB is not the only factor taken into account by private universities accepting new undergraduates. Students without an IB diploma are still accepted. Yet there is definitely a clear connection between the IB's provision within private independent schools and a preference among their students for private university education. That is, recognition of the IB is not merely about the likelihood of academic ability; it is also works as a signifier of cultural familiarity. In other words, Caledonian graduates' qualifications are easily recognisable to the public and private universities of Argentina and elsewhere around the globe.

The IB, for all its global credentials, is just as valuable in the Argentine context as it is overseas. Few Caledonian students go straight to tertiary study overseas; those who do, usually do so having once received an undergraduate degree from a local university. But the desire for overseas legitimation continues in Argentina. In a nation that has long been enamoured with European-ness, the IB works as yet another mode of distinction within the local setting. The IB's value is thus overinflated by elite schools in comparison to the state curriculum. That is, the IB is a marker of eliteness within the local context, if only among certain groups like the corporate elites that choose to send their children to schools like Caledonian.

No doubt this is not merely the case in Argentina and, as such, the IB deserves further scrutiny in the hands of elite schools around the globe. Resnik (2008, 2012) has started such probing, by pointing out how the IB works as a means of idealising global workers and leaders. But much of these global ideals circulate more effectively at the local level. The IB's popularity among elite schools around the world should be read as part of this process of differentiation and deserves greater critical scrutiny. As the qualification is picked up by non-elite schools in the future, it will be interesting to see whether elite schools still find it as valuable.

All of this amounts to the further separation of public and elite private education within Argentina. The IB's prestige is part of the elite appeal of schools like Caledonian, and this flows into the growing reputations of a key number of private Argentinian universities (Zelaya, 2012). That said, these universities do offer a range of scholarships to students from around Argentina and are thus not completely exclusive. Nonetheless, whereas in the past a majority of Caledonian graduates went on to study at UBA, with a few attending universities in the US or the UK, today the majority attend the private universities that emerged during the neoliberal 1990s. The consumption of elite education is a distinct marker of social class and opportunity for improving mobility capital within Argentina as much as outside it (Kaufmann et al, 2004).

Conclusion

The Caledonian School offers a case study for the situation of educational corporatisation as well as the education of corporate elites in Argentina. The school's formula has become a desirable commodity among the corporate elites from the northern suburbs of Buenos Aires. When positioned within the educational landscape of the greater Buenos Aires region, the peculiarity of such high-fee private education is pronounced: these schools represent an alternative education system for elites for whom the public system was never considered as an option. Free from any public obligation, independent private schools like Caledonian have the means and the scope for innovation that far exceed the stymied anti-neoliberal public system.

Elite private schools like Caledonian are therefore establishing their own trajectory. To some, this may not be a bad thing. Independent schools are truly independent when their coffers are not reliant on state subsidy. But the corollary to this scenario is a form of social segregation, in which future opportunities for elites are assured thanks, in large part, to their ability to interpret, navigate and capitalise on global educational trends. Such educational market-savvy goes hand in hand with the leverage that allows for the paying of high fees to schools like Caledonian. In short, educational choice is just one cog in the social formation and reproduction of elites.

In Argentina, elite private schools of Caledonian's calibre cater to corporate elites in a way that legitimises and reinforces their eliteness. This process may not be anything new when it comes to dominant classes asserting their positions. It is important to see how such assertion takes place in a political climate that has been at odds with neoliberalism since 2001. Thus, in the study of elite schools – or other institutions – quotidian policies and practices taken from the corporate sphere serve elites by strategically responding to social and political circumstances of the day. The resulting double standard strengthens the ongoing social segregation of corporate elites from Argentina's education system and its society more generally.

Notes
[1]   The examples I provide are based on six months of fieldwork at the school and in the city of Buenos Aires during 2011. (This work was under the auspices of the Australian Research Council-funded 'Elite Independent Schools in Globalizing

Circumstances', based at Monash University and led by Jane Kenway.) Such examples seek to highlight the way that elite schools in Argentina function. Like all site-specific research, my points do not necessarily apply to all schools considered 'elite' by Argentine society, but they do offer some sense of the educational context in which private schools that cater to corporate elites are increasingly different, if not completely independent, from their state and quasi-state counterparts.

[2] I have explored the issue of elites and class elsewhere (Prosser, 2016). Here I follow the lead of Savage and Williams (2008a, p 9) by 'side-stepping the debate about precise definitions of elites' and focusing instead on how the very wealthy have prospered under contemporary capitalism.

[3] State curriculum means that decided by the Province of Buenos Aires, which is overseen by a federal Ministry of Education. This means that there are regional differences within the Argentine education system.

[4] The school had also been considering the IB for some time before its implementation – the earliest mooting on the IB appeared in the school principal's reflection in the 1975 yearbook.

EIGHT

(Re)producing elites: meritocracy, the state and the politics of the curriculum in Singapore

Leonel Lim

Introduction

Meritocracy today is no longer as Singaporeans have come to know it. In the wake of what the Prime Minister of Singapore himself admits as the city-state's 'watershed elections' of 2011 (Lee, 2012) – which saw, among others, the ruling People's Action Party (PAP) capturing a historically dismal 60% of the popular vote and two cabinet ministers losing their electoral seats – the founding ideology of the world's most successful marriage between high capitalism and modern authoritarianism has come under increasing strain and disapprobation.

Critics charge that the logic and practice of meritocracy have, over time, engendered an elitist class that narrowly (re-)fashions 'merit' in its own image, and whose considerable growth in influence in matters of social and economic policy runs afoul of its diminishing ability to represent the perspectives of the 'broad masses' (K.P. Tan, 2008; Lim, 2013; see also Desker, 2013). The government has responded, in part rhetorically, by injecting into the public discourse on meritocracy a dizzying slew of compound terms – 'inclusive meritocracy', 'compassionate meritocracy', 'meritocracy of equals', 'continuing meritocracy' (Goh, 2013; Tharman, 2013) – all aimed at recovering the egalitarian dimension of what was once taken boldly as an article of faith.

As this chapter will show, however, at least in the education system wherein lies the colloquial starting point, these tensions – as well as attempts to mitigate them – are not new. After first briefly discussing how in Singapore the concept of meritocracy captures both elitist and egalitarian aspirations, the second section considers the ways in which Singapore's education policies have historically vacillated between these conflicting dimensions. This broad survey paves the way towards reframing understandings of meritocracy as not just an inherently unstable concept but also, as developed in the third section, an ideology that is negotiated and contested by dominant social groups as these seek to legitimise a given distribution of social power.

It is, however, important to recognise that dominant ideologies are not only produced in the education system; they are also *reproduced* through it, often in far more complex ways. To see how these ideologies and their tensions animate the very mechanism that sits at the centre of the reproduction of (in)equality – the curriculum – this chapter concludes with an account of how one particular subject area is differently taught in an elite school and a mainstream school. For two reasons this conceptual engagement with a number of themes central to the modern predicament of meritocracy becomes important in any analysis of corporate elites and education reform. First, it illuminates how elite knowledge and dispositions – often drawn from the funds of social, economic and cultural capital of elites in society – become reified in the school curriculum and the forms these take. Second, it accounts for the role of high-status knowledges in the elaboration of class formation and post-developmental state initiatives linked to the parable of modernisation in increasingly corporatised nations such as Singapore.

Meritocracy, elitism and egalitarianism

Meritocracy commonly involves the assumption that 'people with the same level of merit – IQ plus effort – should have the same chance of success' (Swift, 2003, p 24). In thus focusing on 'careers open to talents' (Rawls, 1971, p 65), meritocracy, in its egalitarian moment, signals merit as the rule or principle that governs how limited resources and rewards in a society are to be distributed (Jencks, 1988). This ensemble of ideas central to our understandings of meritocracy, however, remains potentially contradictory. Equality of opportunity requires as well a principle of non-discrimination: individuals should be selected based only on their talents and qualifications for the position and not on their race, class or gender. Yet, as has been multiply demonstrated in the US and elsewhere, categories of race, gender and class do afford unequal social benefits, both within and outside schools (Apple, 1995).

This contradiction is aptly demonstrated in Singapore. Historically, at the time of independence in 1965, the principle of non-discrimination (or multiracialism) was foundational in establishing the 'fairness' of Singapore's sociopolitical system vis-à-vis the affirmative action policies of Malaysia (from which, following a brief merger, Singapore was bitterly expelled). More recently, however, the same principle has been leveraged to 'explain' (away) the subordinate role of the large population of non-Chinese minority races who lag behind in areas of life such as politics, income, language dominance and education (Rahim, 1998). But naive appeals to a categorical good faith in non-discrimination can give meritocracy the veneer of equality, while simultaneously masking the real advantages and disadvantages that have been differentially distributed across a society (Jencks, 1988). Or worse, it can lead to the privatisation of blame – as biological/cultural determinism (Barr, 1999) – among groups that have traditionally been underserved by society. Indeed, to the extent that such a 'charade of meritocracy' (Barr, 2006) evacuates a concerted focus at a politics of difference – one that foregrounds what Fraser (1997) calls needs recognition and needs redistribution – the egalitarian dimension of meritocracy is not left unthreatened.

This moves us to another understanding of meritocracy, one that is, however, less interested in providing everyone with equal *rights* to resources, and more concerned about revealing the *right* person to manage resources in order to maximise the average level of wellbeing in a society (Jencks, 1988; K.P. Tan, 2008). This rendering of meritocracy involves motivating individuals to do the best they can. Implicit is the idea that through a fierce competition for educational resources and, later, material rewards, human talents may be developed to their fullest potential (K.P. Tan, 2008). Given, however, the ways in which the economic and cultural capital of one generation are often converted into the educational capital of the next (Bourdieu, 1984), such a focus on efficiency and competition can displace the egalitarian aspects of meritocracy as well. The then Singapore Prime Minister Goh Chok Tong once warned that if social disparities and unequal rewards did not exist, those with initiative and skills 'will lose the incentive to contribute their utmost to the economy. Then everyone will be poorer off. Do not begrudge them their high salaries ... for getting the big prizes in the free market' (cited in Kang, 2005, p 3). Understood thus, as pointed out by K.P. Tan (2008, p9), meritocracy in practice often translates into 'an ideology of inequality', a belief that an unequal distribution of resources will ultimately be beneficial to the general – if not entire – population. Indeed, in all this the state and its elite leadership have played no small role in articulating and re-articulating the forms and meanings embedded in its discourse of meritocracy and, as we will see in the next section, fashioning a range of education policies in its image.

Tensions in the education system

In Singapore, this emphasis on developing a small group of talented individuals who will eventually work to maximise the overall wellbeing of society clearly shows itself in the workings of the education system. Beginning at the primary level, for example, the *Gifted Education Programme* identifies and tracks the top 1% of nine year olds into a special and separate academic route, in order to 'develop [in them] intellectual rigour, humane values and creativity [and] to prepare them for responsible leadership and service to country and society' (Ministry of Education, 2011a). To be sure, the ideological resources regularly marshalled to justify these elitist impulses often allude to such (putative) facts as that 'Singapore is a small nation with only human resources to rely on for its progress and prosperity. It is to the advantage of the nation that the gifted are helped and nurtured' (Ministry of Education, 2011a).

At the secondary level, the *Integrated Programme* allows students who are 'clearly university-bound' to enrol into separate tracks that bypass the standard General Certificate of Education Ordinary Level examinations at the end of secondary school and proceed directly to the Advanced Level examinations at the end of high school (Ministry of Education, 2011b). Such a provision further demonstrates the elitist strand in the education system; schools offering the Integrated Programme, by optimising the time freed up from preparing for the Ordinary Level examinations, will be able to 'stretch pupils and provide greater breadth in the academic and non-academic curriculum' (Ministry of Education, 2011b). For this crème de la crème, yet another option consists in bypassing the Advanced Level examinations altogether, obtaining instead the more prestigious International Baccalaureate diploma or a diploma from the local National University of Singapore High School of Mathematics and Science.

Other measures that clearly articulate the system's elitist orientations include:

- the Independent Schools scheme, under which selected academically top-performing schools enjoy greater financial and curricular autonomy, which translates into the school-based development of niche programmes that, in turn, heightens the prestige of the schools and their students;
- the families of schools structure that allows well-established secondary schools and junior colleges to provide preferential admission for students from their feeder schools, effectively making

it more difficult for students from mainstream schools to gain a place of study;
- the Special Assistance Plan schools, where academic high-performers may enrol into schools designed to immerse students in Chinese culture and values, triggering concerns of ethnic segregation, as well as the apprehension that, in a multicultural society, these Chinese-cultured elites will find difficulty in connecting to non-elite and non-Chinese counterparts in their professional and social adult lives – indeed, in a poll by a major local newspaper, 82% of students from these schools admitted to having no close friends of other races (Yong and Zaccheus, 2012).

This meritocratic drive to nurture a pool of elites, however, takes place largely in the absence of a level playing field and, as pointed out earlier, when coupled with an overt principle of non-discrimination obscures the fact that students in Singapore stem from different socioeconomic backgrounds and go to school differently prepared. As a survey conducted in 2007 by the same major local newspaper reveals, wealthier students from English-speaking homes predominate in the elite schools (Kwek, 2007). Seventy-one per cent of students from these schools speak English (the major medium of instruction in all Singapore schools) at home, while only 34% of students from non-elite schools do so. From 2001 to 2005, one third of the government's Public Service Commission scholarship holders in Singapore came from families with household incomes of more than S$10,000 (US$8,000) a month, while only 7% came from families with monthly household incomes of less than S$2,000 (Lim and Kwek, 2006). More recently, in noting that up to 70% of parents in some 'brand name' schools hold university degrees (compared to 7–13% of parents in other schools), former Prime Minister Lee Kuan Yew has admitted that such backgrounds figure as a crucial advantage for the students in these schools (Chang, 2011).

Further entangled with the problem of class-based disparities is that of ethnic inequalities. Data from the 2010 population census indicate that the Chinese are significantly overrepresented in local universities, forming 86% of the total enrolment in 2010, while constituting 77% of the overall population. Malays (5.5%) and Indians (6.8%) are correspondingly underrepresented in tertiary institutions (Department of Statistics, 2011). From 1966 to 2005, of the 200 winners of Singapore's most prestigious scholarship, the President's Scholarship, only 14 (6.4%) were non-Chinese (Barr and Skrbis, 2008). While we note that Malay and Indian students have made significant improvements in educational attainment over the last decades, their public examination results continue to lag behind those of their Chinese counterparts (Ministry of Education, 2010; see also Kang, 2005). Indeed, the former prime minister has recently asserted that the Malays would never close the gap in educational attainment with the Indians and Chinese 'because as they improve, the others also improve' (K.Y. Lee, 2011).[1]

These divisive impacts and elitist orientations have, on many occasions, required explicit mitigation by the Ministry of Education (MOE). In a bid to ensure that students from the lower socioeconomic classes would not be left behind, in the early 1990s, the government started providing educational grants to individual students between the ages of six and 16 (recently extended to 17) that could be used towards paying for supplemental school-based activities, and also launched the Learning Support Programme that catered specifically to primary one and two students who lacked basic literacy skills. In 1997 and in the years that followed, several policies under the *Thinking Schools, Learning Nation* framework also aimed to contain the growing disparity in educational provision. Among others, these included the promulgation of an *Ability-Driven Education* philosophy that promised to develop every child's talents and abilities to the maximum; a new National Education curriculum that sought to create a shared sense of nationhood and social cohesion; and the promotion of educational marketisation and competition in schools that was to serve as a catalyst for greater diversity and choice in the educational system in order to – so the argument went – improve overall standards for everyone.

Since 2004, efforts have also been taken to soften the harshness and rigidity of the system's tracking mechanism. These have proceeded by:

- merging the different academic tracks at both the primary and secondary levels;
- gradually abolishing the *Gifted Education Programme* at the secondary level, so that there was no separate track for gifted students;[2]
- encouraging greater interaction between students in the Special Assistance Plan schools and students of other ethnicities, as well as between students in the *Gifted Education Programme* at the primary level and their mainstream schoolmates;
- providing more support and opportunities to students with special educational needs;
- introducing avenues of upward mobility from lower-prestige academic tracks to higher-prestige ones;
- allowing, under the Direct School Admissions (DSA) exercise, select secondary schools (and later junior colleges and polytechnics) the

autonomy to provide preferential admission to a predetermined percentage of students on the grounds of non-academic achievements (such as in sports or the performing arts).

More recently, the reports of the Primary and Secondary Education Review Committees in 2008 and 2010 respectively have continued such a focus on supporting the weakest students in the system. Among other measures:

- language facilitators are now provided to schools, to ease students' transition from their home mother tongue languages to English;
- specialised schools are established for Normal (Technical) (the least prestigious stream in secondary schooling) students as alternative pathways offering industry-focused courses;
- student centres housed in school premises seek to raise the level of in-school support available to students from disadvantaged families, by providing them with a familiar and ready source of advice;
- movements are made towards reducing the traditionally high emphasis on summative assessments in the lower primary levels – especially significant given that students from less advantaged backgrounds possess lesser means of harnessing, through out of school enrichment programmes, a host of crucial examination skills and strategies.

Finally, and responding to the Prime Minister's call in the 2013 National Day Rally address to keep pathways upwards open to all, the MOE has sought to widen what counts as merit for the DSA exercise, by:

- including various personality traits such as resilience, character and leadership;
- ensuring that a number of prestigious primary schools do not become enclaves of exclusivity, by requiring that these schools set aside 40 places each year for new students whose families have no prior affiliation with the school;
- providing opportunities for students in the Normal (Academic) stream to take subjects at the Express level;
- helping to raise the profile of mainstream schools, by appointing to them senior principals previously at the helm of more prestigious schools.

The outcomes of these policies and initiatives, however, have been largely mixed. The National Education curriculum, for instance, continues to reflect the deep divisions of the education system, by prescribing different messages for students of different academic groups (J. Tan, 2008a). Distinguishing between potential leaders and other postsecondary students, the former were to be imbued with 'creative and imaginative capacities' in order for them to 'forge breakthroughs in the knowledge-based economy', while the latter were to be 'willing to strive, take pride in work, [and] value working with others' (Ministry of Education, 1997, p 2). One might also argue that the removal of a separate and centrally regulated gifted track at the secondary level did little to bridge the elite–mainstream divide; most of the gifted students graduating from primary schools are already opting for the elite Integrated Programme schools, most of which have developed their own school-based gifted education programmes. Despite the overtones of fair equality of opportunity and a larger definition of what counts as merit that accompanied the philosophy of an Ability-Driven Education, much of the actual efforts that went into its instantiation – such as the introduction of the Integrated Programme, the International Baccalaureate diploma, and the increase in number of independent schools – remained focused on strengthening the infrastructure for elite education. Indeed, the schools offering direct admissions are mostly well-established schools, and interested students with non-academic talents would still need to score close to the regular cut-off score to be eligible. Also, in admitting such qualities as resilience and leadership into the selection criteria, there is the concern that schools may be turning character into another commodity that middle-class families may be better placed to capitalise on.

Finally, as J. Tan (2008b, p 28) surmises on reviewing the literature on educational marketisation, 'it is highly contestable whether fostering competition does improve the quality of education for *all* students and promote greater choice and diversity for parents and students' (emphasis added). Indeed, the ways in which markets typically respond to the demands of the middle class have been well documented in the US and elsewhere (Ball, 1993), so much so that the possibility that the introduction of neoliberal educational policies in Singapore would instead reinforce the elitist strand in the system remains one that cannot be dismissed. As a case in point, again consider how, within a climate of supposed school choice, the appointment of senior principals to less established schools would likely encourage the active monitoring among parents of the track records of all principals – and the resources (time, networks, and so on) which middle-class parents have at their disposable that would better enable them to benefit from these strategies.

While the state in Singapore retains stringent control over the regulation and provision of education, a number of the reforms discussed earlier provided by the state have sought to offer greater latitude in how schools are administered and the curricular options available. Yet much of this increased autonomy is in fact only available at schools that have produced sterling academic results: such schools, like those under the Independent Schools scheme mentioned previously, can provide a higher level of curricular customisation that responds to its students and their discerning parents, a larger proportion of whom hail from wealthier backgrounds (J. Tan, 2008b).

In delving deeper into the production and reproduction of elites, then, it becomes imperative to understand the forms that such curricular differentiations and customisations take, and the ways they both connect to the forms of intellectual and academic capital that are privileged in the corporate and state arenas (Bourdieu, 1996), as well as the subjective identities and aspirations that they encourage. The next section turns to such a discussion.

Meritocracy, ideology and the curriculum

In all this, I have been pointing to the tensions between meritocracy's elitist and egalitarian dimensions, and the ways in which the state and/or other dominant social groups have sought to respond to these contradictory demands, often by emphasising meritocracy's social utility and beneficence. I now want to tie these insights together, to make a number of points about the workings of meritocracy as an ideology – one that, *despite* its tensions, nevertheless projects the partial views of these groups with a sense of public authority and objectivity.

For a start, we might raise (if only to set aside) commonplace definitions of ideology as the imposition of 'false consciousness' (Freire, 1970),[3] or the indoctrination of a stable body of knowledge and beliefs (Siegel, 1988). Rather, I want to propose a more dynamic and nuanced reading. Indeed, it is probably limiting to think of ideologies as beliefs at all. They are instead sets of 'lived meanings, practices, and social relations that are often internally inconsistent if not contradictory' (Apple, 1995, p 14). Not unlike the rendering earlier in this chapter of how meritocracy in Singapore works to rationalise the 'value' of inequality, ideologies contain elements within themselves that see right to the heart of the unequal benefits of a society *and* at the same time tend also to acquiesce in the relations and practices that maintain the hegemony of dominant classes. Because ideologies contain these elements of 'good' and 'bad' sense within them, they are, as Gramsci

(1986) (one of the most astute observers of the relationship between ideology and power) insists, always contested and struggled over. Ideological hegemony thus involves winning people over to one side or the other. It is here that the propagation of terms such as 'compassionate meritocracy' and 'meritocracy of equals' seeks precisely the naturalisation as 'common sense' a set of essentially contested ideas. As the previous discussion readily demonstrates, institutions such as the education system figure as crucial sites, where such struggles take place and where dominant ideologies are produced *and* reproduced.

This last point is worth stressing. In thus reframing meritocracy as ideology, what becomes exposed are the often covert relations between schools and society in sustaining particular distributions of power. To be sure, ideology – and the power relations and categories it speaks to ('elite', 'mainstream', 'merit', 'high-status knowledge', and so on) – depends for its continued legitimacy on the discursive elaboration by various agents and agencies in the form of everyday practices. The curriculum figures essentially here. By prescribing through its forms of knowledge and experiences particular competencies, identities and desires, it functions more than a little powerfully as a 'symbolic ruler of consciousness' (Bernstein, 1990, p 180).

In the remaining space, then, I want to focus on the role of school curricula in the creation and recreation of the ideological hegemony of dominant social groups. Drawing on some of my empirical work from elsewhere (Lim, 2015), I provide a glimpse of how, in Singapore, meritocracy as an ideology endures in the ways that critical thinking is both taught and talked about in two very different schools: the elite Queen's High,[4] an independent school offering the Integrated Programme and whose students go on to enrol into the best universities both locally and abroad; and the mainstream Valley Point Secondary which, like most of the secondary schools in Singapore, offers a mixture of Express and Normal tracks and where a large number of its graduates find their places in the local polytechnics and vocational institutes of education.

Interest in critical thinking among Singapore's schools is hardly new (Tan, 2016). Following what it considers to be strategic directions towards preparing its citizens for the challenges of the 21st century, the MOE has in recent years positioned critical thinking as one of the central tenets of its *Thinking Schools, Learning Nation* curriculum reform. Speaking on the importance of critical thinking in the new century, the then education minister pointed out that:

'[t]he nature and content of work in future will increasingly be knowledge-based. To succeed in this new economic landscape, our students entering the workforce must not only be skilled and technologically savvy, but also be creative and adaptable. They must be able to think critically, come up with innovative solutions to problems, and work effectively as individuals and in teams.' (Teo, 2000, unpaged)

Yet, while all schools are to emphasise the development of critical thinking – which the MOE broadly defines as 'knowing what questions to ask, what information you need and the value of different sources of information' (Ng, 2008, unpaged) – there is a dearth of published work looking at the divergent ways that schools engage in these efforts. The fact that in Singapore the MOE plays an enlarged role in the provision of subject syllabuses and curricular materials does not preclude different schools from taking up a variety of approaches when it comes to the teaching of a subject that, although venerated at the level of policy discourse, does not come under the purview of any one academic discipline – or of any examination offering. On the contrary, given the traditional classification of critical thinking as 'high-status' knowledge (Oakes, 1985), we might well expect significant differences in the way it is taught.

To begin with, consider Valley Point Secondary's approach to 'infusing' critical thinking across its academic subjects. Rather than being taught within the confines of a single discipline, students encounter, in their language, mathematics, science and humanities lessons, teachers' explicit emphases on the need to think critically. This wide focus, however, is underpinned by a narrow instrumental rationality. Not only does the teaching of critical thinking in these classrooms invariably draw upon a set of subject-specific content knowledge (memorisation of formulas, technical details, historical facts, and so on), but in almost every instance the lone criterion of critical thought is the student's ability to answer a specific question with an equally specific response (or a specific way of arriving at that response). With the pedagogic interaction thus strongly framed (Bernstein, 1990), students have very little input as to what they are to think critically about, and are consequently availed of very little room for variation and originality in their responses. Indeed, on such a curriculum, critical thinking is communicated as being a technical skill employed in solving the 'difficult' questions in students' work; the discourse of critical thinking is often explicitly connected to exigencies founded in tests and assignments, with the former embellished and presented as a way of improving one's performance in the latter.

Such an understanding of critical thinking cannot be more different from what the subject stands for at the elite Queen's High. Here, critical thinking is conceptualised and taught through the school's four-year philosophy programme, where particular attention is given to a host of intellectual standards such as logic, clarity, precision, accuracy, depth, and so on. Often revolving around discussions on philosophical and current issues that students profess interest in, the framing of the pedagogic interaction here is considerably weaker. Teachers adopt the roles of facilitators, and students are encouraged from the start not only to employ these thinking standards in their discussions, but also – and perhaps what is most noteworthy about the programme – to be actively involved in the critique of their own and their peers' exhibition of these skills. Taught this way, under the auspices of a discipline that is itself not part of the national high-stakes examinations, critical thinking at Queen's High centres less on the mastery of any given academic content than on the seemingly gratuitous development of intellectual autonomy and the dispositions of inquiry, exploration and reflectiveness – all traits that, we note, are highly prized in leaders.

Yet it needs to be pointed out that this idea of gratuitousness bespeaks the workings of a more subtle cultural politics and is hardly inconsequential to our analysis of the power relations maintained by the social distribution of knowledge/competencies. As Bernstein (1990), Bourdieu (1996) and others have consistently pointed out, elite educational institutions have historically founded their symbolic capital as 'guardians of intrinsic educational values' (Beck, 2002, p 620) on the insulation between the knowledge they consecrate and the 'profanity' of economic rationalities. On the one hand, far from simply adding to the pool of knowledge workers, the critical thinking curriculum at Queen's High aspires towards the nurturing of leaders imbued with such elite rationalities. On the other hand, critical thinking curricula such as those found in mainstream schools like Valley Point continue to respond to the knowledge economy's call for a workforce appropriately skilled and disciplined in what Harvey (2007) identifies as the technologies of information processing – capacities of information analysis, data handling and problem-solving. To the extent that thinking skills are prized in these jobs, workers will need to be outwardly responsive to whatever material they may be asked to think about. Thus driven by an instrumental rationality, the teaching of critical thinking for these non-elites is projected as a practice in some task-based context where the subject takes on a consumable 'property' aspect and is valorised only insofar as it produces an extrinsic exchange value.

From these examples it should be clear that even as – or more accurately, precisely because – the discourse of critical thinking is applied to all students, what requires attention are the covert ways through which the ideology of meritocracy acts to selectively recontextualise both the form and the content of the subject in the process of its transmission and acquisition. Such 'pedagogic recontextualizations', as Bernstein (1990) reminds us, are always emblematic of a constellation of social ideologies and power relations.

Conclusion

In concluding, then, I want to encourage future critical studies of the role of meritocracy in education systems to go beyond grappling with its definitions, political rhetoric and policy discourses. Instead, the focus needs to be on the ways the ideology is instantiated in the quotidian aspects of schooling, in school knowledge and in the social hierarchies that these foster (Lim and Apple, 2015). Meritocracy specifies more than just who learns what; as I have shown, the 'what' surreptitiously feeds back into the very construction of the 'who'. Routes of inquiry are due that seek to better understand how such an ideology works through the curriculum to:

- imbue social meanings into school subjects and to shape the identities of learners;
- establish differences in social relations and social expectations of elites and the broad masses;
- perhaps most significantly, legitimise and revivify the unequal roles and access accorded to different segments of society.

Finally, it is also important to point out that the Singapore state – just like any other – is constructed along class (as well as gender and race) divisions (Dale, 1989; Lim and Apple, 2016). This, as I have argued at length elsewhere (Lim, 2014), means that the decision of the MOE to foreground critical thinking in the national curriculum needs to be appreciated vis-à-vis the interests of particular class factions – in this case, the professional and managerial new middle class. As indicated in Apple (2006a) and Bernstein (1977, 1990), these are people with backgrounds in systems engineering, data and statistical analysis, measurement, standardisation, human resource organisation, logic and argumentation, market research, and so on – what Bourdieu (1984) terms 'scientific capital' – and who often assume positions as managers, scientists, engineers, administrators, business consultants, researchers and accountants. Responsible for putting in place a network of labour and product control mechanisms that generates a constant supply of 'evidence' to both employers and employees (as well as the state) that one is doing things 'efficiently' and in the 'correct' way (Noble, 1979), this new middle class has been instrumental everywhere in the expansion of neoliberal capitalism and the corporate reform of education. Given the Singapore state's culture of elite technocratic governance, the influence of this class extends as well into the social and political spheres.

Consequently, as experts in these techniques, their own – as well as their children's – social mobility depends on the continued expansion and reification of such skills. The move to include critical thinking in schools is therefore one that, in effect – if not also in intention – plays to the interests of this new middle class, allowing for, as Bourdieu (1984) documents, the reproduction and conversion of their capital in both discursive and material ways. For not only does such a move add to their social prestige, by institutionalising their own cultural capital as the 'official' knowledge of the curriculum to the extent that the academic success of their children may be secured by having the school curriculum mirror or extend from their unique class habitus, but it also establishes crucial boundaries to the material gains already made by them for their children.[5]

Notes

[1] Members of Lee Kuan Yew's cabinet had since distanced themselves from these remarks, urging the public to put them – as well as Lee's other remarks on the integration of Muslims into Singapore society – 'in perspective' (Ibrahim, quoted in Hoe, 2011).

[2] Although a separate gifted track was still in place at the primary level.

[3] See, for example, Freire's (1970) writings on 'false generosity'.

[4] Pseudonyms are used for the names of both schools.

[5] We should not underestimate how the anxieties of this class over the future mobility of their children translate into pressures on the state to institutionalise 'their' skills and values in the curriculum (Lim, 2014).

Part 2
Corporatised governance: provision perspectives

Fast-track leadership development programmes: the new micro-philanthropy of future elites

James R. Duggan

Introduction

Fast-track graduate schemes are an established pathway into corporate elites, and fast-track leadership development schemes are increasingly common entry points to public sector professions in the UK. In education, Teach for All is an international network of fast-track leadership development programmes, such as Teach for America and Teach First, in England and Wales (Ellis et al, 2015). In England, the fast-track model has been translated across public sector domains with Frontline in social work, ThinkAhead in mental health social work, and Police Now in the police service. This chapter explores the relationships between Teach First for the teaching profession and Frontline, an equivalent programme for the social work profession.

Previous research has identified the ways in which Teach for All programmes, are re-articulating teacher professionalism, professional knowledge or are implicated in the broader transformation of education (Smart et al, 2009; Labaree, 2010; Ellis et al, 2015). Drawing on Bacchi's (2009) 'What's the Problem Represented to be' (WPR) approach, this chapter explores how fast-track leadership development schemes represent complex social issues, such as educational inequality and child death by abuse, as problems to be solved by individuals identified as highly talented and the application of a repertoire of corporate rationalities, discourses and practices. In particular it is the representation of high-calibre individuals – individuals who would not normally have become teachers or social workers – as the solution to complex social issues that frames their participation in fast-track schemes. I argue that this is a form of new micro-philanthropy, where such entry and participation in public professions, and thus their contribution to the public, is conditional on reworking and reculturing professional practices and commitments in line with corporatising processes.

The case is presented using secondary sources, news reports and organisational communications that were posted on the Teach First (http://teachfirst.org.uk) and Frontline (http://thefrontline.org.uk) websites.

Corporatisation and new philanthropy

This chapter explores processes of corporatisation, where corporate and financial elites are economically and culturally reworking and reconfiguring public education in line with corporate interests, rationalities and repertoires of action (Saltman, 2010). A prominent mode of corporate elite intervention in public education is through forms of new philanthropy and venture philanthropy (Saltman, 2009a; 2010). Informed by established discourses and traditions of philanthropy and charitable giving by wealthy individuals, new philanthropy is characterised by donations that are accompanied by the application of corporate practices and methodologies to public domains, such as education, with the aim of realising 'clear and measurable impacts and outcomes from … "investments" of time and money' (Ball, 2012, p 70). Venture philanthropy extends the application of business rationalities to aggressively realise returns of investments and open new markets for future investments (Scott, 2009).

New philanthropy funds and invests in and across policy communities and networks of think tanks, foundations and innovative programmes such as Teach for America and Teach First (Reckhow, 2013; Savage, 2016). These networks are purposed to rework and restructure education, reorienting educational purposes and practices in line with imperatives for national economic competitiveness and working to open up markets for exploitation (Lipman, 2014). This economic and cultural reworking of education serves to unsettle public and civic values, purposes and commitments to education and reframe them as private and individual (Saltman, 2009a). A key feature of new philanthropy therefore is that corporate elites give, fund or invest in public education but this contribution is conditional on reworking, restructuring and reculturing education in line with elite interests, rationalities and practices.

Fast-track leadership schemes as new micro-philanthropy

In this chapter I seek to extend the focus on new philanthropy from powerful corporate elites of the present to individual prospective members of future elites. Fast-track leadership programmes seek to encourage the so-called 'best and the brightest' into public professions yet this participation in and contribution to the public is *conditional* on restructuring and reculturing of teaching and social work, indicative of new micro-philanthropy.

Fast-track leadership development programmes represent an alternative to traditional routes into the public sector professions. Defining 'public sector profession' is not an uncomplicated task. Notions of the *public* are complex, contested and subject to continual processes of transformation (Newman and Clarke, 2009). Furthermore, *profession* and *professional* are fluid and contested concepts, reflecting in part the power of one group to extract the status from society (Rueschemeyer, 1983; Randall and Kandiak, 2008). Professionalisation conceptualises the processes through which individuals are trained, qualified, inducted and progress into a particular occupational group and develop competence in the relevant nomenclature, theories, tools, roles, responsibilities and values (Loseke and Cahill, 1986). Furthermore, professionals and professionalisation function in relation to broader institutional processes that in turn inform 'how social obligations are forged and how a society recreates itself through the practices that comprise systems of exchange' (Saltman, 2010, p 125).

The following sections explore the ways in which Teach First and Frontline represent complex social problems as tractable by so-called high-talent individuals and rework and restructure professional training and trajectories as conditional for the participation of its participants.

Teach First – ending educational inequality

In the lineage of Teach for America and Teach for All, Teach First was founded in England in 2002 as a leadership development programme with the mission of ending educational inequality. Teach First is both a registered charity and a company by limited guarantee. By 2016, Teach First employed 490 operations staff, worked in 966 schools, and had an annual income of £60.6 million (Teach First, 2015a; Charity Commission, 2016).

Teach First recruits high-calibre participants who train for six weeks at a summer school, in addition to on-going leadership development training, and commit to teach for two years in a school in a disadvantaged community, in order to improve teacher quality and consequently pupil outcomes. Once the participant completes the two-year programme he or she becomes a Teach First ambassador and a 'Leader for Life' (Teach First, 2016a, unpaged), advancing the organisation's mission to end educational inequality while remaining in the education sector or continuing into a career in business, finance, policy or social enterprise.

What's the Problem Represented to be?

Teach First's mission states that 'no child's educational success is limited by their socio-economic background' (Teach First, 2016b, unpaged). Teach First argues that ending educational inequality requires transformational change across society by a 'movement of leaders' constituted by the ambassador network. Quoting Chairman Mao on revolution, the founder and Chief Executive Officer, Brett Wigdortz (2012), explains that this ambassador network will form 'A benevolent tsunami of leadership [that] is about to wash away generations of educational inequity. It's the only thing that can' (unpaged).

Whether Teach First can end educational inequality is an open question. For advocates, Teach First presents a pragmatic and sufficient inducement for high-calibre individuals to try teaching, especially given the evidence suggesting increased pupil outcomes for pupils with Teach First teachers (Allen and Allnutt, 2013). For critics of Teach First the programme drop-out rate after two years varying between 30% and 70% (eg NAO, 2015) characterises Teach First as an expensive distraction, disparaging the teaching profession, and reproducing middle-class privilege through claims to 'natural ability' (Smart et al, 2009). Furthermore, Ellis and colleagues (2015) question Teach First's focus on the classroom and teaching as the site for improving pupils' educational outcomes as this ignores non-school effects, such as societal and structural causes of poverty and disadvantage, as a greater source of variation in children's outcomes (eg Berliner, 2014). Indeed, Teach First's mission statement – that a pupil's background should not affect their educational success – is a laudable aspiration but suggests individualising and neoliberalising discourses and narratives wherein individual success is defined by individual effort and investment (Bailey, 2013). The case that high-talented teachers can end or at least address educational inequality is recurrent but questionable hope for educators the world over (Apple, 2013); nevertheless, it is this claim that legitimates Teach First's location of its participants, to educate but also to learn how to become a leader for life (Bailey, 2013).

Teach First as new micro-philanthropy

As the name implies, in Teach *First* participants agree to teach first and then advance the mission either in the education sector or beyond education. For Teach First the purpose of the participant teaching phase is to hone 'invaluable leadership skills, humility and confidence' to become a 'Leader for Life' (Teach First, 2015c, unpaged). The decisions and opportunities of Teach First participants are structured through the promotion of discourses and training in transformational leadership and innovation and significantly the disruption of professional development in and beyond the teaching profession implicate Teach First in the production of a cadre of neoliberal social entrepreneurs. (Ellis et al, 2015, p1). The participant phase is temporary and incubatory where the Teach First trainee works to transform the life chances of the pupils they teach in addition to transforming themselves, ranging from and including their employment prospects to their ability to influence societal change through the ambassador network (Ellis et al, 2015).

For example, Teach First has established an Innovation Unit to support ambassador projects, launching a total of 36 social enterprises and seven free schools in ten years (Teach First, 2015b). The social enterprises are predominantly education focused, including a pupil peer-mentoring support programme (Franklin Scholars) and a social impact investment in education services (Right to Succeed). Within this programme there is also an equivalent fast-track leadership development scheme for social work (Frontline), to which I now turn.

Frontline – transforming vulnerable lives

Frontline is a social enterprise and fast-track leadership development scheme in social work, with the mission to 'transform the lives of vulnerable children by recruiting and developing outstanding individuals to be leaders in social work and broader society' (Frontline, 2015a, unpaged). The scheme began with a three-year pilot in London and Greater Manchester between 2013 and 2016, training 102 participants. In 2016, Frontline was commissioned to expand nationally and train 1,000 participants by 2019 (Frontline, 2015b).

Frontline recruits high-calibre individuals into social work for a commitment of two years with the potential of participating in a movement to influence societal change in social work or beyond. Once recruited, participants undergo a five-week training course at the Frontline Summer Institute where they learn practices such as systemic practice and motivational interviewing. The first year of training is in

Frontline child protection work in a unit under the supervision of a senior and qualified Consultant Social Worker, following the 'Hackney Model' of 'best practice' (Cross et al, 2010). In the second year of the programme the participant is a qualified social worker, working in child protection within children's services, while developing their leadership skills and studying for a master's qualification. After the two years the participant becomes a Frontline Fellow and advances the mission within or beyond social work.

What's the Problem Represented to be?

For Frontline, social work is a profession with an image problem and thus does not appeal to high-flying graduates whose traditional career paths would normally not be in social work but in finance or higher-status professions such as law, journalism or the civil service. For example, a Frontline report questioned the academic background of social work master's courses, that, 'of the 2,765 people starting social work masters-level courses last year, only five completed their undergraduate degree at Oxford or Cambridge' (MacAlister et al, 2012, p 7). Once social work is 'rebranded', high-calibre individuals will be appointed and trained, becoming 'outstanding social workers [who] can transform life chances for vulnerable children' (Frontline, 2015c: unpaged).

Frontline's rationale, therefore, neatly associates the dire consequences for children failed by child protection or the care system with the potential for 'life-changing' social workers to transform children's life chances. In this the initiative builds on evidence-based sector reviews questioning the quality and capacity of social workers (SWTF, 2009; Munro, 2011; Narey, 2014). In addition, Frontline aligns with arguments for increasing trust in professional judgement and therefore seeking to improve the quality of social worker ability to make decisions (Munro, 2011).

There are, however, alternative perspectives on the problems facing social work and the children and families they work with. High-profile media discourses and processes of children's services transformation in line with performance-accountability logics have worked to blame individual social workers for failing to prevent child death by abuse in high-profile media cases of the tragic and untimely deaths of a series of young children (Franklin and Parton, 1991; Garrett, 2009). The location of blame for 'preventable' child deaths with social work practice has been extensively critiqued (eg Munro, 2005). Alternative perspectives encourage understanding and engaging with root causes of family dysfunction and breakdown, in terms of the socio-economic causes of inequality, violence and poverty (Pemberton et al, 2012; Parton, 2015). Nevertheless, the UK Conservative government (from 2015 onwards) has sought to engender an ideological shift in social work education, away from sociological understandings of the societal causes of social problems and towards an emphasis on individual agency (Garrett, 2016). The state currently frames the issue of child protection narrowly in terms of, for example, improving the efficiency of child protection processes in social work practice (eg HM Government, 2013). Social work operates within the neoliberal authoritarian state, defined in part by the reduction in state benefits and preventative services, and an increase in statutory intervention and placing children at risk in care (Parton, 2015). Finally, the sole emphasis in Frontline training on child protection practice and single interventions (eg systemic practice) risk narrowing and replacing more complex and critical forms of social work (Higgins et al, 2016).

Frontline as new micro-philanthropy

The Frontline leadership development programme has redesigned social work education. Frontline functions to recruit and train high-calibre individuals into social work. News articles on Frontline often feature students at elite universities, such as Charley from Oxford University and Charlotte from Edinburgh University, who would not normally have applied to become social workers but changed their mind on learning about Frontline when they decided to try social work (Brindle, 2015). The compression, reculturing and reorientation of entry in social work can be understood as the conditions on which participation in the scheme is presented by Frontline and participants' acceptance is structured.

The compression of the training period prior to entering social work is foundational to fast-track schemes. Frontline participants spend five weeks at its Summer Institute whereas master's-level courses typically involve one year of study in a university prior to one year spent on placement. Frontline's academic lead, Professor Donald Forrester, explained the rationale for a compressed training process is expressly to present a competitive offer to high-calibre graduates:

> In an ideal world a five-year qualification would be fantastic, but we have to be realistic about the options open to graduates and the funding available for social work education. The most academically able have a lot of options,

so we need to make this as attractive as possible for them.
(McGregor, 2013, unpaged)

A second condition is the reculturing of social work practice so that social work becomes a leadership profession. The attempt to remake social work as a leadership profession was recognised as controversial within the social work profession (eg Forrester, 2013). Frontline trains and positions its participants to perform numerous forms of leadership, both in the participant phase to 'constructively "disrupt" and challenge within their systems' and then '*as a driving force in participants' lives wherever their journey takes them*' (Frontline, 2016, unpaged).

The third condition is that participants join the programme under the obligation to commit to working in social work for only two years, before advancing the mission within or beyond social work.

Fast-tracks to elite transformation

Fast-track leadership development programmes, such as Teach First and Frontline, are indicative of re-professionalising projects, supported by and interpolated with corporate elites and corporatising projects.

The claim that corporate – and indeed policy and social – elites supported the emergence of and continue to work with Teach First and Frontline is not controversial. Teach First emerged from an engagement between Charles, HRH Prince of Wales, headteachers and business leaders to address the poor performance of inner-city London schools. The global management consultancy McKinsey and Company produced a report identifying Teach For America as a potential approach for recruiting high-calibre individuals and locating them in the inner-city schools. Brett Wigdortz, a McKinsey employee, became the Teach First founder (Wigdortz, 2012). Teach First lists among its corporate sponsors some of the richest and most prominent financial, industrial and charitable organisations in the world, from Google to Goldman Sachs. Frontline's 'founding partners' include Big Change, Boston Consulting Group, The Queen's Trust and The Credit Suisse EMEA Foundation and ARK – an international educational charity founded by hedge fund financiers which runs 31 Academy schools in the UK (Frontline, 2015b). There is a case that, for these corporations, Teach First and Frontline function as schemes for corporate elite recruitment, producing corporate-ready, transformational leaders.

The emphasis on the production of a network of leaders, a cadre of elite neoliberal social entrepreneurs (Labaree, 2010), however, suggests a more ambitious corporate elite project in re-professionalising public professionals and reworking notions of the public in line with elite interests and worldviews. A significant foundation of the ways in which Teach First and Frontline represent complex social problems is that they are tractable by the agency of an aggregate of individual transformational individuals, oriented by a mission to end educational inequality. These representations arguably align with corporate elite interests in that they are individualising, depoliticising and work to foreclose the necessity of, for example, structural attempts to redistribute wealth (Dean, 2016). In addition, fast-track leadership development schemes inhere and promote a repertoire of discourses, practices and ideals from the corporate world, including the corporate ideal of the transformational leader (Saltman, 2010), a corporate view of the 'war for talent' (Michaels et al, 2001, p 1), and orientations to disruptive innovation opening up new sites and spaces for investment and marketisation (Lipman, 2014).

The representation of social transformation through the individual agency of high-calibre individuals also extends and seeks to entrench corporate rationalities, practices and values by reworking entry points into public professions as a form of new micro-philanthropy. Teach First but especially Frontline seek to encourage high-calibre individuals to become teachers or social workers instead of their expected choices of entering higher-status or better-remunerated careers. It is important that in both programmes participants receive payment while training. However, inspired by the mission of ending educational inequality, the high-calibre individual in choosing Teach First and teaching or Frontline and social work is – at least in the short-term – forgoing a higher rate of pay or increased status that would result from becoming, for example, a financier, barrister or journalist. Thus this counterfactual *loss* becomes a *gift* to the public (Saltman, 2010), and a form of new micro-philanthropy.

We can understand new micro-philanthropy as the conditional transformation of professional training and trajectories so that high-talent individuals will join public sector professions. The rationale is founded on statistical evidence that high-talent individuals, judged by attendance at elite universities, do not become teachers or social workers. The offer to become a teacher or social worker is therefore structured to suit the interests and preferences of the *best and the brightest*. In Frontline professional training is compressed in time, practice is recultured around narratives and discourses of transformational leadership, and commitments and obligations to a profession are reduced to two years with the opportunity to join an elite network of Frontline Fellows.

It is the opportunity to join Teach First and Frontline as a site and process of personal and leadership development that is perhaps the greatest and most seductive condition of new micro-philanthropy. There are, of course, many possible motivations and trajectories for prospective Frontline participants. Nevertheless, fast-track programmes restructure participation in professions, unsettle commitments, reorient professional trajectories, and open opportunities to engage in forms of neoliberal social entrepreneurship for participants.

The origin of Frontline is indicative of the potential dynamics of the Teach First ambassador network, a movement of leaders oriented to ending educational inequality. Josh MacAlister, a Teach First ambassador co-founded Frontline, with ARK – an international educational charity funded by financiers. MacAlister can be understood as quintessentially the type of transformational, mission-focused leader that Teach First aims to produce and support as part of its ambassador network and movement of leaders. MacAlister's trajectory is remarkable, from a Teach First participant to successfully co-founding and becoming the Chief Executive of Frontline, and is indicative of the potential benefits of locating high-calibre individuals in leadership development programmes.

If participating in fast-track leadership schemes, there is a case that the capacity to transform oneself into a transformational individual and lead processes of societal change may remain within structures of corporatising elite structures. For example, Frontline translates and adapts the representations of complex social problems from Teach First to social work. Teach First represents the problem of ending educational inequality is possible through its network of ambassadors. Frontline is founded on the belief that transformational individuals working in social work and beyond can create societal change. Both programmes emphasise the transformative power of individuals, and therefore individualising and neoliberalising narratives of social processes and narrow forms of professional practice. The adaptation and translation of corporate practices, rationalities and repertoires of action such as transformational leadership from education to social work in part explains how Frontline has secured the support of financial and corporate elites.

Conclusion

New philanthropy and new micro-philanthropy are argued to represent an intersection between corporate elites and the corporatising project and the ways in which so-called high-talent individuals are positioned in relation to participating in public sector professions and contributing to the public. No one would sensibly argue for less talented teachers or social workers. Fast-track leadership development schemes such as Teach First and Frontline, however, represent complex social problems as tractable by the agency of high-talent individuals to transform society, whether working in education or social work or in business and finance. It is the claimed potential of these individuals that would become 'leaders for life' but not teachers or social workers *for life* that materially and symbolically locates their participation in the programme as a philanthropic act. Yet, in line with a corporatising project, the contributions of elite, powerful or high-talent individuals to the public are conditional on and conditioning in seeking to rework, reculture and restructure the public and public professions in line with corporatising interests, rationalities and repertoires of action.

TEN

Corporate consultancy practices in education services in England

Helen M. Gunter

Introduction

The seismic shift in public education services is well charted by researchers, but examining the realities of everyday speedy neoliberalism is little explored, largely because the tracing, evidence collection and codification of meaning is a demanding undertaking (see Hall, 2011). I take up the challenge by focusing on the realities of what it means for salaried professionals in public services education to live and work precariously at the edge of the rolling back of the state. Specifically I locate my analysis in England, where public services education is being privatised through corporate elites shaping policies that are marketising provision, and are seeking to invest for profit and/or by philanthropic benefaction in schools as businesses.

As politicians and manifestos declare that the market can and should provide, there are consequences of this, as highly qualified educational professionals find that their work and workplace change beyond recognition, and they may even find their jobs made redundant. So I focus on dispossessed experts who are seeking to reposition themselves productively within a turbulent system, and specifically I give attention to those who have relocated as corporate knowledge workers by rebranding their practice as consultants who do consultancy for fees.

I begin the chapter by providing some contextual information, before going on to examine the corporate approach to the relocation of the self and work within the marketplace. I then go on to provide meaning to these changes, whereby forms of corporate hegemony are interrelated with the agency of these consultants through using Gramsci's (1986) work on conjunctural crises. The contribution from this analysis is located empirically in the revealing of these accounts, combined with theorising that seeks to relate meta-narratives of neoliberalism with the realities of people who are marketised.

All change?

My starting point is to ask: who do educational professionals who work in schools turn to for support and advice? From the 1980s till the 2000s a teacher in England could turn to another teacher as their 'colleague', to advisers in the local education authority and to experts in national government units or agencies, and in universities. There has been a strong tradition of experienced professionals relocating their employment from schools into local and/or national services, and into higher education, in order to develop and share expertise with the profession variously through advice, training and research. These sites of support have faced major changes.

Government institutions and agencies

A shift has taken place in the status and contribution of the local authority as an advisory service staffed by teachers on short-term secondment or through a career shift into inspection roles. Local advisory services are being dismantled. Schools run themselves as businesses and buy in services, where schools have been removed from local authorities (for example grant maintained, academies), and schools have been set up outside of local authorities (for example city technology colleges, free schools).

New Labour governments (1997–2010) provided additional nationally coordinated advisory services for the profession through specific investment in:

- technology, for example the British Educational Communications and Technology Agency – BECTA;
- workforce training, for example the Teacher Training Agency – TTA;
- school leadership, for example the National College for School Leadership – NCSL – where professionals relocated to provide professional development and support.

Austerity cuts from 2010 have led to the closure of some units (for example BECTA) and to the scaling down and merging of other units (for example the formation of the National College for Teaching and Leadership).

Those who relocated their careers into national and local advisory work have found themselves made redundant through closures, outsourcing and commercial takeovers of local and national advisory services. Some have found themselves working for a company that has been set up to run local services. Headteachers who are offered early retirement but who do not want to stop making a contribution have found themselves without clear routes beyond headship, and hence the redundant and retired have had to rethink their occupational location and contribution to the profession and to education.

Higher education

A major change has taken place in the status and contribution of schools of education in higher education as a site where educational professionals could locate to undertake teacher training, professional support and research through postgraduate degrees and through partnership programmes with local authorities and national agencies. The school as a business requires particular training and knowledge that may be different to primary research and the knowledge claims underpinning postgraduate studies. In addition, there has been a combination of the corporatisation of higher education in regard to pressures for income generation along with the demands of high-stakes external quality audits for teacher training and research. Those who have relocated their careers into higher education, from lecturers to professors, have found themselves facing contract termination, or have read the changes and have considered occupational relocation through planned business ventures.

I have been capturing the stories of those who have experienced such transitions, where I have begun to map the growth in consultancy services by collecting the professional biographies of 30 people who have relocated their work as consultants: some who have been pushed through redundancy or retirement and some who have responded to the pull of the private sector (see Gunter, 2012; Gunter and Mills, 2017).

The portfolio of work that these consultants describe shows that each person's story is different, where the skills and knowledge that they trade can shift over time:

> '... at the moment I'm running leadership programmes for eight local authorities ...' (PC06)

> 'Most of the time I'm working on training and consultancy for individual schools ... In addition to that there are about three companies that I do work for, as an associate consultant. I do other things as well, with the odd inspection thrown in.' (PC18)

'... at the moment I am the Executive Principal of [name] Academy.' (PC19)

'... I do quite a bit of work acting as Director of HR and Governance in a Multi-Academy trust ...' (PC20)

What is interesting about the narratives is how education professionals negotiated the changes to their occupational location and identities. These people make a living but they are not members of a corporate elite in the way outlined in the Introduction to this book. However, the data are an important site, where non-corporate elites engage with corporate elite dispositions and practices. Or in Ball's (2015) terms, this is an illustration of how neoliberalism works as "little-n, 'in here' in our daily life and our heads" (p 10).

Hence I am going to focus on those who proactively shifted from higher education through the *pull* of consultancy work, and those who where *pushed* and found themselves redundant from local authorities and national agencies, and so had to reposition themselves very quickly in order to survive economically.

Corporate 'pulling'

The data show a shift from working in higher education and government into major international consultancy firms: this enabled access to a globalised brand, infrastructure and the potential to develop new markets in the increasingly privatised schools. This exerted strong 'pull' factors in regard to status and opportunity, which have created an imagined way of working that has structured revealed dispositions regarding how forms of 'bureaucracy' are not conducive places in which to meet the needs of the taxpayer. The development of educational services by major companies (see Mourshed et al, 2010) and the movement of personnel between public services and private consultancies (see Barber et al, 2011) has generated and embedded entrepreneurial dispositions. This can be witnessed through the accounts given by those who had worked in a university and had set up their own 'solo' or partnership businesses, and sought to build up a personal reputation for services. The rationales are that client-oriented work in schools is not valued in universities:

'And that was something higher education never did, and (practitioners) were fabulous researchers and they added value and they created knowledge and that's something that's so fundamental from my perspective and it also meant that research became part of school life.' (PC06)

Working with and for the profession is regarded as vitally important, where consultants found that in a world that focused on basic research, with quality judged through the auditing of research excellence using indicators such as competitive funding from UK research councils and world-leading outputs, the place of 'applied' or 'real life' research was not given recognition.

Juxtaposed with this is another frustration that is encapsulated in a 'breakaway' discourse:

> 'I feel I have total freedom as a freelance consultant, I can choose which projects I want to do, I can choose who I want to work with, I will only work with colleagues who I respect ...' (PC08)

> 'I suppose one of the reasons I went independent was because I wanted to do the kind of work I do ... And therefore I'm lucky because I choose and am able to say yes in a way that I couldn't do, if I was working full time in a university, and therefore I am very much able to exploit my situation. And I make a good living, but also I do the work that I really want to do.' (PC06)

The university as a site of research and as an organisation with multiple demands does not command their support. Central to the escape narrative is how the former academic does not need to do certain types of work any more: 'I don't go to university meetings, for heaven's sake, I don't have course administration to worry about, I have no bureaucracy in my life. It's bliss.' (PC06). In addition, PC06 has come to understand the value for money costing and funding processes within the university:

> 'I can go to a local authority and negotiate a contract with them, and a big contract, and they know that all that money will be devoted to their contract. If I were working full time for a university, the university would slice it, and some universities are slicing forty, fifty per cent. Well, that's a major disincentive.' (PC06).

It seems that strategic location of the self and project in higher education no longer 'pays', where negotiations with clients have enabled this person to realise that salaried employment does not meet the needs of that client or the person who is operating on behalf of the university. The view is that the overheads of a university as a bureaucracy are too great in comparison with an individual, who can work without the encumbrance of funding the campus (such as library and student services) and research infrastructure.

Corporate 'pushing'

The data show how consultants who have set up their own businesses have arrived at this point through being made redundant, or have been headteachers and have taken early retirement but have not wanted to retire. Here is one story:

> 'Local authorities were looking to cut and close teams down and government agency work was disappearing and really the only opportunity I could see would be to attempt to go and work for myself. That's what prompted me to start ... most of what I'm doing is running CPD and training for schools ... because there's been a lack of support from their local authority and more traditional sources, schools are starting now to look elsewhere for support.' (PC10)

Interestingly, within the narratives there are examples of how consultants have learned to be corporate while in salaried public services. Local advisers and headteachers had learned to relate support and training to costing, budgets and value-for-money assessments, and to position within a wider 'edu-business' (Mahony et al, 2004) market with other providers and clients:

> '... my title technically is Lead Consultant for [subject area] with [consultancy company] ... this Company is becoming an arms-length traded service under my local council but only commissioned by the council for doing very specific pieces of work with specific schools ... sometimes an individual school gets in contact and they want some support, maybe a training session run or lesson observations and feedback done.' (PC13)

This means that some local advisers have avoided (or delayed) redundancy by being relocated in a company, and have taken on the risk of delivering in the marketplace. Some of those who have been made redundant are doing work that they previously did in the local authority, but for a fee rather than a salary:

> '... when we first started talking about redundancies I was quite new into the job and I think if that had it all kicked off a year earlier, then I wouldn't have chosen to go as a consultant because I wouldn't have had the credibility and the reputation from having worked in that area to do it ... I think the fact that schools were keen to buy me in to do that gave me the confidence that actually I could give it a go ... The other side of that, of course, is that we got quite a generous pay-off ... that allowed me to take the risk ...' (PC14)

Hence skills and knowledge as salaried state consultants could continue to be used in the private sector:

> 'Well, thirty years I've been working in consultancy work, but employed by a local authority, well more than one local authority .... I enjoyed that full role with a number of schools and not just one school and that's what I enjoyed doing. I liked the variation ... but when that all started to close down because of government cut backs and initiatives – they were political changes not educational changes – I took my chance to take early retirement ... I started to do the things that I thought made a difference.' (PC15)

The data from educational professionals who have held salaried occupational roles in public service institutions and who are now private consultants demonstrate some important trends:

1. There is the contention that the work they did within the public sector can be done in the private sector, and indeed aspects of their work that they did not want to do any longer could be dropped and new opportunities could be developed outside bureaucratic rules.
2. They have come to the conclusion that there is something seriously wrong with the public service institution that they have been employed by, and this judgement is linked to a perceived failure of the organisation to recognise and respond in the right way to

what they think matters in regard to meeting the needs of fellow professionals as clients.

3. They are clear that their knowledge was, and remains, valid and relevant, and that the profession needs it – and that their continued involvement in schools and with the profession will make a difference for children.

The *push* and *pull* data reveal a generative corporate disposition in a number of ways, not least that 'going private' is rationalised as *the only* option, in ways that resonate with Bobbitt's (2002) argument of the inevitability and logic of a market state that 'exists to maximise the opportunities enjoyed by all members of society' (p 229). While working for and with children and teachers is the underpinning value base for their practice, there is some differentiation. Some see the private sector as the place where public values regarding all children having access to learning can be retained, at least for a while, so they can continue with their practice; whereas others see the winning of contracts and projects as being a site where they can flourish as entrepreneurs, enabling the children and teachers to thrive in marketised educational organisations. This is evident not only through the discourse of new freedoms and self-evaluation through giving better value for money for the client, but also through how none of the respondents regarded their experiences as being ones that required a politically activist approach regarding the 'public' nature of their job and how it is linked to democratic forms of accountability. No one talked about working with the profession locally to renew and revitalise publicly owned services.

What seems to have been learned through the corporatisation of the school, the local authority and the university has been how to locate and position the self within financial exchange relationships, where entering and exiting different contracts and organisational arrangements is based on the agency of new freedoms and what this means in terms of their portfolio of work, their income and who they do or do not want to work with. Interestingly, the narratives show that while the transition was risky and fear-inducing, it was normally smoothed through the investment of redundancy and retirement financial packages into private sector services, where the personal need to keep on working was supported by accumulated public money that was released and made profitable through new forms of trade.

Conjunctural crises?

The data and analysis have generated evidence and insight into a personal experience of a process that is very real in the corporate changes taking place in public services in England, and it is happening to people who would not normally be regarded as corporate elites. The sample of respondents are clearly professional elites, in the sense that they have trained and gained accreditation as educators, some with leadership and management credentials, and they have received high salaries with good pension/redundancy packages. They have espoused and recognised knowledge and skills, with positive reputations for their work through networks, where they are known and can be vouched for by like-minded others.

However, while there are examples of former teachers becoming millionaires (see Clark, 2014), they are not (at least not yet) CEOs of their own companies that demonstrate a turnover that puts them in the same league as major consultancy companies such as PwC or McKinsey, or equivalent to other private businesses in the media, retail, banking and manufacturing. But their accounts reveal shared dispositions and outlooks that are corporatised, where the conditions in which they undertake risk and negotiations are similar to those who own and lead internationally recognised corporate businesses. In Bourdieu's (2000) terms, they have engaged with the *doxa* of privatisation in regard to the self and others, have joined the game where the logic of practice speaks to them and where their enthusiasm for playing has been self-generating. As they have shifted from salary to contractual fees, they have recognised the potential of their new situation, and how they can continue to work on what they think matters. For example, one respondent talks about the change from working as an adviser in a local authority to setting up as a consultant:

> 'I took redundancy when they shrunk our very large team of over 100 down to about 20-30 people and it meant I've been able to develop my work with schools ... so, it's really quite exciting to be able to draw on other skills creatively. It began when I was with the authority but I've evolved it since then and re-shaped it with the schools really creatively over the last nearly three years now ...' (PC17)

This respondent goes on to illuminate this further, where the state steps in when the market fails or where the market does not want to invest:

'The schools that are in difficult circumstances, they tend to be worked with by the authority ... I've worked with a lot of schools that are "good" or "outstanding" as well as those who are now in "requires improvement", so you know, it's quite a range of schools and they don't necessarily want what the authority wants to give them.' (PC17)

In other words, the market is creative because it enables work with schools that are doing well and where improvement can be a reasonable expectation, but the schools that this respondent (and others in the sample) used to work with as public experts are in such difficult circumstances that the residualised state is left to rescue and support. There are trends in the data that further illuminate this, through forms of hysteresis, mimicry and misrecognition.

Hysteresis

The data illustrate a breach of the public services field through the corporatisation of politics and the media (see Thomson, 2005), where public values and expertise are no longer acceptable in thinking, doing and speaking. Using Bourdieu's (Bourdieu, 2000) thinking tool of *hysteresis*, I would argue that the data show how the respondents realised and engaged with the lag between the corporatisation of the public institution and their espoused contribution. It seems that the habitus revealed through thinking, talk and action while at the edge of the rolling back of the state, can be one where there are 'critical moments when it misfires or is out of phase', and this generates '*practical reflection*' (Bourdieu, 2000, p 162, original emphasis).

Some, like PC06, were ahead of the game and so moved proactively, and PC08 was not going to go back, whereas others, like PC14, sought to get ahead when they 'read the writing on the wall' and recounted how repositioning is about realigning their identities and skills with the demands of the market. The long antecedence of the corporatisation of local and national governments and agencies had structured their practical reflections – they had learned through forms of 'consultocracy' (Hood and Jackson, 1991, p 24), where consultancy identities, language and practices had been adopted by those within public service or they worked alongside those who had been bought in from consultancy firms to deliver within the public sector (see Coopers and Lybrand, 1988). However, the shock of the change is tangible, and when combined with speedy manoeuvring, it still meant that they had to catch up in order to be tradable in the new knowledge economy. There are glimpses of the damage done to those who play and fail in the game (see Beckett, 2007), but what I have not yet collected are the stories of those who have disappeared into retirement or unemployment, where dispositions deemed to be anachronistic could not be invested.

Mimicry

The adoption of new freedoms from particular work and people within a formal organisation is strong within the data, with a sense of a break with an old system and the opportunity to work with better and/or new systems. Integral to this is a shared disposition that the consultant can pronounce on a problem: identify, outline, solve. In doing so, there is recognition of affiliation and solidarity with those who do this from a position of corporate dominance. There are examples of how consultants in large corporate businesses have a process of working that enables them to be billable, and how corporate philanthropists use their wealth as an example of new freedoms to fund and control educational purposes and knowledge (Saltman, 2010).

Those who are new to the game through changing their occupational location and taking on corporate exchange relationships engage in a form of what Bhabha (1994) identifies as 'mimicry', where agency is scripted in relation to powerful interests, who are separate but who play a game that is perceived to be worth staking a claim for and is regarded as being within reach. The complex decisions to be made when the letter arrives informing the person that their job is terminated – impacting on the everyday security and wider aspirations of the family – can both 'appropriate' the person through the discipline of clear and obvious routes to follow, and can be 'inappropriate' for the person through how what has been 'normal' is rendered obsolete (Bhabha, 1994, pp 122-3). The narratives show struggles within such decision-making, where respondents are grappling with making the self legible and readable, and hence legitimate within the market.

Misrecognition

Self-identification by professional elites with corporate elites could be interpreted as a form of 'misrecognition', whereby Bourdieu (2000) argues that agents engage in a form of self-deception regarding the structuring of the conditions in which exchanges take place. In taking action in relation to the *doxa* of privatisation, then the *illusio* – or belief in the value of the game – means that it is worth playing through the staking of *capitals* (knowledges, skills, experiences, reputation, redundancy cheque).

Those who espoused how they were pulled by the allure of corporate opportunities misrecognised that spurned university bureaucracies made important demands on their practices, such as primary research and peer review with shared responsibilities for infrastructure, that they could not meet. Those who experienced the push into the private misrecognised how they had been prepared for the corporate world through becoming business-like through forms of 'endogenous' privatisation, and how the private sector had entered public services by 'exogenous' privatisation (Ball and Youdell, 2008, pp 9-10). Playing this modernisation game means that these dispossessed experts are seeking control of identity and worth through a form of 'collective self deception' (Bourdieu, 2000, p 192) where 'everyone knows – and does not want to know – that everyone knows – and does not want to know – the true nature of the exchange' (p 192).

In the stories, there is strong evidence of a struggle for agency in a world where the structures and cultures have shifted. Where the rules and regulations of organisational bureaucracy designed to deliver universal services – according to transparent rules with accountability to the electorate through representative systems at local and national levels – are presented as failing and necessary only to deal with market failure, where the more productive alternatives are through private ownership of capital and marketised services. The failings of bureaucracy to deliver the espoused goal of equity, not least through cultures that often 'othered' gender, sexuality, race and class, is not seen as a site for reform but of complete transformation, where the *doxa* of privatisation is that equity can be resolved through market processes that are deemed open to all. A core feature of the misrecognition of the potency and inevitability of marketised social justice is that of depoliticisation, where the relocation of the idea and actuality of public education into families supported by charity and philanthropy, means that areas of concern regarding access and achievement become a private matter, where private business is the site for recognition and resolution of problems (see Courtney and Gunter, 2017).

Thinking through the data by using these interconnected thinking tools illuminates Hall's (2011) account that neoliberal hegemony is rooted in the generation of 'unfocused anxiety' (p 212), where the new freedoms enabled through depoliticisation run hand in hand with rationalities and narratives that are about seeking control through sense-making. The stories are replete with accounts of people finding themselves in risky situations, and explaining how they have overcome

– or are overcoming – these through how they are playing the game that is not named but is being learned. They do not use researcher coded language or attribute causal connections with corporate interests, but they are living a situation in which a significant shift is taking place in regard to their lives; it is what Gramsci (1986) identifies as 'moments' within 'conjunctural' crises (p 180). Hall and Massey (2015) build on this, by arguing that: 'a conjuncture is a period when different social, political, economic and ideological contradictions that are at work in society and have given it a specific shape come together, producing a crisis of some kind' (p 60).

The crisis is one of the state, encoded and popularised through Thatcherism (Thatcherite governments 1979–97), whereby public sector workers were vilified by claims of greedy and unaccountable 'provider capture' in regard to their expert knowledge and contribution, and where the rolling back of the state released such labour to the discipline and responsiveness of the market. New Labour's (1997–2010) approach was to 'do marketisation better than the Tories' not least by 'letting the market buy out most of the public activities that were profitable, while the state concentrated on the technical management of the consequences' (Hall and Massey, 2015, p 63). Those in public services experienced vacant posts not being filled, relocating work to others who already had a full schedule, appointing cheaper non-qualified people to do the job, making people redundant and granting early retirement, while at the same time maintaining demands for standards. This continued to work its way through under the Conservative-led Coalition from 2010 to 2015, whereby austerity accelerated the relocation of services and expertise into the market and where contradictions continued to surface. Not least, that education for the public would be more efficient and of a higher standard through private means, at a time when the state had to bail out and protect the banking system. In other words, neoliberalism needs a strong state. This is clearly lived by the respondents, where they needed a strong state in order to generate the funding to support their shift in employment.

In summary, Hall et al (2013) argue that 'conjuncture' is 'not just a date in the calendar' (Hall et al, 2013, p 2), but is:

> the development of contradictions, their fusion into a crisis and its resolution. Resolutions to the crisis can take different forms: there is no preordained result. They may allow the historical project to continue or be renewed, or they may provoke a process of transformation … Conjunctures have no fixed duration, but so long as the crisis (and its

> underlying contradictions) remain unresolved, further crises
> are likely to proliferate and echo around different domains
> of the social transformation. (Hall et al, 2013, p xv)

The data show how public sector experts lived through, were produced by and attempted to resolve the contradictions in the crises through corporatisation. Their accounts show simultaneous moments of confusion and clarity as they talk about how they understand their situation, and how they have come to be there and see it unfolding, and what they now need to do, think and say as they reposition themselves.

This is not to say that the stories demonstrate determinism, particularly since there are resilient residues of public service values within the stories that are potentially counter-hegemonic through the commitment to all children obtaining access to learning through productive pedagogic relations within schools. Indeed, Apple (2006a) notes that neoliberalism is plural through how it plays out locally, and how those who espouse these ideas make alliances with other interests in order to secure approved-of practices (for example with neoconservatives regarding the emphasis on individuals and families).

Consequently, neoliberal activities are not based on a fixed blueprint, but are constructed within and against practices, where Hall (2011) argues that neoliberal hegemony 'has constantly to be "worked on", maintained, renewed and revised' (p 127). It seems that the key point is 'where hegemony is won or lost' with the argument that is 'in the civil, political, juridical and ideological complexes of the social formation – in the "superstructures"' (Hall et al, 2013, p 215).

What is on show in the narratives as a form of 'theatre' are dispositions that the situation has been awful but is now much better, where being in business means that there are huge gains, and so 'the relations of class forces, given their fundamental form in the antagonistic relations of capitalist production, appear and work themselves through to resolution' (Hall et al, 2013, p 215). Consequently, neoliberal hegemony is energised and sustained through such position-taking and where day-to-day work is ennobled through affiliation with corporate elites.

Acknowledgements

The data on which this chapter is based are drawn from two funded projects, and I would like to thank the British Academy for funding the *Consultancy and Knowledge Production in Education Project* (Award Reference: SG121698) and the Economic and Social Research Council for funding the *Knowledge Production in Educational Leadership* project (Award Reference: RES-000-23-1192).

ELEVEN

The business of governorship: corporate elitism in public education

Andrew Wilkins

Introduction

In this chapter, I examine the role and ideology of corporatisation and the image of the corporation as a dominant policy technology guiding different aspects of school governance in England. Corporatisation can be defined as the regulation of public organisations and utilities by specific interests, laws or rules intended to subsume the 'public' within the logic of the 'private'. This does not necessarily mean that public organisations are fully privatised since they remain publicly-owned and intensively regulated by their owners, the state. Instead, it points to the transformation of public entities as business-like organisations governed by managerialist practices of securing productivity, efficiency and value for money through internal audit, performance evaluation and enterprise activities. That is to say, corporatisation is not privatisation but refers to the performance and regulation of public organisations as if they were for-profit organisations.

Corporatisation also requires certain techniques, shared values, social relations and practices to predominate over others in order for the above conditions to be made legitimate and desirable. This is because, under corporate ideology, means can always be justified where they are commensurate with the fulfilment of certain ends. Therefore, value differences or value divergences tend to be regarded as risky business. In this chapter, I consider the extent to which corporate strategies are evident in the kinds of everyday work performed and inhabited by agents of school governance, namely school governors. Moreover, I consider whether 'corporate elitism', rather than corporate elites per se, is implicit in decisions concerning who and why certain people get to enter governance roles.

For well over six hundred years, governors in England have played an essential role as the 'custodians', 'stewards' and 'wardens' of schools, in essence bringing judgements to bear upon the 'performance' or 'quality' of schools as publicly accountable institutions. Governors refer to parent, staff and community volunteers who are either elected or co-opted to their position and who have traditionally occupied a lay role as 'critical friends' to the leaders and managers of schools. Today, however, that role is changing significantly, and increasingly governors find themselves being trained and made responsible in new ways that mirror elements of corporate aspirations and principles.

Central to the reform of governing bodies in England since 2010 and their complete disbandment in some cases (Coughlan, 2016), is the promotion of risk-based approaches to regulation that seek to subordinate the work of governors to a strict corporate focus on financial probity, internal auditing, compliance-checking and risk absorption. These reforms have produced cultures of school governance that are increasingly 'corporate' rather than 'charitable' or political. To be more specific, those forms of charitable giving (or volunteering) that underpin school governance have been co-opted to serve a myriad of corporate ends (see Wilkins, 2016). To evidence these trends, I draw on evidence taken from my three-year research project funded by the Economic and Social Research Council (ESRC) (Grant Ref. ES/K001299/1, 2012-15) to highlight the movement by which governing bodies in England are undergoing change in response to wider, structural reforms linked to disintermediation and decentralisation, and related, internal pressures linked to the necessity for governors to performance manage themselves and senior school leaders.

When we consider the different actors and knowledge that have come to influence forms of policy-making and enactment in England – from philanthropic organisations (Ball, 2008) and consultants (Gunter et al, 2014b) to school business managers (Woods, 2014) and policy innovation labs (Williamson, 2015) – governors can be conceptualised in similar ways as central figures in the 'modernisation' and 'corporatisation' of state education.

Creeping corporatisation

Over the last six years there has been an unprecedented acceleration in the number of academies and free schools to open in England. Unlike 'maintained' or 'community' schools overseen by locally elected politicians and state-employed bureaucrats, academies and free schools, better known as 'state-funded independent schools', possess certain freedoms and flexibilities over the running of the school. This includes making decisions about budget spending, curriculum and pedagogy, staff pay and conditions and length of school day. According to statistics released by the Department for Education (DfE) in June 2015 (DfE, 2015a), 4,679 secondary and primary schools have converted to academy status, 1,404 schools have opened as academies under the guidance of a corporate sponsor and 201 schools are in the process of converting to academy status. Recent statistics also indicate that 154 free schools have opened since 2010 (DfE, 2015b). Identical to academies, free schools are granted powers to operate outside the politics and bureaucracy of local government, albeit on the agreement that those powers are exercised responsibly and not contrary to the public interest. Central government therefore appears relaxed about schools operating outside local government control, so long as those schools are sufficiently 'modernised' and mirror the kinds of arrangements found in corporate settings, where continuous improvement is managed through self-monitoring, risk assessment, performance evaluation, budget control, succession planning, target setting, and the like.

At the same time, central government appears anxious that many schools are not populated by the kinds of people who are capable of remaking – or willing to remake – their governing body in the image of the corporate board. Hence the government is keen for schools to be taken over by an academy chain or 'multi-academy trust' (MAT) as 'sponsor academies'. These schools are governed by a single board of trustees, who employ teams of experts from education, finance, continuing professional development training, information technology and human resources to improve and monitor quality of provision. In cases where schools are academies but not part of a chain (sometimes called a 'converter academy'), central government intends for those schools to be monitored internally by bands of experts or 'professionals', so that performance management of senior school leaders is forensic and stringent in the absence of local government intervention (Wilkins, 2015, 2016). This has implications over who is included and who is excluded from the business of school governance.

In 2014, I interviewed a group of governors who were overseeing the development of a new free school in a very affluent area of London. The journey from free school application to school opening was a testing time for the governors. To support their case for a free school, the governors were involved in running public meetings, attending community events, writing articles in the local press, utilising social media, developing a website and holding regular steering groups and advisory meetings with legal experts, curriculum specialists, governance advisers, local authority officials, and senior leaders and teachers from some of the local primary schools that would later act as feeder schools to the proposed free school. As one of the governors of the free school, Gill, remarked at the time:

> 'It's fair to say it's a relatively middle-class governing body and with the skills. One of the things I always think about with the free schools thing is the sense that it could happen in any community just isn't true. You do have to have the perfect storm of people with the right sort of skills and some available free time and not every community has got that actually.'

Free schools were launched in 2010 to enable groups of parents, teachers, private organisations and charities to open schools in areas where there was evidence of 'need'. The caveat to these arrangements is that a free school application to the DfE requires all kinds of social, economic and cultural capital for it to be successful. It is therefore not surprising to learn that the majority of free school applications are not submitted by groups of parents but by headteachers and middle managers, private schools, faith organisations, educational management trusts and philanthropic organisations (Higham, 2014b), namely persons and organisations with sufficient resources, expertise and contacts to demonstrate capacity and capability as school proposers. In 2015, the DfE requested that free school applicants provide evidence of 'necessary experience and credentials to deliver the school to opening' (DfE, 2015c, p 2), such as 'access to individuals with specific and sufficient time commitments and relevant experience in … managing school finances, leadership, project management, marketing [and] human resources' (DfE, 2015c, p 24). Funded by the DfE and advocate of free schools, the New Schools Network (NSN) makes the point that: 'The most successful Free School groups are those with a diverse range of individuals, skills and contacts' (NSN 2016).

During 2012, when I was conducting fieldwork, the above free school was halfway through its first year of opening. It was therefore a very busy time for the governors, many of whom were preparing school policy documents for ratification, outlining the terms of reference for different committees, conducting a skills audit of the governing body, embedding quality controls to enhance long-term sustainability, setting targets according to Ofsted-approved benchmarks, monitoring pupil premium spending, commissioning consultants to carry out external evaluations, designing and implementing delegation of authority, outsourcing contracts to private bidders, perfecting the use of data coding and tracking instruments, generating business links and sponsorship, hiring new staff and scoping premises for a new school building. This level of administration, oversight and strategic design is now typical of the 'corporate work' performed by many governing bodies in England today, especially those functioning outside local government control and with responsibility for the financial and educational performance of the school. But this governing body was not exactly typical.

Unlike schools situated in deprived, low-income areas, where co-opted governors tend to be bussed in from outside the immediate area, the governors at this particular school reflected the local community, where the average house price is £1 million. Among the governing body were members of the professional and managerial class, specifically people with skills and experience in marketing, communications, business development, accountancy, town planning, investment funding, project management and advertising. The types of creative, strategic work undertaken by these governors were suggestive of people who are mobile, calculative, tech-savvy and business-driven. There were elements of entrepreneurship to how these governors conducted themselves and their approach to governing schools. In many ways, their actions echoed and redeemed elements of the corporate world, namely people who view problems as challenges and opportunities and who adopt a positive attitude to change and risk-taking. It is precisely these kinds of people who the government wishes to see populating governing bodies. As the Parliamentary Under Secretary of State for Schools, Lord Nash, argued during his speech to the Independent Academies Association (IAA) in 2013:

> 'I'm certainly not opposed to parents and staff being on the GB [governing body], but people should be appointed on a clear prospectus and because of their skills and expertise as governors; not simply because they represent particular interest groups ... Running a school is in many ways like running a business, so we need more business people coming forward to become governors.' (GUK, 2013)

Remaking school governance

As Sallis (1988) shows, governors – the principal agents of school governance – can be traced back over six hundred years to the Winchester School in 1382, where their primary responsibility was to scrutinise the teaching and progress of schools with a view to attesting the 'quality' of provision and giving some assurance to the funders of the school on matters of financial probity and continuity of vision. During this time, however, schools were either maintained and funded by religious organisations (in the case of charity schools) or privately funded by town or city corporations by means of endowment or subscription (in the case of public schools and independent schools, which were limited to the most privileged or 'deserving poor'). This meant that school governance, or 'stewardship' and 'trusteeship' as it was known then, was voluntary for the majority of schools except for those schools in receipt of public subsidy (grammar and charity schools specifically). The 1902 Education Act was therefore significant for the development of school governance, to the extent that it shifted power away from church authorities and towards state-centred control driven by county councils introduced in 1888. Up until this point, the notion of 'individual schools, individually governed' (Kogan et al, 1984, p 3) was therefore commonplace within the English school system, albeit realised in different ways and sometimes not realised at all due to the resistance among some school boards and city authorities to delegate powers to a body of governors. It was not until the 1970s that power began to shift towards governors.

Against the backdrop of a diminishing post-war 'rationing culture' and the changing expectations of burgeoning 'consumer culture', public discourse on the role of parents in education was changing. In England and the United States in particular, 'parents were pressing for increased decentralization of educational decision-making to local community school boards' (Kogan et al, 1984, p 5). A key turning point in the development of school governance came in 1975 with the organisation of a Committee of Enquiry organised under the chairmanship of Tom Taylor (later Lord Taylor of Blackburn) and the then Secretary of State for Education. The outcome of this enquiry was the publication of the committee's report, *A New Partnership for Our Schools* (Taylor, 1977), which recommended among other things the duty of local authorities to delegate powers to governors and for governors to exercise those powers on their behalf. These recommendations would not be fully realised until the introduction of the Education Act 1980 and, more importantly, the Education Act 1986, which sought to overturn politicised nomination procedures by granting schools freedom to co-opt members to the governing body.

Schools were also permitted at this time to opt out of local authority control and to become independent planners and managers of their services in the role of grant-maintained schools. Take the example of city technology colleges (CTCs) introduced under the terms of the Education Reform Act 1988 and the local management of schools.

These schools operated outside the purview of local authority control to enable the maximum delegation of financial and managerial responsibilities to the governing body (Whitty et al, 1993).

As Sallis (1988, p 137) shows, the structure of feeling among many headteachers, teachers and local authorities at the time was that the Education Act 1986 represented 'attacks on local authority independence, teacher status and morale, and free and fair schooling for children'. However, Sallis (1988, p 137) goes on to argue that the Education Act 1986 'affords opportunities to strengthen the concept of local responsibility, enhance teacher status and morale and restore free and fair schooling for children'. For example, the Education Act 1980 strengthened the notion of a stakeholder model of school governance, by confirming the statutory right of parents to be elected as governors. Contradictory forces were also at work during this time. In 1987, the then Conservative government introduced a national curriculum, in effect centralising state power and removing the responsibilities of governors to shape the curriculum. What this amounted to was less local authority interference but more centralisation of state power. As Dean et al argue:

> 'In recent years (effectively since the 1988 Education Reform Act), the degree of direct control from central government has increased, at least for state schools, while the degree of local authority control has declined. The majority of schools, therefore, have gained a high level of independence of action, but only within a highly prescriptive framework of national regulation.' (Dean et al, 2007, p 3)

Devolved management

Following these trends, the then New Labour government introduced academies in 2000. These were originally designed to offer 'radical and innovative challenges to tackling educational disadvantage' (DfES, 2005) among underperforming schools in disadvantaged urban areas. Academies in effect constituted the wholesale expansion of CTCs established in 1988 under the then Conservative government. The basic legal model for CTCs (state-funded and privately run pursuant to a contract with the Secretary of State) is the same model for academies today, albeit funding agreements for academies post-2010 are variable (Wolfe, 2013). This includes free schools introduced by the Conservative-led government in 2010 which, similar to the legal set-up of academies, operate under conditions of devolved management as public–private hybrid organisations: state-funded schools operating outside local authority control and run by private sponsors and academy chains, or in a small number of cases by local parents and teachers.

While there is nothing about these reforms to suggest something new about the trajectory of English education policy over the last thirty years, the scale and pace of these reforms is undoubtedly something very new. Consider that New Labour opened three academies in September 2002 and 14 academies in 2003 and 2004 combined. As the architect of the academies programme, Lord Andrew Adonis, recalls: 'the tipping point came with Tony Blair's commitment in July 2004 to establish at least 200 academies' (Adonis, 2012, p xiii). Between September 2002 and May 2010, New Labour oversaw the creation of 210 academies in England (BBC, 2012). The accelerated pace of these reforms occurred in May 2010 when, under the instruction of the Conservative-led government, new legislation was rolled out, making it possible for all 'good' and 'outstanding' schools (schools judged by the school's inspectorate, Ofsted (2015), to be exemplary in terms of effective teaching, assessment, learning, management and leadership) to become academies.

Subsequent to these reforms, underperforming schools were systematically targeted by the government for academy conversion or 'improvement'. In some cases, schools were forcibly converted under the instruction of government-employed 'academy brokers' (Holehouse, 2013). In tandem with these trends has been increased 'disintermediation', namely: 'the withdrawal of power and influence from intermediate or "meso-level" educational authorities that operate between local schools and national entities' (Lubienski, 2014, p 424). However, the diminishing capacity of local authorities to intervene as key middle-tier players in the organisation, delivery and monitoring of education services does not necessarily mean a missing middle but rather a shift towards public–private partnerships, in which the 'informal authority of networks supplements and supplants the formal authority of government' (Rhodes, 2007, p 1247). These trends reflect the creation of a heterogeneous, intermediary space occupied by different voluntary and private actors and organisations, including 'local authorities, teaching school alliances, federations, chains and partnerships, the National College, private companies and other school improvement initiatives' (Hill, 2012, p 22). As I will go on to show, governors also occupy a key role in this space.

The hollowing out and repopulating of the middle therefore represents 'a shift away from formal local government structures and institutions as the principal locus of policy shaping and service delivery to what has become known as local governance' (Atkinson, 2012, p 40). Also known as cooperation, co-governance or co-management, these trends denote a shift from government to governance, from a 'logic of structures' (defined by hierarchies and top-down bureaucracy) to a 'logic of flows' (defined through interdependence between organisations and interactions between network members) (Lash, 2002, p vii). It can also be read 'as the latest in a dishonourable history of strategies of "depoliticization" of politics that attempt to conceal the problems and conflicts of politics behind an appeal to forms of knowledge and varieties of technical expertise' (Clarke, 2008, p 142). But to say these trends represent the removal of political control and influence over strategic decisions would be misleading. New forms of political control intended to guide the actions of others are evident through the rise of a performance culture among governors (Wilkins, 2016).

Under new inspection guidelines introduced by the school's inspectorate, Ofsted, in 2012, school governance is now considered integral to both school leadership and school improvement – so much so that governors are judged by Ofsted on how effectively they hold senior school leaders to account for the financial and educational performance of the school. Announcements and statutory guidance from the DfE (2013) and Ofsted (2011) also highlight the key responsibilities to be undertaken by governors, which include providing scrutiny of direction, enabling strategy and ensuring accountability. As I will go on to show, these trends have tightened government focus on the role of governors, now increasingly imagined in policy and instrumental terms as subjects whose function is to produce schools that are intelligible to the funders and to the regulatory body as self-sustaining, expert-handled, performance-driven, 'high-reliability' organisations. This means that governors are required as a condition of their role to embody and celebrate certain attitudes and orientations take to be vital to 'strong governance', namely rigorous checks and balances weighted and assessed against set targets and long-term goals. These corporate sensibilities – or corporate elitism – not only provide the ground logic or deeper frames guiding the day-to-day activities of governors, but they also set limits on what it means to govern and who is 'fit for purpose' in terms of supporting the realisation of these aims in practice.

The data presented in this chapter are taken from a three-year research project funded by the ESRC (Grant Ref. ES/K001299/1). A key focus of the project concerned the changing role and responsibilities of governors under recent education reforms and the necessity for governors under conditions of devolved management to enhance corporate, contract and performative measures of accountability. Data included over 100 interviews with headteachers, senior school leaders, school business managers and governors, together with 42 observations of governing body meetings.

Risky business

It is evident from the way many governing bodies conduct themselves today, especially with the roll-back of local government and the roll-out of devolved management, that financial probity is key to strong governance:

> 'They [governors] have to make sure the money's right ... they didn't tell me how to run a thirteen million pound turnover business, and some of the guys in there have run thirteen million, so there is that level of making sure that that works ... in the end as an academy there isn't a nice big local authority behind you if you don't make the budget balance and you can't afford to pay your staff in July.' (Christopher, Headteacher, Child's Hill)

Another key role of governors is to performance manage those with operational responsibilities for the day-to-day running of the school – the delivery of the curriculum, maintenance of premises, safeguarding of children, and so forth. The roll-back of local government oversight and intervention has produced a regulatory gap and related concerns that some schools are failing to govern themselves properly. Hence the importance of governors to central government. As functionaries of the state, governors are central to the formation of quasi-autonomous entities such as free schools and academies. The day-to-day practices they undertake constitute vital relays for linking the formally autonomous operations of schools with the 'public' ambitions of government:

> 'By making us answer those questions and making sure that we have answers to those questions, they [governors] are having an impact. And there's no doubt for me the fact that I will have to explain things to the governors. It does affect my work.' (Christopher, Headteacher, Child's Hill)

'I wouldn't want the governing body to be directing my work, and dictating my work, or the school's work, but you want them there as, you know, somebody to kind of like just remember you will have to explain this to me at some point.' (Robert, Assistant Headteacher, Wingrave)

In many ways, governors today mirror the function of parastatal agents and bodies such as the school's inspectorate, Ofsted: 'They provide the information that will allow the state, the consumer or other parties – such as regulatory agencies – to assess the performance of these quasi-autonomous agencies, and hence govern them – evaluation, audit' (Rose, 1999, p 147). Governors open up schools to new grids of visibility and therefore cultivate the kinds of spaces and practices through which the internal operation of schools can be subject to new methods of scrutiny and control. But in order for governors to successfully temper these specific arrangements, internal school processes must lend themselves to audit and measurement so that they can be ranked, sorted and graded by external evaluators. Specific types of skills and knowledge therefore tend to be privileged over others – data mining and analysis, accountancy, performance evaluation and risk management in particular (Wilkins, 2016). Governors therefore find themselves engaged in the kinds of 'corporate work' where the 'core business is educational outcomes' (Wendy, Governance Manager, T-ALK, Sponsor of Richford) and 'the only thing that really counts are the outcomes' (Herman, Diocese Representative, Richford).

Corporatisation of school governance is also evident in the way that governors make explicit the connections between school governance and a business approach:

'So when you are a governor of a school you are basically running a business ... And you've got to run something like that on a business-like basis. Now it's not a business but it has to be run in a business-like fashion.' (Alex, Vice Chair of Governors, Moorhead)

'I think going to, once you make that move as a school, to go to academy status, as a headteacher of that school it is quite daunting in the sense you are going into much more of a business.' (Liz, Assistant Headteacher, Canterbury)

'I'm not a curriculum person as such but the business of the school interests me … Well, pupils equals pounds, you've got to provide a first class education.' (Dominic, Chair of Resources Committee, Ballard's Wood)

The legal and financial responsibilities underpinning academy conversion means that governors face pressures to rethink and revise traditional, 'stakeholder' models of school governance, once described to me as a 'bums on seat' culture. The growth of disintermediation and decentralisation in the education system over the last six years means that central government now looks to governors as enablers of reform on the ground and, more importantly, as agents willing and prepared to absorb the risks and insecurities once managed by local government:

'Well if you don't perform in the private sector you lose your job typically … I think in my experience the private sector there's less room for error. And I think that forces a discipline and attention to detail, which is less prevalent in the public sector. … One of the reasons why the academy concept came to play was this very idea of bringing private sector into this space.' (Sam, Deputy Chair of Governors, Richford)

'Just imagine yourself in business. You've got a problem in business you can't just slide home. You've got to sort it out. You've got to sort out the balance sheet. That's gonna be an issue and things like that. You can't just assume that someone else is going to sort it out for you. It's not like that. But that's the price you pay for the additional responsibility.' (Larry, LEA Governor, Wingrave)

This has direct consequences for the types of people who get to enter governance roles. Specifically, the types of people who are considered 'fit for purpose' tend to be those with the skills and knowledge relevant to, and generative of, the conditions and materiality of devolved management:

'It would be an advantage to have, or in the finance sector, those kind of businessy-type skills. They are quite invaluable as well I think when you are making those decisions and for someone to have that kind of knowledge.' (Liz, Associate Headteacher, Canterbury)

'I think she [the chair of governors] hopes that with the move to academy status that we can professionalise the governing body and move up a gear.' (Mark, LEA Governor, Canterbury)

Governing bodies are also actively seeking people who are trained and skilled in the art of compliance monitoring, namely people who are familiar with embedding systems of scrutiny and control to future-proof the sustainability and integrity of organisations in the face of public investigation. This includes the ritual undertaking of procedural imperatives and of compliance-checking internal processes against targets set by regulatory bodies and against statutory requirements and contractual obligations issued by government.

'So compliance is a big issue and ultimate responsibility, which is why it's very important that the relationship between the governing body and the senior relationship team is a strong one because unless you are hearing everything you need to hear, you know, something could be going on that suddenly becomes a public issue, with potential media involvement, and you as a governing body say well we didn't know this was happening.' (Gregory, Foundation Governor, Child's Hill)

In their study of governing bodies, Deem et al (1995) observed that it is difficult for governors to behave as 'critical citizens' (to engage as political subjects with potentially conflicting interests and modes of participating) when they are conscripted to behave as 'state volunteers'. We might argue that today governors do more than the work of the state. Under conditions of devolved management, the conduct of governors appears to be shaped by the logic of the market and the rationality of business. The suggestion is that governors occupy a role that stands at the intersection of the state and the market.

Corporatisation?

In this chapter, I have briefly discussed the relationship between wider political trends affecting the state school system in England, namely disintermediation, depoliticisation and decentralisation, and related changes to the role and responsibilities of governors. The rapid spread of devolved management across the English school system means that, in the absence of local government monitoring and oversight, governors have been spotlighted by central government as key to enhancing accountability, namely by opening up senior school leaders to greater forms of scrutiny and control. As purveyors of corporate work, governors tend to be interpellated and organised as monitors, assessors or appraisers, so that external regulators can be assured of the performance, legality and efficiency of the internal operations performed by senior school leaders.

In some cases, governing bodies that were once made up of local voluntary associations are being replaced by professionally managed, translocal organisations, such as academy sponsors. In other cases, governing bodies are seeking guidance on how to reconstitute themselves in the image of corporate boards, so they may adapt to the challenges of school autonomy on their own terms. In a small number of cases, some governing bodies appear to require little or no change to their practices, because their existing approaches are sufficiently 'modernised' or 'corporatised' to meet the requirements of devolved management. These trends indicate both the corporatisation of school governance and the hollowing out of democracy.

Since 2010 the Conservative government has attacked some of the normative preferences guiding school governance up until now (see GUK, 2013, 2015), namely proportional representation and wider community participation where it does not contribute to smooth oversight of educational and financial performance. Opposition to a stakeholder model of school governance can be discerned among government and many quangos and private and third sector agencies (Stuart, 2014), where it is framed in anachronistic terms as not fit for purpose, as something inappropriate, unwieldy and counterproductive to the tasks and responsibilities now facing governors. Arguably this is true – democracy lends itself to possibilities of difference, deliberation and even dissent. Such possibilities are not exactly complimentary to discrete, technical practices and expert regulatory measures designed exclusively and narrowly instrumentally to ensure smooth bureaucratic administration and evaluation of organisational performance. Hence the dominant discourse now appears to favour a skills-based model of school governance, one that promotes conditional participation subject to skills and technocratic efficiency led by professionals, expert handlers and research people (Wilkins, 2016). As Leo et al (2010, p 77) argue: 'Appointments [to the governing body] need not be based on any representational niceties or on any ideological links to local democracy'.

However, we need to be aware that the desire to privatise decision-making in this way has ideological links and implications of its own. Consider that the appeal to neutral expert administration over politics serves to make school governance a microcosm for government regulation. This is because, strategically, central government stands to gain more influence over the formation of schools where corporatisation and attendant concepts of 'performance' and 'productivity' predominate. Politicised nominations to the governing body are not necessarily counterproductive to these aims, but they certainly present a risk to disrupting and derailing what the government intends governors to be and to do.

TWELVE

The courtier's empire: a case study of providers and provision

Steven J. Courtney

Introduction

In this chapter, I present data and analysis regarding how headteachers and principals[1] in England are increasingly being hierarchised, and their space for agency constrained, by newly powerful regional actors. The latter may either belong to a corporate elite or succeed through adopting their methods, and are achieving newly exalted positions within an education policy landscape of corporate-inspired structural reform. These elite system-leaders are building empires of education provision, and are defining what is possible as a headteacher for others in such empires and even what is meant by school leadership.

The neoliberal and neoconservative reform agenda to which education has been subjected since the mid-1980s in England has enabled a corporate elite to open or acquire publicly funded schools. This elite embodies the ideal, entrepreneurial leader, constructed through policy and lauded by policy makers. In England, for instance, from 2000, 'under-performing' local authority (or district) schools have been replaced by independent, business-sponsored, state-funded *academies* (homologous with charter schools in the US). Their architect, Andrew Adonis, lavishly praised elite corporate leaders of academies' forerunners as 'highly capable sponsor-managers, who ran their schools free of the shifting sands of local and national education bureaucracies' (Adonis, 2012, p 56). Some, such as Peter Vardy and Harry Djanogly,[2] see this preferment formalised through a knighthood or through membership of key networks.

So, the phenomenon of *elite, corporate education providers at the state court* is not new. These courtiers market key state policies through embodying their objectives, means and privileged status. What is new, and what is explored here, is how the subjectivities and practices of headteachers and principals are being structured and subordinated by corporatised elites. This is happening in and through the regional empires that these elites are establishing, which draw on corporate structural models facilitating expansion and acquisition, and through their personal contacts with powerful actors. These arguments make a contribution to the literatures concerning how headteachers position themselves, and are positioned, in relation to external change (for example Grace, 1995; Gunter and Forrester, 2009; Thomson, 2010) and/or within a local field (for example Coldron et al, 2014; McGinity, 2014). To make this contribution, I discuss and typologise three responses to headteacher/principal subordination to corporate elites: the 'follower'; the 'acquired'; and the 'excluded'.

The empirical data and arguments are illuminated through Bourdieu's (1990, 1998) concepts of capital, misrecognition and symbolic violence. The two latter concepts explain how agents interpret the effects of arbitrary power relations which may subordinate them iin ways that make that subordination seem natural, or to use Bourdieu's term, *doxic*. I interviewed nine school leaders in the north-west of England as part of a project funded by the Economic and Social Research Council (ESRC) (Courtney, 2015b), three of whom raised these issues unprompted. Through the case of England, I aim to illuminate how – and with what effects – neoliberalism internationally is facilitating business–derived models of organisational expansion within education 'systems' (for example Saltman, 2010).

Gaining elite status as a system-leading headteacher

Responsibility for the strategic oversight of local state-school systems in England has historically belonged to democratically accountable local authorities (LAs), thereby enabling claims to 'publicness'. The English instantiation of a global education reform movement aiming to dismantle welfare-state education systems has consequently targeted LAs on several fronts over the last thirty years. For instance, LAs' role in directly managing schools' budgets was eliminated through local management of schools in 1988; and new school types have been created, with forerunners such as grant-maintained schools and city colleges paving the way for the contemporarily dominant academies and their subtypes, including free schools, studio schools and university technical colleges (Courtney, 2015c). These are funded directly from central government and exemplify also how LAs' role in governance and administrative support has been supplanted by corporate sponsors (Courtney, 2015a). New structures have been required to replace these systematising (formerly LA) functions. Two are particularly important and feature here as alternative 'systems' in a neoliberal landscape: the multi-academy trust (MAT); and the teaching school.

In England, by 2014, 21.6% of state schools (including around 60% of secondary schools) were academies (DfE, 2014). Late capitalism favours in education provision, as elsewhere, the concentration of capital and the consequent emergence of elites – academies are therefore increasingly subject to legal, cultural and organisational mergers into *chains*, whose most common form is the MAT. This is an independent legal entity, which enters into a contractual arrangement with the Department for Education (DfE) to provide education across multiple sites in return for state funding.

While the MAT is commonly understood as the 'sponsor' and these sites known as 'sponsored academies', in fact these latter have no distinct legal status; their relationship is rather one of *merger* and presently they cannot legally disassociate from their MAT 'sponsor'. MATs consequently structurally facilitate aggressive expansionism by canny CEOs. A major concern has been the prospect of education's privatisation through academy sponsorship by elite corporate actors (Saltman, 2010; Courtney and Gunter, 2017). However, poor performance and governance in some academy chain sponsors (see, for example, Downs, 2013) has opened a new front, whereby (previously) public sector actors are corporatised through adopting the purposes and methods of the corporate elite, even reconstituting their identities to succeed in a corporatised policy environment. This success is exemplified through elite system-leader status as CEO of a MAT. All academy chains with a business or charitable sponsor share a MAT governance structure: the arrangements therefore come with state approval, owing largely, according to Deborah Perry[3] (in a document which has been removed from the public domain), to their 'clear lines of accountability' and, exemplifying *the tail wagging the dog*, to their offering 'a structure within which the role of an Executive Head can be readily utilised'. The hierarchisation of those leading schools may therefore be seen as a policy goal – and the creation of elite members a corollary.

Leading a teaching-school alliance is another way for headteachers or principals to increase their operational range and is another indicator of elite membership. Teaching schools were developed from 2010 to assume responsibility for:

• initial and early-career teacher education;
• leadership development;

- designating, accrediting and brokering teacher-consultants, known as *specialist leaders of education* (SLEs), who provide school-to-school support;
- research and development.

The teaching school operationalises these functions through its formal network, called an *alliance*, of schools and other institutions. Schools may bid for teaching-school status if they receive 'outstanding' in at least three (the overall rating, leadership and teaching) of the five categories rated by the school inspectorate in England, Ofsted. The purposes and effects of teaching schools fit within a neoliberal policy framework, which autonomises schools by transferring educational responsibilities within the alliance from the 'expert knowers' in universities (teacher education) and LAs (school support) to 'practitioner knowers' in schools. This knowledge is packaged and sold through a consultancy model, whereby needful schools inside and outside the alliance bid for support from SLEs, and teaching-school leaders manage those bids (Courtney, 2015a).

Teaching-school alliances and MATs constitute new, market-ready systems in education policy. A headteacher or principal seeking competitive advantage must embody this new policy construction of best practice in leadership privileging systems over education. Such 'system-leaders' are to play a key role in future reform aiming to further reduce the role of the public through LAs, as exhorted by Lord Nash, schools minister and MAT CEO:[4]

> 'Huge change is taking place enabling us ... to convert the school system into a genuinely school-led system, not run by central or local bureaucrats but by school leaders themselves.' (Nash, 2014, np)

So, echoing New Labour from 1997 to 2010, a neoliberal reform agenda is operationalised through appealing to a reconfigured leadership which constructs an elite cadre of *believers* (Gunter, 2012), but here to lead whole systems and whose purpose is to replace LAs in delivering those systemic functions. This *turn* empowers new actors; and the provenance of some of these in the public sector blurs the public/private boundary, permitting corporatised leadership to flourish and disguising the significance of social capital through extensive private sector networks. An example of such a 'system-leader' is Brian Sykes CBE,[5] CEO of a MAT here referred to as Eckersley Trust. Sykes, along with other elite academy principals, has obtained MAT and teaching-school lead status and is using them to leverage increasing symbolic and economic capital at the expense of regional competitors. His achievement of these statuses signals his greater symbolic capital (Bourdieu, 1990) to peers as well as parents-as-consumers.

System leadership, while discursively privileged, is insufficient to achieve Sykes' elite status: the final criterion is *greater social capital* demonstrated by *access to the political-cultural elite*, constituted of, for instance, ministers and their aides, high-ranking civil servants along with certain people from business, the media and the arts. McKelvoy (2015, np) calls this elite 'the new network-ocracy [whose members] float between different spheres of influence, with a handy web of friends and contacts in similarly lofty positions'. In education, affiliates and (near) members of this elite attend or chair national committees or councils, gain honours or other official recognition, and are designated 'preferred bidders' in acquisitions and tenders. The line between the corporate elite and those who mimic them is consequently blurred (Gunter, 2015).

Leading in a courtier's empire

The data from three headteachers and principals demonstrate how their identities and practices are structured by Sykes' activities. I have typologised their positioning as the 'follower', the 'acquired', and the 'excluded', through which I offer a partial, empirical answer to Thomson's (2010) challenge to the field to identify when and how heads work collectively, when they are 'prepared to cede decisions to a networked organisation' (Thomson, 2010, p 17), and which decisions they retain. These positions are structured responses to a neoliberal policy context producing corporatised elites as a means of achieving education reform, where acquisition, outbidding and market dominance are normalised features.

The 'follower'

Phil Ormerod heads a selective grammar school that recently academised. These features, along with the school's 'outstanding' rating by Ofsted, mean that he has significant symbolic capital (Bourdieu, 1990). Fifteen years ago, these qualities would have sufficed to indicate elite status, but in a policy context where advantage accrues to those who demonstrate the capacity and ambition to lead *multi*-academy trusts, Phil is obliged to acknowledge his (and his school's) subaltern status through joining Sykes' teaching-school alliance.

Phil is suspicious of powerful, charismatic MAT CEOs, describing them as 'doing a little bit of empire-building', with questions about whether the 'over-riding moral purpose is ... to improve the overall shape of schools, which a lot of them will say, or is it about making sure that you're at the heart of what's going on?' Sykes' success is attributed not to expertise, but because he 'is a personal contact of Michael Gove [then Secretary of State for Education], and is his favourite headteacher of all time'. With only small differences in choices taken, preference, leadership qualities or circumstance, the ingredients existed for Phil to be like Sykes. Instead, his positioning is reactionary:

> 'We had this discussion at the governing body; I was kind of saying to them, '"ook, we need to get involved somewhere, we can't be an island". You can't be. We're good, and we're confident, but even for us, to not be involved somewhere would be seen as weakness.'

This involvement is cautious; 'I feel like we're in the game, but ... I'm kind of playing around at the edges rather than diving in full speed ahead'. This approach to Eckersley Trust's teaching-school alliance comprises semi-detached participation, whereby Phil is 'on the inside' only 'to find out exactly what is going on'. This is partly to escape sanctions:

> 'It's almost ticking the Ofsted box; it's ticking the, we have a system-wide responsibility as a school to make sure we're part of system improvement. And if you're not, you're going to be criticised for it ... The playing a game thing is actually almost covering our back, because that's the political agenda.'

Phil frames these alliance-related activities as being necessary consequences of his strategic decision to join rather than as contributing to a wider vision for educational excellence:

> 'We've had people on outstanding teacher programmes, improving teacher programmes, doing the School Direct [school-based teacher education conducted through the alliance]. We've been involved in the research ... So that kind of thing is happening.'

These are passively described as *things which are happening* rather than *things which he is initiating* to benefit pupils or staff. In another example, Phil describes his participation in Eckersley Trust's bid for an important contract to lead a regional curriculum hub as being 'sort of on their paperwork'. What is missing is any talk of Phil's own vision work, contemporarily constructed through policy as equating to leadership itself (Courtney and Gunter, 2015). So, Phil's association with Eckersley Trust with its market dominance, despite his symbolic capital, relegates him to one of the led rather than permitting significant expression of agentic leadership. He misrecognises this loss of agency as his active dismissal of performative and insubstantial empire-building:

> 'It's a bit of an Emperor's clothes situation … I think it's all gloss and underneath there's no real substance to what's going on … People are doing stuff, but it's not co-ordinated in the teaching-school framework as people think it is.'

This misrecognition is articulated as phlegmatic acceptance of not being in the top-tier of school leadership: 'we can't have 3,000 Brians running around the place, you know … A lot of heads don't always take that approach. They're not all ego-centric expansionists.' Phil anticipates too that Sykes will encounter other elite system-leaders: 'I don't think they'll be working together, I think they'll be carving it up, separately. It is a much more business, free-market world we're living in. Whether that's a good thing or not, time will tell.'

The 'acquired'

At the time of our first interview, Will was about to open a new type of academy called a university technical college (UTC). These were conceived by the Baker Dearing Educational Trust, which owns and manages the brand, to offer technical education to 14–18 year olds with:

- a corporate pattern of working hours;
- sponsorship by corporations represented on the governing body;
- a curriculum co-constructed with industry partners and partly delivered by industrialists;
- close university links.

In our second interview, Will spoke of his concerns about recruitment to the new UTC. Owing to its entry age, which is out of sync with surrounding schools, pupils intending to go there would have to leave their current school at age 14, which would lose the funding accompanying them. This was one of the reasons which disinclined local headteachers to support Will's UTC. Furthermore, he reported that the UTC's educational partner/sponsors' 'capacity to support in the way that we needed support wasn't there'. Six months later, in our final interview, Will announced that the UTC was 'in the process of becoming part of Eckersley Trust'. This acquisition had been facilitated by the UTC being plugged into networks where key relationships are formed:

> 'Were there other options? Yeah. There were a couple of other organisations that we probably could have talked to if Eckersley hadn't come about. But Eckersley had the edge because of their relationship with our governor and being a known quantity from that point of view, I think.'

As it was a new academy, Will had been (discursively at least) an *autonomous* leader, free of the LA's 'bureaucratic' control. His autonomy in practice did not exceed the ideological limits of neoliberalism, which encouraged in him the *relentless leadership* of a school he liked to think of as 'an education establishment that is being driven and directed by business'. Nonetheless, following the acquisition of his UTC by Eckersley, Will has been subordinated as a leader. There is now an executive headteacher hierarchically over him, parachuted in from Eckersley to resolve its operational problems. Will's interpretation of this is influenced by his difficult experience of the UTC's first year, insisting, for example, that the executive headteacher 'is a good thing because we need that extra capacity'. On the possibility of his being made redundant by Eckersley, he responds:

> 'I'm open to it. My view was, and I got asked this by their director of secondary education, I don't at all feel threatened because I've got to the point in my professional life where something had to change. And my view is that if my face doesn't fit within Eckersley, I'll take it on the chin and I'll move on.'

The acquisition is thereby depictable as salvational. Eckersley has saved the UTC from public failure and probable closure; has saved Will from professional burnout; and has saved the UTC brand from contamination – Baker Dearing Educational Trust being, in Will's view, concerned with 'making sure it's just good news that's coming out the door'.

These data demonstrate one way in which the tension between a marketised 'system' and the political and educational need to avoid market failure can be reconciled: these near-failures are instead opportunities for entrepreneurial and ambitious MAT CEOs to acquire millions of pounds' worth of assets in land and often renovated buildings. Not only is failure averted, but the market is also strengthened through the use of its technologies to achieve it.

Bourdieu's concept of symbolic violence is useful for thinking about how power is operationalised in the school-led system revealed in Will's account. Symbolic violence 'allows force to be fully exercised while disguising its true nature as force and gaining recognition, approval and acceptance by dint of the fact that it can present itself under the appearances of universality' (Bourdieu, 1990, p 85). Will's story exemplifies the misrecognition of the imposition of an arbitrary set of conditions that subordinates him. For Bourdieu:

> to say that certain agents recognize the legitimacy of a pedagogic agency is simply to say that the complete definition of the power relationship within which they are objectively placed implied that these agents are unable to realize the basis of that relationship... (Bourdieu and Passeron, 1990, p 14)

So, it is not universally or historically the case that school leaders' exercise of headship/principalship may be thus interrupted; nor that the leader is rendered a deputy; nor that the process be understood as salvational; nor that schools be rebranded and relaunched. These are specific conditions, made intelligible to, and normalised among, actors in the field through a market logic whose conditions are partly maintained through misrecognised symbolic violence. In inviting Eckersley to take over his school, Will shows the 'largely below-conscious complicity' that James (2015, p 101) argues is fundamental to Bourdieu's conceptualisation of subjugation.

The 'excluded'

Like Phil, Bridget has several characteristics positioning her as *near-elite*. Although her school is not an academy, as a voluntary-aided Roman Catholic school it is jointly governed by the Catholic Church and the LA. Its faith status constitutes a successful brand (Courtney, 2015c), whose benefits to her own symbolic capital as headteacher are reinforced by her long-lasting and successful leadership there.

Moreover, she leads a teaching-school alliance. Nonetheless, she lacks the social capital demonstrated through elite contacts, disqualifying her for *courtier* status. She is certain that this matters:

Steven: 'What kinds of school and school leader are on those teaching-school councils?'

Bridget: 'Ones that are very pally with Mr Gove [then Secretary of State for Education], if you want my honest opinion.'

Bridget competes directly with Sykes for high-status contracts in the region, but her perception that insider status is privileged over expertise and experience leads her to conclude that 'it's developing into the most corrupt system that I've ever known in education'. Below is Bridget's account of the bidding process that prompted her conclusion; I have altered some elements to maintain her and Eckersley Trust's anonymity.

> 'The teaching schools were asked to apply to be a science hub of expertise. And I think probably our reputation for being a leading school for science and the support we've done is national. There are very few comprehensive schools like us, and we've done considerable school-to-school work with our SLEs. So we thought that perhaps this should be something that we should go for because we've got all the credentials. So I put in an expression of interest and didn't hear anything. And two schools rang me up to ask me if I'd not applied. And I said "yes, we have". And they said, "we're on the short list; we thought you'd not applied because you were better than us and you're not on the short list". At which point I wrote a three-page letter to the DfE to say, "why aren't we on the short list? Or I'm going to take it higher? To the Secretary of State?" At which point, we ended up being on the list for the next stage, and that appalled me. It shouldn't be that because you write a letter, that you end up on the list. And the other people on the list had had the regional training for writing the bid or whatever. Had a day. We had a webinar. And we had an interview. And I knew we weren't going to get it, but I went ahead for the interview, because I knew that it would be Eckersley Trust. This was just one example that I was involved in where it was a stitch-up from day one.

> And there's no transparency. It's an odd [situation], it's grace
> and favour now, not on merit at all.'

Bridget interprets this as a performative invocation of due process, a cynical manipulation of democratic processes to legitimate the expansionism of the *preferred bidder*. For her, it means that the badges and statuses she and her school have acquired are not universal currency: they might position her advantageously in the eyes of many (see Coldron et al, 2014), but not, crucially, in those of the political elite, whose own networks ultimately produce and name the winners and signal openly to the losers that this is happening. Bridget's leadership skills and the symbolic capital of her amassed statuses do not allow her to progress beyond this point and step over the 'glass cordon' into the courtiers' VIP area, where social capital is the entry criterion.

Bridget's experience offers a case where symbolic violence must operate differently because misrecognition is impossible – Bridget is not complicit in the operationalisation of power. Since, unlike Will, her subordinate position to Sykes cannot be assumed, he is 'obliged to win and endlessly rewin the social recognition that PAu [Pedagogic Authority, or arbitrary power] confers from the outset' (Bourdieu and Passeron, 1990, p 20). Importantly, having no established basis for doing so, and in the manner experienced by Bridget, this is achieved through 'usurping the direct or inverted appearances of legitimate practice' (p 20). However, in openly engaging in questionable practices, the underlying power relations of dominion become visible and open to challenge.

Conclusion

These data reveal that powerful regional elites, such as Sykes, are structuring what is possible as a school leader and thereby defining and embodying successful school leadership. These elites' appearance is a product of the confluence of several elements. Two of these are the disposition and means to benefit from a sympathetic policy context, where new actors are being sought to adopt established, corporate technologies for removing both state and public from education provision. A further contributing element is the renewed importance of elite networks in devising and enacting policy. Their origins as education practitioners and leaders in the maintained sector both legitimates them in the field and belies their adoption of these corporate strategies and identities in order not just to play, but also to win convincingly the modern school-leadership game. Consequently, it is school-led MATs' CEOs and teaching-school leaders who will play a significant role in the next phase in the replacement of LAs in their school-support/improvement role, and who illuminate how similar policy agendas may play out internationally.

Those who applaud this development as at least a 'pause' in the corporatisation of English education provision are mistaken. This emergent elite succeeds because of its facility with corporate discourse and practice: it engages in mergers and acquisitions; obtains high-status contracts to deliver regional services in return for economic and symbolic capital; and performs (and sells) a form of *system leadership* constructed as superior. Success in corporatised leadership privileges reach over quality; growth is about *expanding* rather than *deepening*. The neoliberal project to transform the very souls of actors in the social world into calculable, calculating entities (Ball, 2003b) appears to have succeeded, the most successful contemporary embodiment of corporate leadership residing not just in incoming business people, but also in transformed school leaders themselves. Such approaches are legitimated and normalised in intellectual work in the school-improvement field (see, for example, Hargreaves, 2012; Greany, 2014).

The analysis presented here is significant because while changes to how heads position themselves and are positioned owing to the encroachment of the corporate field onto the educational are well documented (for example Grace, 1995; Thomson, 2005, 2009, 2010), what is new is how such changes are being produced through the widespread imposition and impact of corporate organisational structures. These processes are exemplified by the expansionism discussed here and embodied in elite actors. In other words, headship has long been a 'risky business' (Thomson, 2009, p 1), but those risks have not previously included to such an extent the activities of competitors made strong through the apparatus and technologies of neoliberal structural reform. In explicating the risks to heads and headship in 2009, for example, Thomson was able to conceptualise federations and federating as a possible structural solution to the problem of headteacher workload. What is revealed in the chapter is how the effects of schools coming together under one CEO is part of a new and growing problem for headteachers' agency and subjectivities. This chapter has presented three of the myriad positions possible: the 'follower' – subordinated to a corporatised elite in the market of provision; the 'acquired' – swallowed whole by this elite, expansionist provider; and the 'excluded' – outbid in a process where the social capital distinguishing this elite supersedes her own expertise.

The implication of these positions is that leaders attempting to do leadership in someone else's empire are inevitably structured such that not only are their practices constrained, but also the policy construction of leadership as agentic and all-reaching is shown to be problematic. Further, the logic of practice governing education leadership and education reform is rooted in competition and market positioning. Bourdieu and Passeron (1990) shows us here the way in which education policy, as an instrument of pedagogic authority, has constructed the limits experienced by a majority of headteachers out of another elite group's hierarchical, organisational and discursive supremacy, weakening rather than strengthening the system they are meant to be leading.

Acknowledgements

The research reported in this chapter was funded by the ESRC, award reference: ES/J500094/1.

Notes

[1] Those leading academy-type schools are called *principals* to differentiate them from their maintained-sector equivalents, *headteachers*.

[2] Sir Peter Vardy was CEO of a car dealership in the north-east of England and sponsored one of the first City Technology Colleges (CTC), Emmanuel College. He then created the Emmanuel Schools Foundation, an Academy Trust. Sir Harry Djanogly is a textile manufacturer who sponsored Djanogly CTC in Nottingham, and then established the Djanogly Learning Trust.

[3] Then Head of Programmes, Academies at the Specialist Schools and Academies Trust.

[4] Nash, a former venture capital worker, is simultaneously Parliamentary Under Secretary of State for Schools with responsibility for academies, and CEO of Future Academies Trust, both as at October 2016.

[5] Brian Sykes, research participants and organisations are pseudonymised.

THIRTEEN

Political and corporate elites and localised educational policy-making: the case of Kingswood Academy

Ruth McGinity

Introduction

The purpose of this chapter is to present data and analysis in order to theorise the role that both corporate and political elites played in the development and enactment of localised policy-making at Kingswood Academy, a secondary school in the north of England (anonymised name). The analysis offered here reveals how a single case-study school provides an important site to explore the ways in which the educational policy environment enables the conditions for elites to play a significant role in the development and delivery of localised policy processes in England.

The theorisation of this single case study speaks to and advances the findings of a range of studies in this volume and elsewhere (Apple, 2004; Rizvi and Lingard, 2010; Gunter, 2012; Ravitch, 2013a; Au and Ferrare, 2015). Notably, such research examines how and why globalised, marketised neoliberal approaches to education reform have led to 'organisational recalibration' (Ball, 2012a, p 94), where there are now visible multifaceted and multitudinal 'policy entrepreneurs' involved in public sector policy processes trading on and developing 'various forms of social and network capital which translate into the right to speak and the necessity of being heard' (Ball, 2012a, p 69).

In the case of Kingswood, there was a core triumvirate of policy entrepreneurs involved in a range of activities that will be described and analysed as an instantiation of how, through localised policy-making, political and corporate elites are influencing the field of education, not as incidental bystanders but as integral and central policy actors. In this sense, Kingswood's approach to localised policy-making is reflective of, and speaks to, the changing nature of educational provision in England and elsewhere, as the terrain is re-formed to privilege certain actors, networks, and ideological and political positions where a crucial tenet of the intended consequences is the privatisation of public assets and services.

The contribution is to offer an empirical account of how influence flows within a single network, thus identifying the essentialising and privileged nature that social capital plays in the exchange relations revealed through the work of policy entrepreneurs. While there is a growing body of work that focuses usefully on the spread of corporate influences on educational policies, with a particular methodological interest in using social network analysis (Au and Ferrare, 2015) and policy network analysis (Ball, 2012a), this must not be at the expense of developing localised empirical and conceptual accounts of how corporate and political elites are involved in the development of localised policy-making. Thus this chapter makes an empirical contribution in responding to the challenge of Jessop et al (2008) for more *contextual* and *specific* variations of social relations within critical policy analysis.

The analysis offered in this chapter is of significance, because the field needs to empirically extend understanding of the impact of such networks on the localised development of policy. Such analysis contributes to revealing the exchange relations within elite networks and thus the power of such networks in the conception and enactment of localised education policy in a neoliberal state. This chapter addresses this gap, and in so doing brings greater conceptual clarity through a careful tracing of how networks occurring at the localised level reflect globalised and discursive constructions of education policy as a commodified and increasingly privatised activity. Bourdieu (1986) provides the thinking tools to undertake this theoretical and intellectual work, and I deploy his conceptualisation of misrecognition as a means of interrogating how the involvement of corporate and political elites in the processes of localised policy-making reproduces the hierarchised power of particular networks, which ultimately contribute to the privatisation of educational 'goods' as marketised commodities in an era of a 'Global Educational Reform Movement' (Sahlberg, 2013).

Localised policy-making at Kingswood Academy

The data presented here are drawn from a three-year ethnographic project, funded by the Economic and Social Research Council, at Kingswood Academy between 2010 and 2013. The project involved a multilayered, qualitative approach to data generation, in which 18 students, five parents, 22 teachers, seven school leaders and two governors were interviewed on multiple occasions in order to construct 'in-depth accounts as to how school leaders, teachers, students and to a lesser extent, their parents were positioned and position-took in the production and enactment of policy processes at a local level during a period of rapid educational reform in England' (McGinity, 2014a, p 3). The data for this chapter draw on the accounts given by the principal, the deputy principal and the chair of governors to illuminate the discursive privileging of corporate and political interests in the development of localised policy-making.

During the fieldwork, in 2012, the school converted from the maintained sector to an academy – an independent state-funded school (Glatter, 2011). The Academies Act 2010 was a significant legislative intervention brought about by the Conservative-led Coalition UK government (2010–15). The Act was illustrative of the acceleration towards 'autonomy' in England, where schools are either voluntarily or forcibly removed from local authority maintenance (or control) and enabled to set up as either converted, standalone institutions or are absorbed into academy chains, in which, often corporate, sponsors are involved in the governance of a number of academies branded together into chains (Courtney, 2015a). The 2010 Act was of particular significance because, prior to this legislation, it was schools that had been identified as 'failing' by the government (through the inspectorate Ofsted) that were required to reopen as academies, whereas after the 2010 Act, schools that were deemed to be 'good' by the inspectorate were enabled to convert to academy status. It was under this legislation that Kingswood converted to academy status on the grounds of the school's record of achievement (both through the inspectorate system and standardised test results[1]). In itself, the Kingswood conversion can be understood through a reading of the changing role of the state in the development and delivery of public services (Clarke and Newman, 1997; Gewirtz, 2002), and how specifically in education the increased diversity of provision (Courtney, 2015c) demonstrates the scale and pace of change, in which the state gives way to privatised forms of governance as a means of providing policy solutions to educational problems.

The solution to remain distinctive in a competitive and diverse 'quasi-marketplace' for the principal of Kingswood was to 'opt out' of the local authority, in order to develop a set of localised policies and practices to overhaul the organisational structures and to bring in corporatised influences into the development and running of these new structures. The autonomy granted through conversion to academy enabled Kingswood to develop two pathways of provision on its single site as a means of sorting and selecting students. Between the ages of 11 and 13, all children would be educated together in a lower-school provision. Following this, there was to be a 'Professional School', which would take children from the age of 13 and would focus on academic subjects; and a Studio School, which would have a more vocational focus. (For a more in-depth explanation of this type of discrete academy, see Courtney, 2015c.) Connecting these new provisions would be an explicit emphasis on 'employability skills', embedded into the curriculum but also delivered discretely with the input developed by a global management consultancy firm. Alongside this, the school was to develop a number of employability pathways running parallel to the provisions developed, where the students would access curricula connected to a large international bank, an international airport and other smaller 'professional' firms. The governance of the school shifted during 2012, when the various partnerships were being developed with this range of corporate and professional sponsors, who were in turn invited onto the board of governors.

Networking, social capital and field theory

An additional and significant aspect of the context is the role that the local constituent Member of Parliament (a cabinet member of both the 2010–15 Conservative-led Coalition government and also of the 2015 Conservative government) played in the development of the restructuring of provision at Kingswood:

> 'Yes, it was through him [MP and Cabinet Member], he was the one that routed it through to [name of Parliamentary Under Secretary of State] … One of our industrial partners is the [name of a national business support group], which is the biggest employers' organisation for small and medium sized businesses … and the guy who's the chief executive by the end of this afternoon is going to be one of our governors … he came to the meeting with [MP] and said what we were doing is truly brilliant and all schools should be doing it …' (Principal, Kingswood Academy: Interview May 2012)

Through the development of a network between these political and corporate policy actors, a process of 'exchange relations' is visible. In this process, it is possible to conceptualise the emerging network as occurring within a social 'field' that:

… may be defined as a network, or a configuration, of objective relations between positions. These positions are objectively defined, in their existence and in the determinations they impose upon their occupants, agents or institutions, by their present and potential situation (situs) in the structure of distribution of species of power (or capital) whose possession commands access to the specific profits that are at stake at the field, as well as by their objective relation to other positions (domination, subordination, homology, etc). (Bourdieu and Wacquant, 1992, p 97)

The specific profits at stake in the developing network of relations outlined previously are high, because there is an opportunity for the principal to demonstrate 'entrepreneurial' leadership, where in England, 'successful' leadership has been located within a praxis of innovation (Gunter, 2016) and to draw on symbolic capital previously accrued in order to legitimate the localised policy activities he is developing (see also McGinity, 2014; Gunter and McGinity, 2014; McGinity and Gunter, 2016). Legitimation is via the MP, in his representation of the power that might be bestowed when the favour of the political elite is ignited. The power itself, in this particular instance, is visible in the breaching of the fields, where capital obtained in one field (for example in the political field, the educational field or the corporate field) has value in additional fields (Thomson, 2005). Fields are hierarchised, and so the breaching into the political field by the principal of Kingswood is significant, because the accumulation of symbolic capital is translated into social capital that enables the principal to hold a legitimated position in a high-profile and high-stakes network. This, of itself, is significant, because the influence of political elites in the development and delivery of localised policy-making in education is not often remarked upon, yet, as in the case of Kingswood, it plays an integral role in supporting the organisational recalibration of Kingswood, in which corporatised versions of public education are increasingly normalised.

Exchange relations in the policy process

The process of capital exchange requires an exchange relationship to occur, and so in this case it might be worth considering what sort of capital accumulation the data suggest the MP might expect to accrue in this process. The breaching of the education field is seemingly less of a legitimising activity for an MP and Cabinet Minister, yet in this case, the process of opening the doors to the principal of Kingswood –

and becoming a central policy actor in the network created as a result – matters because, as the deputy principal put it to me:

> 'So [MP] is being used, but then no doubt at some point [MP] will want to be associated with it if it does grow really big so, [MP] is not stupid. He knows that there is political gain in it if things go well.' (Deputy Principal, June 2012)

The crux of exchange relations is that there is value to be had in and through the trading of capital (whether it be financial or symbolic, for example). This is true also when it comes to the involvement of corporate elites within the processes of localised policy processes. As Ball (2012a) points out:

> Commercial consultants and public service companies ... are eager to provide and enact radical and innovative 'solutions' to policy problems, solutions which almost always take the form of inserting into public sector organizations technologies of 'modernisation' and 'transformation' and metagovernance ... as well as changing the relations between organisations – as in the deployment of the 'market form'. But also via the development of partnerships, consortia and contracting. (Ball, 2012a, p 113)

The involvement of the global corporate consultancy firm in the development and delivery of the school's localised policy processes points to the centrality given to such policy actors within educational reforms across the globe (Junemann and Ball, 2015). As such, the capital available to policy actors representing the corporate field is vast. Through processes of privatisation, enabled through governmental and legislative interventions such as the Academies Act 2010 in England or charter schools in the United States, there is a redistribution of power within the field of education, in which certain activities undertaken by certain policy actors are both privileged and legitimated. Ball's (2012a) work illustrates this point with a number of powerful examples; one such is the review of the education policy work undertaken by PricewaterhouseCoopers (pp 102-4). Importantly, Ball (2012a) focuses predominately on how the influences of multinational, corporatised policy entrepreneurs have a globalised reach. A Bourdieusian approach would draw on field theory to identify the workings of the hierarchies of power within this globalised field as a means of furthering this analysis. Grenfell and James (2004) identify that the process of thinking with field theory gives rise to analyses in which:

> What is thinkable and unthinkable, expressible and inexpressible, and valued or not, is the product of the field structures within which they arise and the principles of legitimation operating there. This legitimation establishes an orthodoxy – or doxa. (Grenfell and James, 2004, p 509)

In other words, the doxa refers to the architecture of assumptions that we take for granted and which are subsequently rationalised and privileged in hierarchial ways. The neoliberal turn in educational reform – and the positioning of corporate elites within the development and delivery of a vast range of educational policy activities, services and consultancy work – has reconstituted the field structures in which localised policy work is undertaken, and so reveals the orthodoxy of corporatism within educational reform processes. The contribution here is that through the establishment of a network in which the political, the corporate and the educational fields are breached in the development of localised policy processes, the legitimation of such activities becomes not just common sense. The field structures operate in such a way that those principals unable or unwilling to 'play the game' find themselves in precarious and vulnerable situations (Courtney and Gunter, 2015).

The misrecognition of localised school policy-making

The exchange relations are such that the triumvirate of policy entrepreneurs in the case of Kingswood Academy are revealing their implicit understanding of the doxic narrative in the field. This reading goes beyond a process of accumulating capital *per se*, but extends to the place that social capital specifically plays in the 'right to speak and the necessity of being heard' (Ball, 2012a, p 69). The chair of governors demonstrates his own implicit understanding of the neoliberal *doxa* in how certain human–capital approaches to educational provision are privileged within educational policy in England, and subsequently the centrality of the social capital afforded through the networks developed in the successful implementation of policy activities that reflect this:

> 'If you listen to CBI [Confederation of British Industry] or the Forum for Small Businesses employers are saying that they see kids coming out of the educational system without

those basic sort of softer skills that kids need in order to be effective in terms of competing for jobs and within the work place ... So I guess what we are trying to do is respond to that both in terms of putting something formally in to specific training in that area so that's the [input from the global management and consultancy firm] on employability and so forth ... So [MP] has been very helpful in terms of us trying to get access to the DfE [Department for Education] and getting them interested in what we are doing.' (Chair of Governors, June 2012)

In this account, it is apparent that localised policy-making at Kingswood has become a corporatised process. The breaching of fields in this network makes these entrepreneurial activities thinkable, expressible and above all valued (Grenfell and James, 2004). These processes of exchange relations are not about financial acumen (although of course in processes of privatisation, the economic privileging of transactional relationships is crucial), but rather go beyond this position:

In contrast to the cynical but also economical transparency of economic exchange, in which equivalents change hands in the same instant, the essential ambiguity of social exchange, which presupposes misrecognition, in other words, a form of faith and of bad faith (in the sense of self-deception), presupposes a much more subtle economy of time. (Bourdieu, 1986, p 24)

In this reading, the principal of Kingswood Academy, in his role as both policy architect and entrepreneur, has worked carefully and strategically, drawing on accumulated symbolic capital and his own innate understanding of the *doxa* in the field. He has thus utilised the 'subtle economy of time' in order to develop a network built on social exchanges with powerful political and corporate elites. Ball (2012a) argues that: 'one of the defining characteristics of many of the key participants in policy networks is their ability to move between social, political and business words – they practice [sic] what they preach by breaching traditional boundaries and by being flexible and adaptable' (p 50). The principal of Kingswood demonstrates his 'policy entrepreneur' credentials in this process. He shows that these traits are important not just at the global level of policy actors derived from corporate elites, such as PwC or Pearson, but in fact can be – indeed the doxic narrative presupposes *should be* – embodied and enacted by local actors, such as those occupying places in school leadership teams. This matters because, as Thomson (2005) posits:

> a doxa works as misrecognition; doxic narratives deliberately obfuscate how the game (re)produces social inequality through the (re)production of the hierarchy of positions and capitals ... [T]he doxa provides a teleological rationale through which failure is able to be attributed to poor playing, rather than the nature of the game itself. (Thomson, 2005, p 746)

The development of networks in the case of Kingswood Academy, in which corporate and political elites interplay and are part of a privileged discourse within the development of how schools operationalise localised policy-making, speaks to global reform agendas developed elsewhere by and through particular interest groups (for example through the Bill and Melinda Gates Foundation in the US), in which the stated goals of such involvement are of higher standards, greater efficiency and better accountability in the delivery of educational provisions (Ravitch, 2013c). The misrecognition occurs in this discursive construction through the (re)production of hierarchies imported from the political and corporate fields and breached into the field of education. There is no outward acknowledgment or *recognition* in the data that the involvement of the corporate elite in the guise of the global management consultancy firm's development and delivery of an employability curriculum at Kingswood, and the significance of the support of the political elite embodied by the involvement of the MP, are deeply connected to the 'recalibration' of public services along neoliberal and privatised lines. Corporate elites are invited, and indeed lobbied, by governments to become involved in developing policy solutions to policy problem. This is true in other public sector organisations, and as Thrift (2005) argues:

> These companies are used by governments as a policy device, a way of trying things out, getting things done, changing things, and avoiding established public sector lobbies and interests, in an attempt to 'routinize innovation' and incubate creative possibilities. (Thrift, 2005, p 7)

There is permanence involved in these exchange relations, where the outcome of such fundamental changes in the delivery of educational provision will affect a large number of children coming through the system in Kingswood. The principal of Kingswood announced in one interview that:

> 'I've got all sorts of devious schemes that would take me too long to explain, with this Professional School. I am very wedded to it, certainly for this school, but I think it's something all schools should be doing.' (Principal, May 2012)

The principal as a policy innovator and entrepreneur misrecognises the conditions that have been created through the structured and structuring processes in the neoliberal turn of educational reform processes over the last forty years in England. The role of school leaders within the field is to deliver on these centrally derived policy objectives, in much the way that Michael Barber (2007) envisages in his product of 'deliverology', developed under the Blair administration in the early 2000s.[2] The misrecognition is visible in how the principal locates these policy activities as innovative and distinctive, when in fact they are what we would expect to be the next logical step in the delivery of localised versions of education as a result of the neoliberal *doxa*. The importance of belonging to a powerful network, and the social capital this confers, has, in some respects, blinded him to the possible interpretation that a place at this 'table' has, in fact, enabled the extension of corporate interests into the delivery and ultimate recalibration of public education. In this sense, the social capital available through the network with the corporate and political elite represent empirical support for Ball's (2012a) assertion that such involvement in education policy processes is intended to 'change the subjectivities, practices and discourses of these providers' (p 113).

Conclusion

The accumulation of social capital through networking with political and corporate elites may still only be an option for some policy entrepreneurs at the local level. Where schools are forced into academy status as a result of 'failing', or more recently in England as a result of 'coasting' (McGinity and Courtney, 2016), principals are often replaced – and often by people who are better placed to enact the vision of the academy chain to which the school has become subsumed – embodying the changed subjectivities, practices and discourses required within the neoliberal *doxa* of education (Courtney, 2015a).

The case of Kingswood Academy also illustrates that access to elite networks is dependent on the ability of the principal both to exploit previously accumulated symbolic capital from the field of education and to strategically position himself in relation to powerful actors to which he has access, in the case of the MP, because of the geographical coincidence that the school is located in the MP's constituency. There is an element of pragmatism, as well as an element of providence, that such a powerful political elite is accessible, but it is not through chance or luck that the principal was ultimately granted access to such a high-profile network of political and corporate elites, as the following extract from the deputy principal points out:

> '[The principal] is strategic and really enjoys doing the sort of work that he's doing. He gives very good dialogue ... I think that – the meeting he had with the bigwigs of [the global consultancy firm] one of the first things that came up was [the principal] having gone to Cambridge [University]. It's just pathetic that that still exists. [The principal] hates it. It's just ... we all know that still exists but it irritates him beyond belief ... you use everything you need, don't you, to move an idea forward and [the principal]'s just been pragmatic all the way through this. Like with the use of [MP] as well. [MP] is a canny operator.' (Deputy Principal, June 2012)

Here is another side of the *elitism* that is visible in such networks, which helps to explain the social-capital stakes involved in the educational field breaching into the corporate and political fields. There is a sense of 'an old-boys network' in the way that political and corporate entities operate. In England, at least, where you went to school (Eton, in the case of the MP), which Oxbridge college you attended (the 'bigwigs' in the case of the corporate sector and the principal in the case of Kingswood) matter, not because the education itself is superior in these institutions (although it is discursively constructed as superior across a range of fields), but because attending gives you heightened access to the type of social capital that is legitimating and legitimated in networks such as those described in this chapter. So the misrecognition that occurs is all the more violent, where being a policy entrepreneur involves embodying the privileged status of the elites to which success is attributable and necessary, and where the recalibration of education at Kingswood Academy provides 'a model for other schools around the country' to be reproduced (School Leader, February 2012).

Thus the localised policy-making at Kingswood Academy, and the privileging of certain policy actors within this 'vision' for education, is illuminating of the changing nature of educational provision in England and elsewhere. In this instantiation, there is a misrecognition of the innovative approach that such recalibrating represents – in the neoliberal *doxa*, the school is *following* rather than *leading* the discursive terrain of policy. While the social capital developed as a result of the strategic and pragmatic principal has undoubtedly exposed the importance of political and corporate elites in making this happen, ultimately the localised policy-making has become part of an 'epistemic policy community' (Ball, 2012a, p 50), in which exchange relations form the basis of centrally – indeed globally – derived policy solutions; that is, the privatisation of public education.

This chapter has offered an empirical and conceptual analysis of elite corporate and political influences on localised policy-making as a means of responding to the call of Jessop et al (2008) for greater exploration of *contextual* and *specific* variations of social relations within critical policy analysis. Within this approach there is also apparent a methodological contribution, where this study is the first regarding an embedded primary researcher undertaking ethnographic work as the academy conversion unfolds in a school in England where elite corporate and political actors operate in, and influence, everyday policy enactments. This is significant because there is an imperative to develop in-depth cases of the influence of corporate elites in local educational processes, in order to reveal the breadth and extent of private – and privatised – activities in state schools in England and elsewhere.

Acknowledgements

The research reported in this chapter was funded by the ESRC, award reference: ES/GO39860/1.

Notes

[1] The school achieved year-on-year improvements in its General Certificate of Secondary Education (GCSE) results between 2007 and 2011. GCSEs are the exams used as a standardised benchmark of pupil and school attainment, and are taken by students at the end of Year 11 at the age of 16.

[2] Michael Barber as a 'policy entrepreneur' was Head of the Policy Delivery Unit under Prime Minister Tony Blair in 2001 and latterly Head of McKinsey & Company's global education practice. He now sells policy solutions for public sector 'problems' globally.

FOURTEEN

The usual suspects? Free schools in England and the influence of corporate elites

Rob Higham

Introduction

The recent history of education policy in England has featured a plethora of attempts to increase institutional diversity among state schools. As part of the promotion of choice and competition in quasi-markets, diversity policies have allowed or incentivised varying degrees of overt and covert student selection, including by 'ability', faith, curriculum specialism and governance type. One consequence has been the reproduction and expansion of segregation between schools, particularly by socioeconomic status (Gorard, 2014). Diversity policies have also created explicit opportunities for new agents to enter the state education system as dominant school governors or, more accurately, as private providers of state schools (Higham, 2014a). As Woods et al (2007) show, the original academies – set up under the New Labour government from 2001 – were opened predominately by business philanthropists and the Church, reflecting and deepening their wider structural advantages in society. The subsequent growth of multi-academy trusts (MATs) has allowed non-state actors influence over chains of schools.

'Free schools' add a new dimension to these policies of diversification. Linked to Prime Minister David Cameron's 'Big Society' agenda, the background to free schools is instructive. Before entering government, Cameron (2009, p 5) argued that by becoming 'too big' the state was crowding out civil society responsibility, promoting 'selfishness' and 'perpetuating poverty'. The remedy was for communities to take more ownership of 'persistent societal challenges' and for government to shrink, while supporting civil society groups with funds 'from existing state budgets to deliver public services' (Cameron, 2009, p 9). In taking office in 2010,[1] Cameron invited communities and civil society groups to apply to the central UK Department for Education for the right and the funding to open and govern a new free school in England. The outcome of this 'demand led process', the government declared, would depend on proposers coming forward with 'the vision, drive and skills to set up a new school' (DfE, 2010, p 59). The guiding aim, Cameron (2011, p 4) argued, was to: 'break open state monopolies and open them up to new providers, saying – "if you've got the ideas and the people and the commitment to tackle our most deep-rooted social problems, come and play a role in our public services".

Responding to these opportunities, the first 24 free schools opened in September 2011. The number has increased in annual waves to over 300 in 2015, with a further 100 proposals accepted prior to opening. In May 2015, Cameron committed to opening a further 500 free schools by 2020, which, if fulfilled, would mean that free schools would comprise about 1 in every 25 state schools in England. Notably, free schools (and academies) are legally independent of local government. Proposers are required to create a company limited by guarantee (with exempt charitable status). If accepted as proposers by government, the company signs a funding agreement with the Secretary of State for Education. The company directors also appoint, and have a controlling interest in, the free school's governing body (Higham, 2014a).

In this context, several pressing questions about free schools can be identified:

- Who has entered the state education system as a successful proposer?
- What policy processes have supported their entry?
- What patterns of influence and advantage are emerging as a result?

Exploring these questions, this chapter argues that corporatising elites have come to dominate the governance of free schools, enhancing the processes of corporatisation in state education. Corporatisation concerns public services taking on the practices and instincts of the private sector, including through state institutions being reformed as independent companies that contract with the state (Courtney, 2015a). As Saltman (2009b) shows, these processes can redistribute control from public to private interests. In the case of free schools, this chapter argues that three differently positioned, but economically and socially interconnected, elite groupings have become particularly important agents of corporatisation. These are:

- a corporate elite within the private sector;
- a socioeconomic class elite within civil society;
- a state school elite within the public sector.

While attending to counter-currents and non-elite actors where they exist, the analysis progresses as follows. First, the features of these elite groupings are outlined. Second, the entry and expansion of elite influence in state education via free schools is explored. Third, the wider consequences are considered.

Identifying elites in state education

Elites can be understood as individuals and institutions that have 'disproportionate access to or control over a social resource' which afford significant social power and advantage (Khan, 2012, p 1). In the context of free school policy, these structural advantages work to position three interconnected elite groupings as being particularly well placed to open and control new schools.

The first of these elite groupings consists of private sector corporations. Reviewing corporate influence in state education, Gunter et al (in Chapter 10 of this book) show how the pervasive use of consultants in policy implementation has supported the ascendancy of corporate language, practices and identities in schools. These ongoing processes reflect the wider power and influence of corporations. Maclean et al (2010) show, for instance, how corporate actors have entered governance networks at the intersection of the private and public sector. Through these networks, corporate actors are able to negotiate institutional change, promote their goals and influence the distribution of resources in their favour. Tracing these networks in state education, Ball (2007, 2009b) demonstrates how elite corporate actors have developed a range of public service delivery roles and gained access to sites of policy development in the state. These actors include for-profit educational services companies, philanthropists and a plethora of social enterprises.

The second grouping consists of a socioeconomic class elite within civil society. Savage et al (2013) identify three advantaged groups in Britain who account for a third of the population. 'The elite', comprising 6%, is defined by its extreme economic wealth and is typically corporate CEOs, senior managers and directors. The 'traditional middle class' (25%) is the 'comfortably off bulwark of society', typically professionals and managers constituting a non-metropolitan elite. A 'technical middle class' (6%) comprises a science, research and senior educator class. These groups exert and gain influence and advantage through state education, including through voice, choice and exit. The 'elite' has historically exited to attend private fee-paying schools (Maxwell et al, 2014), which account for some 7% of pupils, but are schools which exert significant symbolic power, including in political arguments that their 'autonomy' in markets should provide the blueprint for state schools (Glatter, 2012). The 'middle classes' have predominately attended state schools, but used 'their social and cultural resources', through voice and choice, 'to escape from class "others", and to maximise their children's ... future opportunities' (Ball, 2013, p 16). These actions have mutually encouraged the widespread adoption among state schools of private sector marketing, branding and PR techniques.

The third elite grouping consists of well-positioned state schools within the public sector. The inclusion of these public sector actors may seem surprising given the intentions of free school policy, but state schools in England have been located by policy into quasi-markets since the mid-1980s. The competitive relations that result have the potential to create and reproduce local hierarchies of schools, but a school's hierarchical position is rarely simply a function of 'quality' (Ball and Maroy, 2009). Rather these reflect wider societal values that ascribe status, including the importance placed by advantaged parents on the degree of academic focus, attainment and the composition of the student body (Woods et al, 1998). The contemporary roll back of local government, furthermore, has encouraged the rise of particularly powerful headteachers (Coldron et al, 2014). These leaders are able to entrench the local positioning of their school, including by progressing favourable alliances and mergers, taking on chief executive roles and pursuing market advantage. These practices can deepen processes of corporatisation in state education. As Coldron et al (2014) argue: 'there is clearly room for action by schools with high levels of capital to adopt conquest and profiting strategies ... at the expense of less advantaged schools and stakeholders' (p 399).

In outlining these three elite groupings, it is argued their different but relative power and advantages make them particularly well placed to access the resources required to own and govern free schools. This is not, however, considered inevitable. There are reasons why elites may choose to not engage with free schools. Corporations are profit seeking, but – as explored later in this chapter – it remains illegal to make a direct profit from governing a state school in the UK (Ball, 2007). Socioeconomic class elites, strongly overrepresented in fee-paying private schools and high-performing and selective state schools, may conclude that free schools offer little additional advantage. Well-positioned state schools have typically been unwilling to increase pupil numbers in response to demand, due to fears that this would dilute their advantaged intakes (Allen and Burgess, 2013). As such, there may be room for other less privileged actors to access free school ownership. Moreover, the role of the state will be significant, in terms of which actors are incentivised by policy, what practices are permitted and what other opportunities non-state actors gain by working closely with ministers and civil servants. It is these processes of entry and gatekeeping that are now explored.

To consider who has entered the state education system as a free school proposer and what policies and processes have supported their entry, three phases of research were undertaken as part of the project *An Investigation into Free Schools in England* (Higham, 2014a, 2014b). The three phases analysed, respectively: civil society proposers of free schools; corporate consultants and sponsors; and state school proposers. These are explored in turn.

Civil society proposers

With the ambition to devolve state funds to civil society, the Coalition government initially encouraged four civil society groupings to develop free school proposals. These were defined as 'teachers, charities, parent groups [and] faith organisations' (DfE, 2010, p 59). In the first research stage, 50 semi-structured interviews were conducted with a sample of these actors. The sample was representative of the distribution of open, accepted and rejected proposals mapped during an earlier research phase (see Higham, 2014b) and contained 15 parent, 15 teacher, 13 faith group and 7 charity-led proposer groups.

Respondents described a range of motivations for working to open a free school. These included responding to perceived local need – given demographic pressures – and responding to perceived demand for a better or specific type of school. The majority of proposers also recognised that they were pursuing their own self-interests. Across these motivations, however, two distinct analytical clusters emerged that described the majority of the sample. This distinction was between, on the one hand, proposers accepted by government and, on the other hand, rejected proposers located in the highest quintile of disadvantage.[2] Analysis of each cluster highlights the dominance of a socioeconomic class elite among successful civil society proposers.

Cluster 1: accepted civil society proposers

The demography of proposers in the first 'accepted' cluster was found to consist almost entirely of advantaged social groups. Ninety-five per cent of core proposal team members were recorded as 'senior managers, directors and officials' or 'professionals' – the first and second major occupational groups defined by the Office for National Statistics (ONS, 2010).[3] This profile was also illustrated qualitatively. Parents readily described themselves as middle or upper middle class. Teachers pointed to the importance of their Russell Group university networks in recruiting private sector and corporate professionals into their proposal teams. Charities described their influence within local or national policy-making and the balance, for many, between their social and entrepreneurial missions.

Progressing their applications, proposers made good use of the capitals they possessed (Bourdieu, 1986). Economically, proposers committed time and financial resources to cover the costs of travel and public meetings. Proposers' social and cultural capitals helped them to fulfil two key government tests – on evidence of demand for the school and proposers' expertise. On demand, proposers drew on existing social networks to build alliances of support. This meant news of their proposal spread quickly by word of mouth and email, and led to well-attended meetings, enabling proposers to register the demand of hundreds of parents. For teacher proposers, this marketing was harder work, in part as they were entering areas in which they had fewer established ties. For the majority of proposers, however, evidencing demand often had the effect of drawing in relatively homogeneous communities of parents, who were supportive of the potential advantages that a free school might provide.

Proposers' social and cultural capital also supported the recruitment and demonstration of their team's expertise. The government requires proposers to set out an educational vision, detail their curriculum and staffing plans, and provide evidence of their own capability as proposers. This includes specific 'expertise, such as ... successful experience of setting up a new organisation or business, school governance, human resources, ICT, property/construction, marketing and project management' (DfE, 2011, p25). In this first cluster, proposer teams could readily display knowledge and credentials from across a range of private and public sector professions. Crucially, proposers reached out to recruit specific individuals whose corporate management, finance or business skills were judged to convey particular prestige.

There was also strong alignment in the educational aims that proposers advanced. These were focused on 'excellent academic' schools and coalesced around two themes:

- The first was for traditional conservative values on behaviour, dress and ethos, a curriculum privileging academic subjects and extracurricular provision for arts, sport and music. These aims were often modelled on the symbolic advantages of private independent schools and typically promoted by parents in advantaged contexts, but also with faith-related variations.

- The second, less numerous, vision was for a school with an academic focus and high expectations on attainment located in an urban context with above average disadvantage. Typically proposed by teachers and charities, this was suggestive of a slightly lower reputation or advantage, but aligned closely with the status given to academic subjects by the Coalition government.

Cluster 2: rejected proposals in the highest quintile of disadvantage

By contrast the second cluster, of rejected civil society proposers, located in the highest quintile of disadvantage, had a very different set of characteristics. While a majority of team members were professionals – working in charities, as teachers or attending faith groups – over a quarter had occupations within the ONS's third, fourth, fifth and sixth major categories of: associated professional and technical; administrative and secretarial; skilled trades; and caring, leisure and other service occupations. The profile of proposals was also qualitatively different. Very few proposals originated among local parents. Teacher proposers tended to be older and longer serving in the communities they hoped to work with. Charities reported being less securely funded.

A defining characteristic of this second cluster was the focus on serving particularly poor urban areas. This informed a diversity of educational aims. Several had an urban academic focus similar to that described earlier; others focused on child development in primary schools. For the majority, however, the focus was on a vocationally influenced curriculum, combined with an ethos enabling students to understand the connections between school and the world of work. Local employer engagement was seen to be important in curriculum design and providing transitions to work, although the destination was usually envisioned as labour in, rather than management of, corporations. While this was often a response to local unemployment, it also aligned with the lower status widely attributed to vocational and technical education in England.

To build evidence of local demand, proposers engaged in a wide range of outreach. This included awareness campaigns and leafleting outside schools. For many proposers it was hard work to reach out to local parents, including because of a perceived lack of trust in existing schools and less awareness about, or interest in, the forms of advantage that a free school might provide. Work on demand rarely led into the recruitment of a local reservoir of expertise. While proposers often partnered with teachers, they were much less successful in recruiting expertise from across the business, professional and corporate spectrums that government requires. A further obstacle, keenly felt, was the time and costs that proposers faced in making an application.

In distinguishing these two clusters, it is clear that proposers in each cluster had on average significantly different capitals at their disposal. This is not represented as a simple dualism (see Higham, 2014b).[4] Rather, it highlights how the government's free school process interacts with the distribution of advantage in civil society. While the government argues that its selection method is designed to judge the quality of proposals, the consequences have significant effects on the interests brought into state education. Accepted civil society proposers in the sample were drawn, almost exclusively, from the 'traditional' and 'technical middle classes' identified by Savage et al (2013) as well as, to a lesser extent, their 'elite'. They were also much more likely to be economically and socially interconnected with corporate elites, and this mattered to their success. The majority saw free schools as a means to gain or maintain their own advantage, rather than serving disadvantaged communities.

Corporate consultants and sponsors

In the context of these selection processes, the DfE funded the charity New Schools Network (NSN) (www.newschoolsnetwork.org/) to provide advice to proposer groups and to help accepted proposers open schools. For direct and detailed support, however – having excluded local government from the set-up process – the DfE turned to and endorsed the corporate consulting and educational services (ES) sector, both as advisers *and* school providers. This second section explores this private sector involvement. In addition to questioning the 50 civil society proposers about their engagement with corporate actors, five representatives of widely cited consultant and ES companies were interviewed. Two events at which proposers and ES companies were networked together by the NSN were also observed. These corporate activities are explored through the processes of consultancy and school 'delivery'.

Consultancy

A range of for-profit companies has worked to support the development and operation of free schools. This activity is stimulated by the set-up funding released to accepted proposers by government to open schools. The majority of accepted civil society proposers have used these funds to contract services from consultants, who win contracts worth up to £300,000. To simplify the tendering of these services, the DfE developed two frameworks of 'pre-approved suppliers', from which proposers choose 'project management' or 'educational services'. The companies appointed to each framework in 2011 included Babcock 4S, Capita Symonds, Deloitte, Edison, Mouchel, Novatia and Tribal (EducationInvestor, 2011). As Ball and Junemann (2012) demonstrate, these are companies that have accrued, over the last two decades of public sector privatisation, detailed knowledge of social ties with and legitimacy in government, thereby embedding their self-interest in both networks of governance and public sector delivery roles.

In supporting civil society actors to open free schools, corporate consultants often impact on a school's structures, systems and organisational goals (see Gunter et al 2014b). For example, one parent proposer described how the consultant she contracted not only 'managed regular meetings with the DfE' but also 'oversaw the staff recruitment process and the creating of the curriculum' (Interview 03.05.13). Consultants also sought out longer-term work. One consultancy respondent had signed up proposers to the company's procurement service. Another had sold free schools ongoing management services. These services were on display at the NSN's 2011 conference, which had a 'networking exhibition' where proposers could visit company stalls. Observing the event, I met one for-profit company's representative who explained how she could provide any service from project management to 'actually delivering the school'.

School 'delivery'

For many companies at NSN conferences, the line between consultancy support, management contracts and even corporate control is increasingly blurred (Newman and Clarke, 2009). Free school policy offers corporations new tools and spaces in which to shape-shift organisationally, so as to best deploy their capitals in search of profit. In return, the state gains willing partners able to invest in the policy process.

One outcome is that companies providing set-up support to free schools have created a new market in school delivery – that is, the opening and running of free schools. To date, companies have been encouraged by government to exploit two distinct delivery pathways:

- The first, termed 'school provider' (NSN, 2012, p 10), involves a for-profit (or indeed a not-for-profit) organisation being contracted by a civil society group to deliver and run their proposed school. This has not proved popular to date, especially given the complicated tendering process.
- The second, increasingly common, pathway is for a company to become a 'sponsor' (NSN, 2012, p 8). Where a civil society proposer group does not want long-term responsibility for the school, and is willing to allow another organisation to take control, it can seek a sponsor. The sponsor puts in the proposal to the DfE and governs the resulting school. As a governor, the sponsor is not allowed to make a direct profit from the school (although see Mansell (2015) for resulting controversies and malpractice). Given these restrictions, sponsors have taken the following forms: existing academy chains run by corporate philanthropists (such as ARK or Harris); charitable ES organisations (such as CfBT); and also, new not-for-profit arms of for-profit corporations. Edison Learning Ltd, for instance, a subsidiary of Edison Learning Inc, created The Collaborative Academies Trust, which claims to be establishing a network of 'outstanding' free schools (Edison Learning, 2013, p 1).

These organisational innovations open up a range of opportunities for corporate sponsors. First, sponsors commonly aim to enter or expand as state school providers, by developing chains of schools. In these chains, individual free schools purchase services from their multi-academy trust (MAT), which the sponsor controls. As one not-for-profit ES organisation respondent described:

> '...there was an opportunity for us ... to work in partnership with local parent community groups to ... manage state-funded schooling. ... The schools are then as it were married to us ... The schools pay a membership fee which covers a range of core services ... the financial ... and core services to do with property, HR, legal.' (Interview, 13.05.13)

Second, these opportunities to build and control state-funded networks of schools through free school proposals run on, particularly in the case of for-profit companies, to creating additional market entry points. As The Key (2013, p 1) notes, 'while a sponsor cannot make a profit from the school it sponsors, it may undertake profit-making activities that are separate from the school'. With capital and recurrent school costs provided by the state, a MAT is able to pay for the at-cost services of its sponsoring for-profit company, while the sponsor gains the opportunity to refine and market its wider services to other schools. As one for-profit ESO respondent argued:

> 'For-profit providers … are happy to go into a not for profit academy trust … it's about getting a base of operations here, running schools, and you know those schools run curriculum models and I would imagine there's no better marketing tool for a curriculum model or a curriculum approach than having outstanding schools running it.' (Interview, 16.05.13)

While the resulting issues of transparency and oversight are manifest (Greany, 2014), the deeper processes revealed are how corporate organisational hybrids are able to move and convert capital and resources across sectors, within themselves. Sponsors deploy their existing organisational capital to build knowledge of state schools, seed innovations and establish symbolic prestige, as these are also strategies that help to develop new markets. The resulting not-for-profit arms of corporations can even be held up as constitutive of the 'Big Society' agenda. In Newman and Clarke's (2009, p 93) terms, they 'face both ways' – they play multiple and conflicting roles and are 'able to legitimize themselves both as profit-making enterprises and as public bodies; or as voluntary/not-for-profit enterprises and as businesses'.

Well-positioned state schools

Another set of implications of this expansion of corporate elites in state education is that they may 'further diminish the role of public sector organizations, qualified practitioners and elected local government' (Ball and Junemann, 2012, p 43). There is evidence for this among free schools, particularly the diminishing role of local government. At the same time, however, there is also the potential of new roles and influence for well-positioned state schools.

Figure 14.1 sets out the main categories of proposers to have opened free schools between 2011 and 2015. State schools are shown to be the largest single category, opening one fifth of all free schools. Drawing on interviews with five headteachers who have opened free schools, this final section explores the new roles that state schools are taking on and the policy processes encouraging them.

Figure 14.1: Free schools opened in the first four annual waves, by proposer category

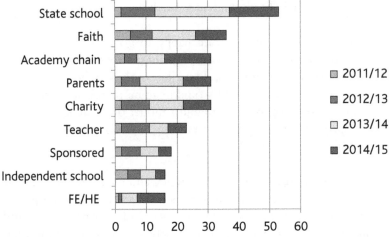

Note: FE/HE denotes Further and Higher Education Institutions. Independent schools are private fee-paying schools that have used Free School proposals to convert into state schools.

While free schools have been opened by universities and further education colleges and independent schools (see Higham, 2014b), as Figure 14.1 sets out, the largest group of educational institution proposers is state schools. Schools opening free schools are not, however, a representative sample of the total state school population. Of the 53 free schools opened before July 2015 by state schools:

- 43 were proposed by a secondary school (or a secondary school-led consortium);
- 39 were proposed by schools that were judged by Ofsted to be 'outstanding' (with the remainder judged 'good');
- 44 were proposed by schools that have converted to academy status (including consortiums containing an academy converter).

An important distinction, then, is how school proposers are drawn from a particular stratum of state schools, comprising predominately secondary converter academies judged to be 'outstanding'. These characteristics align with two other recent studies. First, Higham and Earley (2013) report on a survey of over 800 headteachers to show that while the majority of heads were concerned or cautious about contemporary policy, just over one fifth were notably positive. This latter group – in which academy principals and heads of 'outstanding' secondary schools were overrepresented – expected to gain greater school autonomy through lighter-touch regulation and opportunities to build MATs. Second, Coldron et al (2014) report on interviews with 15 heads to show how well-positioned schools are increasingly able to use their power and influence to construct favourable alliances through executive leadership of multiple schools, joint school governance and/ or MAT building.

Investigating the motivations of five state schools that opened free schools, several similar aims could be discerned. Local needs were identified, but two uniting threads were evident. First, proposer state schools were seeking to extend their influence over a formal chain of schools. Similar to corporate sponsors, free schools helped schools to create or expand the MATs they lead. Typically, this involved a lead secondary academy opening new primary or secondary free schools, but also included the opening of special or alternative provision schools and 14–19 colleges. Second, state school proposers commonly believed that in an increasing fragmented system, it was better that they took on new positions of power than corporate or philanthropic organisations. One CEO of a large school-led MAT argued that the post-local government system was 'better driven by educationalists than corporate foundations' (Interview 03.02.12). Similarly, an executive headteacher of a newly established MAT argued that for his school this was:

> '... an increased remit for an evolving organisation. ... If the Free School model was not available, [local government] would have had to commission a new school [given demographic need]. ... I'd rather it was [led by] a school in context, with a long-standing service of outstanding quality ... than a removed body that reproduces the [Local Government] differently.' (Interview, 31.01.12)

There is an irony here (Hoyle and Wallace, 2007), in that as school-led MATs become larger, they can take on the ethos, hierarchies and branding reminiscent of corporations (Chapman, 2013; Courtney, 2015a). Indeed, this 'increasing remit' for well-positioned schools is being incentivised in policy as government looks to particular headteachers to take on new executive leadership roles in a 'self improving school system' (DfE, 2010). For Hargreaves (2010, p 5) this system can be constructed out of networks of collaborating schools, guided by the moral purpose of lead schools, which 'accept responsibility for self-improvement of the[ir] cluster as a whole'. Such professional ethics do exist in a range of contexts, but there are also clear competitive advantages for lead schools. These include gaining economics of scale and financial security, building networks in which they are central nodes controlling knowledge and human resources, and securing further status and prestige. Viewed in these terms, free school proposals may more closely reflect the aims of efficiency, competitiveness and managerialism (Gewirtz, 2002) and involve, as Saltman (2009b, p 53) argues, 'the corporate model of organisation being applied to institutions that should not aim for the maximization of profit and growth'.

Conclusion

This chapter has considered three pressing questions about the introduction of free schools in England. These concerned who is entering the state education system as a free school proposer, what policy processes have supported their entry, and what patterns of influence and advantage are emerging as a result.

Reviewing the evidence on free schools that opened in the first four annual waves, three differently positioned but interconnected elite groupings were shown to have dominated free school ownership to date. The first grouping was identified as a private sector corporate elite. Already well positioned as deliverers and influencers of policy, private sector corporations have gained both consultancy work and new opportunities to sponsor – and hence control – state-funded free schools. While corporate sponsors are not allowed to return direct profits on this activity, their schools become sites in which to build knowledge, market innovations and develop new for-profit services.

The second grouping was identified as a socioeconomic class elite in civil society, drawn particularly from the traditional and technical middle classes. While this does not appear to challenge the hegemony of elite, private, fee-paying schools that cater for an aristocratic and economic elite (Glatter, 2012), free schools where shown to enable members of the 'comfortably off bulwark of society' (Savage et al, 2013) to secure new advantages by opening quasi-independent schools.

Finally, the third grouping was identified as a state school elite in the public sector, which comprises the largest category of proposers opening free schools. While this is perhaps the least 'usual' of suspects, free schools are enabling a particular stratum of state schools to take on or expand executive leadership and governance roles that were previously organised by elected local governments.

While the Conservative government argues that a demand-led process to opening free schools means that everyone can potentially gain access to state funds, this chapter has shown how evidence of corporate expertise is crucial to proposers' chances of success. This includes proposers recruiting corporate managers through social ties, evidence of executive multi-school leadership potential or (more simply) corporations demonstrating their willingness to sponsor not-for-profit MATs. For these reasons, each elite grouping can be seen to be enabling new processes of corporatisation. Civil society groups are opening independent state schools supported by consultants and corporate sponsors. For-profit companies are contracting directly with the state to open free schools. Well-positioned state schools are being incentivised to adopt new corporate practices and executive identities. In these ways, a demand-led free school system appears able to prioritise an unequal distribution of corporate expertise while simultaneously concealing processes of corporatisation within a discourse of openness. The consequence is that public resources are diverted towards corporatising elites who are motivated by a complex mix of aims, which clearly include private, self-interest.

Notes

[1] In 2010, David Cameron's Conservative Party formed a Coalition government with the Liberal Democrats. The Conservative Party won an outright majority in 2015. In 2016, following the Brexit referendum, the new Conservative Party Prime Minister, Theresa May, reiterated the Government's commitment to free schools, including by arguing for more universities and independent schools to sponsor free schools. The new Prime Minister also announced her intention to allow the opening of new grammar schools.

[2] Disadvantage was measured by the Income Deprivation Affecting Children Index for the Lower Super Output Area in which the proposed free school was to be located.

[3] Respondents detailed their core team members' occupations and these were classified within the Standard Occupational Classifications (SOC) of the Office for National Statistics (ONS, 2010).

[4] A small number of accepted proposals sought to serve disengaged young people from disadvantaged areas. Separately, a number of rejected proposers in the remainder of the sample shared characteristics with those in cluster 1. Being a team of professionals with academic aims and a range of corporate expertise is not always sufficient to gain state approval, although it appears to be the DfE's preferred model.

FIFTEEN

When students 'speak back': challenging elite approaches to teaching, learning and education policy

John Smyth

Introduction

This chapter comes at an interesting strategic juncture in this book – placed in the latter part – and I suspect placed deliberately so by the editors. It helps to focus attention on how corporate governance and provision are experienced in everyday learning within and out of school. Everything that occurs in the educational policy domain can ultimately be 'read off' in terms of what happens to students, and how they respond. I want to frame the opening part of this chapter around two orienting concepts: the first is the canary in the educational coalmine – a harbinger of the effect of what corporate elite policies are doing; and the second, what Sheehan (2013) refers to as 'callous capitalism' – as a way of depicting how it is that the corporate elite policies do their disfiguring and deforming work. In the second part of the chapter, I will deal with the conditions that are turning young people off school, specifically, the most disadvantaged, followed by a discussion of the very different set of conditions these young people 'speak into existence' when they are permitted to re-engage with learning.

Canaries in the educational coalmine: in the context of 'callous capitalism'

I am invoking the metaphor of the 'canaries in the coal mine', while also borrowing from the title of a book on Australia's economic and social wellbeing, to indicate the existence or otherwise of crucial 'vital signs' that point to a 'vibrant society' (Emerson, 2006) (or not as the case might be). There can be no better indicator of whether a society is 'vibrant' than how it treats its young people, and educationally the signs across most Western countries, especially in places that have most vigorously embraced the ideology of neoliberalism, are far from good.

The distressed young people I am referring to are the ones schools have given up on; they have been 'pushed' out or 'shoved' out of school, or otherwise propelled into some context that, while technically still in school, effectively exiles them by hermetically sealing them off in well-intentioned re-engagement programmes, but in which there is still a heavy intent of preventing them from contaminating other students. The official nomenclature invoked is that they are 'dropouts', 'troublemakers', or else have insinuated themselves in the 'NEET' (not in education, employment or training) category. At best, these young people are seen as 'underachieving' in school. In policy terms, it is alleged that they have become 'disengaged' from school, because they lack 'motivation', are unprepared to make the necessary effort, and overall, are lacking in 'aspiration' because they come from family backgrounds that 'don't value education'. They are referred to as being 'at risk' because of a litany of attributes that make them effectively uneducable in policy terms.

Against this thumbnail background sketch, it is worth returning to the canary metaphor for a moment, because it is helpful in framing the rest of this chapter. Speaking of issues of race and power, Guinier and Torres (2002) regard the canary in the mine as an important signalling device:

> The canary's more fragile respiratory system would cause it to collapse from noxious gases long before humans were affected, thus alerting the miners to danger. The canary's distress signaled that it was time to get out because the air was becoming too poisonous to breathe. (Guinier and Torres, 2002, p 10)

As they put it, as a social metaphor, 'the miner's canary captures the association between those who are left out and the social justice deficiencies in the larger community' (Guinier and Torres, 2002, pp 10-11). By focusing on how clients, of whatever kind, are experiencing something, can 'provide the early warning signs of poison in the social atmosphere ... [and to that extent] it encourages us to do something different from what has been done in the past' (Guinier and Torres, 2002, p 12). The way young people put it, is that schools have become such toxic places, that the only sane option open to them is to tune out or leave. In that regard, the canaries have signalled that all is not well with schooling, but there is another dimension to this as well.

While '[o]ne might say that the canary is diagnostic, [it is also the case that it is] signaling the need for more systemic critique' (Guinier and Torres, 2002, p 12). What Guinier and Torres are pointing to is the need to listen to the voices of the whistleblower. In that respect, those who speak back are not just recalcitrants, but activists signalling 'the need to rebuild a movement for social change informed by the canary's critique' (Guinier and Torres, 2002, p 12). In schools there is a burgeoning literature (some of it underwhelming) around student voice as a counternarrative to the official policy discourse.

As I will indicate shortly, if the difficulties being evidenced by the increasing numbers of 'distressed' non-middle-class young people in schools in Western countries were merely an amalgam of individualised problems, or the collective 'pathology' associated with adolescent dysfunctions, then the 'problem' could be solved relatively simply. But, for the same reasons that Guinier and Torres (2002) advance in respect of matters to do with race and power, what happens in the context of corporatisation, privatisation and the propagation of elite educational ideologies, is that these come with deep dimensions of 'structured power and privilege' (p 12). As Guinier and Torres (2002) colourfully put it:

> These pathologies are not located in the canary. Indeed, we reject the incrementalist approach that locates complex social and political problems in the individual. Such an approach would have solve[d] the problems of the mines by outfitting the canary with a tiny gas mask to withstand the toxic atmosphere. (Guinier and Torres, 2002, p 12)

Bridgeland et al (2006) graphically capture the magnitude and gravity of the issue relating to young people becoming disaffected with school in the US, as comprising 'a silent epidemic' – in which: 'Each year, almost one third of all public high school students—and nearly half of all blacks, Hispanics and Native Americans—fail to graduate from public high school with their class' (Bridgeland et al, 2006, p i). These numbers represent only the students who have made the active decision to dissociate themselves from school. The numbers for those silently, passively or indignantly disengaged could be as many again, or even greater. Putting figures on an issue of alienation like this can be notoriously difficult, and possibly even misleading. There are always nagging questions about the undisclosed motives of those who present such portrayals, usually because they are using them to garner public support in order to argue for more of the same harsh policies that gave rise to, or were implicated in, producing the problem in the first place.

I ought to come clean here and declare my position on this. I believe that the source of much of the alienation and disaffection displayed by students that takes the forms of their disenchantment with schooling, can be directly sheeted home to young people's resistance to what they see as the construction of an alien, elitist and exclusionary institution they regard as wilfully ignoring their backgrounds, lives, aspirations and desires for the future.

My claim is that the most insidious aspect of domination is that it operates in ways that obscure how power works, and the way the ideology of corporate elites has become insinuated into schools and the lives of children, is a classic case in point. There are several aspects to this.

First, one thing that power elites always do is that they are very careful to make it appear as if what they are up to is natural or common sense – and the commodification and marketisation of all aspects of our lives is just the start of it. The misrepresentation perpetrated is that markets are an equitable and efficient way of distributing all manner of resources.

Second, this hoax is legitimated through the construction of 'fake' crises, in which the claim is made, in respect of schools, that they are to 'blame' for all manner of social and economic ills – endangering the economy, because of their inability to provide the correct kind of human capital; as the 'cause' of a lack of international economic competitiveness, due to the absence of innovation and entrepreneurial flair; the breakdown of social discipline, because of permissive and promiscuous child-focused pedagogies in the hands of misguided and self-interested educational professionals and their lack of connectedness to 'real life'; and, most recently, risking national security due to an inability on the part of schools to counter and contain elements of religious radicalisation.

Third, the 'supposed solutions' visited upon schools, are presented as residing in:

- more authoritarian approaches to discipline;
- making education more vocational and 'job-ready';
- standardisation of learning through measurement and calibration, and punishing deviations;
- consumerist approaches, in which market discipline is inserted into schools;

- generally presenting this seemingly unassailable ensemble of ideas, as Thatcher did, by claiming that 'there is no alternative'.

These ideas are held in place by their inherent unchallengeability – there is no space for public debate, and they are presented and packaged in ways purporting to be in the interests of young people and society in general.

I want to turn now to the other part of my opening move, the notion of 'callous capitalism' (Sheehan, 2013). This term has a general meaning that constitutes what Sheehan (2013) refers to as 'an enormous social experiment', where 'soulless corporations' are engaged in the relentless quest of 'managing out' all manner of problems – where staff who do not meet rigorous key performance indicators are 'pushed out' in the context of the 'unforgiving marketplace'. There are very distinct echoes here of the parallel way in which students who are not achieving or not seen to be contributing to the national economic good, are also made surplus to requirements.

Part of the policy ensemble of callous capitalism is its overt deflection of the real issues around the legitimacy of work and its synthetic reconstitution around 'outsourcing', 'offshoring', 'subcontracting', 'casualising', its eulogising of 'private providers', and 'downsizing' the workforce in order to achieve 'greater operating efficiencies and lower costs' (Sheehan, 2013). While Sheehan is clearly referring to practices that have their genesis in the corporate sector, these are the same policies that have been inflicted on schools in varying degrees through the 'self-managing school', the 'autonomous school', the 'public independent school', 'free schools', 'academies', 'charter schools', and the like. The imaginary in common to all is a thoroughly individualistic competitive ethos, and the notion of a self-responsible, self-enterprising individual. These are ideas that may have a modicum of common sense in the business sector, but they come seriously awry in schools – especially when deemed to be applicable in/to the lives of students.

As attributes, notions of corporate elitism fly directly in the face of the relational nature of what schools exist for, and what it is they existentially do. Connell (1996) is helpful on this, when she says:

> Education is both a social process and a creative process. A social transaction occurs between teacher and student, between learner and learner, and an educational relationship is constituted. Children in school mainly relate to education through their personal relationships with teachers ... [and

> it is] in these relationships, something about the student changes … [in which] new capacities for practice come into existence. (Connell, 1996, p 5)

What Connell is arguing is that learning is not simply transmissive or extractive in the sense that the student takes something for private benefit from the teacher, to be used exploitatively in later life. The 'new capacities for practice' that come about through education, Connell (1996) says, 'cover the full range of types of social action: productive capacities used in economic life; symbolic capacities, used in making culture; capacities for collective decision-making, used in politics; and capacities for emotional response, used in personal life' (Connell, 1996, p 5). In that respect, 'good teaching' involves going 'beyond boundaries' where 'there is a (benign) excess: an enthusiasm … [that] inspires a pupil, or communicates a love for knowledge and a respect for the learner' (Connell, 1996, p 5). This 'excess', Connell (1996) says: 'is something given by the teacher. We recognise when it happens; but being an excess, we cannot easily define it in job descriptions, nor account for it in budgets … Good teaching … involves a gift relation. It is a practice founded on a public rather than a private interest' (Connell, 1996, pp 5-6). There we have it, as succinctly as it could be put – the essence of what it is that goes on inside the educative relationship.

The ideas that Connell (1996) is articulating are very much at odds with the ones that have held sway in schools in Western Anglo-countries for the best part of half a century through the alleged supremacy of the market as the sole regulatory mechanism. As Connell argues, the market has to commodify relationships in order for the pricing mechanism to work. Markets require the existence of quite explicit features. They have to: standardise – too much variety makes comparisons impossible; institutionalise – personalisation is too chaotic, unpredictable and uncontrollable; and stratify – it is only by arranging in a hierarchical rank order, that the process of rational choosing can operate. When applied to a social and cultural process like education, the most pronounced effect is that commodification involves 'stripping away of the complexities and specificities' (Connell, 1996, p 10), resulting in the creation of some kind of packaged 'modularisation' (p 10) – something that is rendered saleable.

The perversity, as Connell (1996) notes, is that what is purportedly up for sale – 'educational services' – are paradoxically 'free of charge in the state schools'. In reality, something completely different is being sold and bought – 'educational and social advantage' – or positioning for their children (p 9), which is a direct artefact of the increased 'social stratification' (p 11) produced between schools in order to enable consumers to differentiate. In these situations, the 'main beneficiaries are the already privileged families with money, know-how and mobility' (p 11) who are able to benefit from the creation of the market.

Elitist policies meet working-class students in schools

Neoliberal educational policies – with their mantra of competition, individualisation, meritocracy, aspiration and the virtues of the entrepreneurial self – are, at their essence, elitist. They are blind to the way neoliberalism requires schools to do its bidding, and to the relays by which this operates, in which the central construct is the notion of a learning identity – the way in which young people have to constitute or construct themselves in 'becoming educated' (Smyth and McInerney, 2014). The kind of identity work required of the neoliberal school is very different in its essence to the views of identity held by working-class students.

For an understanding of what is happening here, we need to look to the burgeoning area of research around educating white working-class boys, and the associated aspects of masculinities (Gilborn and Kirton, 2000; Reay, 2001, 2002, 2008, 2009; Francis, 2006; Reay et al, 2007; Reay et al, 2008; Reay et al, 2011; Ingram, 2011; Stahl, 2012, 2013, 2014, 2015; Stahl and Dale, 2012, 2013).

One of the more interesting strands of this work is around the psychic effects of social class and how the working-class fraction intersects with the neoliberal policy landscape of schools (see Reay, 2005; and followers like Allen, 2013; Stahl, 2015). In other words, the neoliberal school seeks to construct a particular kind of learning identity around 'motivation, expectations [and] goal orientation' (Stahl, 2014, p 91) that elevates and celebrates notions of competition, individualisation and self-responsibility.

Davies and Bansel (2007) argue that the neoliberal form is seeking a particular kind of 'investment' in the self, so as to produce 'self-reliance, autonomy and independence as the necessary conditions for self-respect, self-esteem, self-worth and self-advancement' (p 252). The undisclosed intent here resides in 'the shrugging off of collective responsibility for the vulnerable and marginalized' (Davies and Bansel, 2007, p 252). When applied, in particular, to white working-class boys who have become surplus because of the disappearance of unskilled work, the neoliberal perspective is able to locate the problem clearly in the persona of these "underachieving" boys [who are made to] appear to be unable – or worse, unwilling – to fit themselves into a meritocratic educational system that produces the achievement vital for the economic success of the individual and of the nation' (Francis, 2006, p 193). In a very interesting cascading sleight of hand, the progeny of the working class, through their indolence and 'lack of application', are blamed for jeopardising their own futures, 'distracting their classmates and teachers', while impeding the economic advancement 'of the nation' (Francis, 2006, p 193).

Where the 'interactive trouble' (Freebody et al, 1995, p 297) occurs is when the aspirational middle-class dispositions being created by the neoliberal school encounter the 'embodied dispositions' (Nash, 1990, p 432) of the everyday lives of working-class boys that are deeply insinuated in families and histories. The 'way of being' of the working-class boys in Stahl's (2014) research, provided 'a counter-narrative' that served 'to rebuff the neoliberal rhetoric' (p 97).

According to Stahl (2014), what he was hearing from his white, working-class, male school informants was that 'meanings' are drawn from their lives rather than from 'imposed' alien outside ideologies (p 99). Rather than being animated by the middle class 'upwardly mobile' and 'economically comfortable' trajectory that brings with it a capacity 'to marshal resources to position them advantageously' (p 99), instead 'working class masculinity typically values anti-pretentious humour, solidarity, dignity, honour, loyalty and caring, and commitment' (Stahl, 2014, p 99). In other words, the defining 'narrative centred on egalitarianism defined as "fitting in" ... where "no one is better than anyone else" or "above their station"' (Stahl, 2014, p 100). Stahl labelled this 'loyalty to self', or in the words of one of his informants, "I don't try to act like something I'm not" (Stahl, 2014, p 101). His informants, while not openly identifying themselves as working class, 'both through interviews and focus groups', revealed 'discomfort in acting like something they were not' (p 101).

What would have been necessary here for the working-class boys in Stahl's study to embrace the middle-class neoliberal ideology required for them to become successful students, would have been a degree of 're-cod[ing]' (Wilkins, 2012, p 768) that they were not necessarily prepared to make. As Stahl (2014) put it:

> The ability (or desire) for my participants to shift identity was not apparent in my observations and interviews; instead my participants actively employed strategies holding close to what they perceived to be an authentic self ... (or as one informant put it) ... "I'm my own person. I don't follow no one, innit, I'm just by myself". (Stahl, 2014, p 102)

To be successful in school, working-class boys needed to 'reduce their affiliation to "loyalty to self" and accept the aspiration rhetoric of change embodied in an institutional[ized]' neoliberal alternative being presented to them by the school (Stahl, 2014, p 103). That is not to say that these working-class boys were incapable of making the transformation, but rather that they had to weigh up the costs – which meant being 'strategic' about how they played the game. The way they did this in Stahl's (2014) study, was by committing to being 'average', 'ordinary', 'middling' or 'normal' (pp 105-6). They were 'negotiat[ing] a space for their emerging subjectivities within the neoliberal discourse' (Stahl, 2014, p 107).

The conditions of school disconnection and reconnection as heard from those at the margins

Stepping back from this a little, it is possible to obtain a glimpse of how elitist neoliberal policies do their deforming work, by listening to what the most disadvantaged students have to say. I need to emphasise that I am not giving an account here that is essentialist, deterministic or totally pessimistic; the reality in the lives of young people, their teachers and schools is far more complex than that.

I can get to my point most expeditiously by drawing from a study that myself and colleagues did between 1996 and 1999, in which we interviewed 209 young people (mostly who had been officially designated as coming from backgrounds of 'disadvantage') in South Australia, who had either left school early before completion, or were contemplating doing so. Entitled *Listen to Me, I'm Leaving* (Smyth et al, 2000), the study pursued the broader question put to the young people to 'tell us what was happening in your life at the point you left school'. While there was an outpouring of issues, I want to focus here specifically on what they had to say about the context of their schooling. The study concluded that early school leaving, or in contemporary terms, disengagement from school, needs to be understood in terms of: 'how schools help to construct the identities of young people, yet seem to be unable to respond adequately and productively to the complexities of their lives' (Smyth et al, 2000, p 293).

In the process, young people's lives are mediated by the culture of the school. Through listening to what the young informants told us, we were able to piece together three broad kinds of school cultures. We described these as 'archetypes' (Smyth and Hattam, 2002, p 382), and what they represent is the way in which 'power is seen to be exercised in the respective school cultures' (p 382), which gave rise to their respective labelling as being 'aggressive', 'passive' and 'active'. These power relations seemed to have some effect in shaping learning identities, but equally, young people brought their own sensibilities to bear in terms of what they were prepared to accept, and this was not always consistent with the school seeking to make them 'obedient, subordinate … citizens' (Levinson and Holland, 1996, p 29).

In two of the three instances, the young people were telling us that the neoliberal school and its elitist agenda presented 'barriers to [their] full participation' (Smyth et al, 2000, p 297).

Instance 1: an aggressive school culture

The aggressive school, as described to us through the accounts of the young people, distinguished itself by its emphasis on a climate of fear, silence and resentment, usually embodied in a "strong discipline policy" in the school. To put this another way, there was a pervasive absence of a sense of trust and respect for young lives. There was a tendency for the school to frame success in terms of the middle class norm of students pursuing an academic curriculum to university entrance. Students who opposed this norm were labelled "trouble makers". Often these were the same students who had a robust sense of justice, or who were prepared to take a stand against what they regarded as school policies or practices that were disrespectful of them. This action invariably brought them into sharp conflict with the school authority structure. And, it was often students from low socio-economic backgrounds who failed to meet up to expectations, because their cultural capital was not adequately recognised.

These were also schools that affirmed the Competitive Academic Curriculum (Connell 1998), often through processes of streaming that served to further undermine the self-images of particular students. Behaviour management policies and guidelines were enforced in ways that left little doubt as to the consequences for failing to comply. The outcome was often a self-fulfilling prophecy. This was especially notable in relation to the possession of prohibited substances. Students who got caught up in the implementation of these policies were left in no doubt about their authoritarian nature. Such a culture was not especially good, either, at dealing with student emotions; indeed, young people were treated in ways that preferred to assume that all such matters reside outside the classroom door.

This kind of school did not have caring ways of dealing with students who "speak back" and teaching approaches often appeared to embody child-like approaches, enacted by teachers who appeared condescending, over-reacting, and even paranoid. Issues of harassment, sexism, racism and classism were rampant in these schools, with an attitude of indifference on the part of the school, which regarded such matters as not being the rightful domain of the school.' (Smyth et al, 2000, pp 273-4)

Instance 2: a passive school culture

The passive school presents itself as being ... benign in its attitudes. Underneath, however, it is struggling, with limited success, to come to grips with the rapidly changing nature of contemporary youth. Symptomatic of this is an overall failure to understand the importance of curriculum relevance to the lives of students. Looked at superficially, it could be said that these schools have a disposition of appearing to be "nice places" on the surface. The odds of succeeding with large numbers of students are strongly stacked against these schools.

Students find these schools have curriculum, teaching and assessment practices that are boring and uninteresting, and what passes as teaching often more accurately amounts to "misteaching" because of the multitude of lost opportunities for connecting in any real way with young people's lives. Many of the students in these schools describe themselves as having been "eased out" by a school trying to present itself as acting in their best interests, while really denying that it still has allegiance to an elitist curriculum that is satisfying for only the minority of students heading for university. In other words, they ... teach to [what Connell, 1998 called] the Competitive Academic Curriculum.

[There] is an incapacity to operate flexibly, for to do this would require a more mature and sophisticated understanding of young people, which is absent. There are pastoral care programs in these schools, but they amount to ways of handling problems as if they were deficits of individual students, rather than system or social pathologies.

Thus there is an acknowledgment that students have emotional needs, but these are dealt with immaturely by the school.

The overall lack of understanding of young people's lives ultimately produces a culture of dependence in these schools for those who remain in the school. At worst, there is a process of writing over the lives and experiences of students who fit the self-fulfilling prophecy of appearing to be ill-suited to the Competitive Academic Curriculum. At the same time, there is also a fundamental failure to challenge the glossed over or covert manipulative power relations, that clearly exist in such schools.' (Smyth et al, 2000, p 274)

Instance 3: an active school culture

While it was not one of our deliberate objectives to uncover schools that were working well for students, it was inevitable that conversations with young people would reveal some elements of such schools, and although not quite as clearly articulated (because of the happen-chance way it was acquired), we have come up with a tentative archetype of the culture of an active school—active in the sense of reaching out to the lives of young people, and not merely responding to them.

An active school presents itself as stepping out and working reciprocally with students to create an environment in which, regardless of background, all students have the opportunity to succeed. Student voice is the pre-eminent theme in schools with these cultures which is used to construct rigorous curriculum and pedagogy around the lives and experiences students bring with them to the school. Rather than deny popular culture, or relegate it to the realm of "outside of school", these schools see this as an important facet around which curriculum is actively constructed.

Instances of student behaviour management are regarded not so much as requiring discipline, but as instances of students disengaging with curriculum that is inappropriate or propagated in unthinking ways. Curriculum in these schools includes both content and process and, as a consequence, necessarily engages with power relations between teachers and students. The negotiable nature of curriculum and pedagogy flows over into the flexible way they approach timetabling and the scheduling of student commitments, which is important in the way it acknowledges different forms, styles and pace of learning, as well as the complex lives students lead beyond the school.

There is a mutually respectful tone within this school, that winds up producing agency and independence in the way students own their learning and the curriculum. Above all, students are listened to respectfully, and there are high levels of mutual trust between students and teachers. The consequence is that students in this kind of school have enormously rich experiences, and the school is enriched as well, as the cultural map is enlarged for both school and students. (Smyth et al, 2000, pp 274-5)

What is interesting about these three archetypes of school cultures is that they do not come about by accident. While I am not suggesting that any of them exist in a 'pure' form, they do stand as dispositions that in some way reflect the forces that brought them into existence, and that sustain and maintain them. The 'aggressive' school culture (and to a degree its more benign 'passive' counterpart), is the product of a set of tendencies that would have us believe that discipline, fear, conformity and compliance are good for children – it is character-building, and will stand them in good stead in the wider competitive world. What is not revealed, of course, is that having a docile and compliant citizenry – especially in respect of a rhetorical notion like 'vocational education' – is manifestly good for capitalism, in that things occur instrumentally and are not subject to messy contestation and debate. The 'active' disposition, on the other hand, has worked out how to refuse to accept the tenets of the corporate, 'military-industrial-academic complex' (Giroux, 2010), and instead engages in indignation, defiance and resistance in arguing back that elitist corporate interests are not the same as students' interests.

Conclusion

In this chapter, I have looked in general terms at the way in which elite education policy, as embodied in the neoliberal school, impacts young people, especially those designated as coming from backgrounds of disadvantage. Education policy for these young people is mediated through the way students construct a learning identity that is framed around three perceived notions of school culture that form around the working of power relationships. I have argued that some of these construals accommodate to the corporate elitist agenda, while others resist and redefine an identity 'against' the will of such elites.

Where the school culture was less harshly framed around a concern for students and their backgrounds, and tried to involve itself in their lives, it seemed that the school was less inclined to become involved in promulgating a mismatch between the lives of the students and the direction being pursued by the school. In some senses, then, this kind of school archetype had positioned itself as valuing the desires of the students and their families above any desire to pursue externally imposed elitist policies.

Where the school had a 'detached' (meaning hierarchical) view towards students, and displayed more loyalty towards promulgating a conforming corporate elitist view of how students, their lives, families and aspirations should be treated (both as part of an elitist network and as a local variant), then what prevailed was a fairly unproblematic elitist approach – this was a school culture within which there was the greatest resistance by students.

In the case of the archetype of the 'confused' school culture, it seemed that this one failed in its attempt to try to understand the students, but without the deep commitment necessary to develop a mature approach to the relationships with students. It was an orientation that was mouthing the rhetoric of seeming to want to be more progressive, but it ended up – through its lack of commitment– being little different than a benign version its more fearful counterpart. In its effect, it was still keeping students in their place.

CONCLUSION

The challenge of corporate elites and public education

Helen M. Gunter, Michael W. Apple and David Hall

Introduction

The primary research and critical analysis reported in this collection of essays has made a substantive contribution to the field of critical education policy as well as to democratic discourses, through undertaking and accessing fieldwork data and through thinking productively in order to scope and bring meaning to, the relationship between corporate elites and the reform of public education. Our goal in focusing on emerging forms of corporatised governance is not only to add to the growing body of work about the ideas, networks and strategies adopted by corporate elites, but also to reveal – and bring new perspectives to – how this has become extraordinarily ordinary. What our data and insights show is that there is an accepted normality to what is unfolding, where counter-narratives are difficult but not impossible to construct.

In this concluding chapter, we draw together key outcomes from the within-outside analysis, and consider what this means for the ongoing debates, realities and experiences of public education. Within this we put emphasis on what the reforms mean for ongoing research agendas and methodologies.

Mapping corporate elites and the reform of public education

We have set out to uncover and tell some important stories, and we have located those accounts within the wider context of critical education policy studies through drawing on analysis of global trends, the changing role of the nation state, together with the policy processes and the networks that underpin this. But the distinctive nature of the accounts that illuminate corporatised governance is that we have also shown what it actually means for people working in universities and schools, and how people are handling their often confused and contradictory location at the leading edge of corporate activity and influence – some are pushed off the edge into a void, some continue to struggle with what it means, and some leap to embrace attractive opportunities. Here we provide a summary of what our data and analysis are indicating regarding significant shifts in government, in educational institutions and professional practices, and in civil society.

Movement of educational issues from the public to the private domain

Our claim is that we are witnessing the increased dominance of the 'private' within privatisation through how educational issues are increasingly shifting to personal (rational? whimsical?) choice agendas. Corporate elites have both contributed to this shift and are beneficiaries of it.

This is evidenced in a range of ways in our essays and the cases provided. The first illustration is from the chapters by Prosser (Chapter 7), Lim (Chapter 8) and Sinclair and Swalwell (Chapter 6), whereby the private decision to purchase education for your child (and family) demonstrates how advantage is related to commercial exchange relationships. While the case is made that all can achieve and/or that particular needs have to be responded to through exclusive provision, the data offer evidence of how elite schools actually provide insulation and protect particular interests. Hence in Singapore, the case is made about meritocracy, but research shows how the privileged are further advantaged. In Argentina, there are a range of schools that enable private education to be purchased by different income groups, and research shows how corporate elites enable their children to be particularly advantaged in this market. The relationship between cost and price in regard to curriculum is important, where Sinclair and Swalwell present research that examines how a curriculum product is designed to enable consumers to stay ahead in accessing elite higher education, and then onwards into the corporate world.

Such private processes of reading, thinking, talking and deciding are not only related to financial resources. For example, Wilkins (Chapter 11) shows how the corporate world – with the right type of knowledge and know-how – has come to dominate governing bodies of publicly owned schools in England. The setting up of new types of schools by those with the right type of social, cultural and financial capitals, enables the corporate private work involved to be made explicit (see Wilkins, Courtney, McGinity, Higham, Chapters 11, 12, 13, 14). Schools for communities and paid for by the taxpayer but run as a business, means that the decision to set up a school and to seek public funding (see Higham, Chapter 14) and/or to change the legal status of a publicly funded school (see McGinity, Chapter 13), has implications for those who may not have the resources to consume in the way that corporate elites do. The opportunity exists to mimic the advantages that corporate elites display in relation to the private practice of choosing. A key message is that it is only your own children that matter, where a key benefit of choice is to make sure that other people's children in the school of your choice are ones that you approve of.

Relocation of public education issues from government institutions to particular private organisations or individuals

Our claim is located in the construction of the state as 'limited', as regulator (of standards, delivery contracts) rather than provider (of shared, local, free at point of access), where public funding is invested in increasingly for-profit private and outsourced educational products (schools, research, curriculum). Our essays provide a range of evidence and analysis that demonstrate how corporate interests are seeking taxpayer funding to support market gains: for-profit is entering the market, where there is an increased role for not-for-profit interests with linked for-profit business gains (see Higham, Chapter 14). For example, Burch et al (Chapter 1) and Saltman (Chapter 2) provide detailed casework about the student identity and test markets, with particular emphasis on the role of the media and technology. Both chapters report on data that demonstrate the transition features involved in change, where the entry of corporate services and products generates an endemic demand for new products. Importantly, market failure needs to be given attention, where the education of children becomes increasingly influenced by companies that pull out of the market and/or close down, and so the consumer must be a shrewd shopper in order to ensure that such shifts are further opportunities for securing advantage.

How such transitions are taking place is related to the investment of private decisions into education. Indeed, Duggan (Chapter 9) examines the training of teachers as one example of how the private becomes public, and this is linked to corporate demands to open up this workforce to act as consumers (see Saltman, Chapter 2). The challenges to professional knowledge and skills, with the drive to modernise practice, are particularly evident in the chapters by Fitzgerald (Chapter 4) and McGinity (Chapter 13). In universities (see Gaus and Hall, Chapter 5; Fitzgerald, Chapter 4) and schools (McGinity, Chapter 13) there is a process of identity fracture and reworking in meeting corporate demands and investment. Fitzgerald (Chapter 4) engages with how higher education uses its traditions and status to connect with elite demands, while for McGinity (Chapter 13) it is how those who work in schools invest accummulated symbolic capitals to demonstrate corporate complicity. Integral to this is how the curriculum, teaching, assessment and organisational processes are increasingly marketised through the exchange relationships involved in the purchase of consultant and consultancy branded knowledge and skills. Corporate knowledge work has burgeoned through the rolling back of the state and the ongoing privatisation of public institutions (see Fitzgerald, Chapter 4; Gunter, Chapter 10).

Meanings and conduct of professional practices

Our claim is that those who work in public education services are increasingly being required to take on corporate identities, images, languages and practices as leader CEOs or as follower managers and employees, in ways that co-opt or replace existing educational professionals and trade unions. Corporate elites have funded training programmes and provided role models for modernised ways of working.

All of our accounts provide understandings about what it means to do corporate work; to economise values, processes and outcomes – and what this means for identities and practices that have been shaped in different times. Importantly, our authors show the urgency, necessity and vitality of thinking and doing through financial exchange relationships. What is evident is the importance of speedy, and often pragmatic work, where inherent talent and experience interrelate in order to produce workers who join and leave. Hence professional knowledge is a portmanteau of experience, aptitude and training in basic know-how skills. This is evident in the notion of fast-tracking from novice to expert, as illustrated by Duggan (Chapter 9), where the corporate teacher is not held back from doing what is necessary by being required to spend time engaging with the learning and development of professional knowledge and skills.

Those already working in schools and universities must succumb to corporate thinking and practices, so that student outcomes are efficiently and effectively delivered at a time of high competition (see Gaus and Hall, Chapter 5). Those who cannot or do not adapt are either disposed of, or will seek out opportunities to take on board new corporate work (see Gunter, Chapter 10), and those who see the necessity of risk are able to realise new ways of working, as illustrated by Courtney (Chapter 12), who shows how headteachers in England take on elite status as corporate middle managers through investment in regional provision of new forms of schools.

Meanings and engagement of teaching and learning

Our claim is that those who work in classrooms in schools and higher education (adults and children) are required to understand and engage primarily with the purposes of education as being about economic productivity and outcomes. Corporate elites have intervened within and shaped the discourses about why people go to school and university, and who pays for it.

Our co-authors present cases where they identify how corporate elites can buy the type of curriculum, pedagogic processes and outcomes that can benefit them, and how differentiation within elites shows how private choice and resources can be used to control the advantages they want for their children. While these 'super' elites can lead separate lives (global mobility, gated communities, security cordon) and espouse the cosmopolitan and economised dispositions that enable this (for example discourses about world-class education), they can help to create the conditions in which the left-behind middle classes can strive to achieve the same. Through portable expertise, projects and the ever-increasing demand for good managers and flexible networkers, there are opportunities for repositioning by those 'in the middle' to gain advantages in relation to those who only have residualised provision to fall back on within the nation state. The building of advantage, not least through accessing technology and media-linked products and learning packages, means that the person and the family are enabled to think and position the self in relation to corporate productivity (see Saltman, Chapter 2). Expert teachers and teaching become the essential luxury that has to be paid for, while the majority experience education that is increasingly teacher-proofed through curriculum and assessment delivery packages.

Smyth (Chapter 15) makes a contribution by examining what it all means for those who have experienced corporate practices as 'other people's children' who are 'outside of the middle'. Notably he provides examples of what happens when a child's understanding of success does – and does not – match up with the aspirations that the school promotes. Smyth's lexicon is different to the corporate one adopted by taxpayer-funded schools that are readied for private takeovers. He is concerned with respect, how children are spoken with and listened to, particularly through cultures of care that underpin access and participation in teaching and learning.

What our cases and evidence illuminate is a complex picture of entryism and distancing, expansion and defence, and reform and replacement. For example, Schirmer and Apple (Chapter 3) in the US and Higham (Chapter 14) in the UK provide detailed accounts of how this is happening within and through the usual channels within government; how systems that everyone has access to (for example voting, representative assemblies, legislation, courts) are sites where wealthy and powerful activists are able to secure control in order to influence laws and policies that protect and expand their interests.

Following Harvey (2005) we are witnessing 'accummulation by dispossession' (p 149), whereby 'surpluses of capital ... lie idle with no profitable outlets in sight', and where public assets (schools, houses, transport, water, and so on) are a site for new freedoms, and where 'overaccumulated capital can seize hold of such assets and immediately turn them into profitable use' (Harvey, 2005, p 149). The logic of capital flows is seemingly rational with inevitable consequences, but as Thrift (2005) argues, trends can go in different directions, and it seems that 'many of the ways in which it has proceeded on are the cumulative result of "small" events that, at the time, no doubt, seemed to have little significance' (Thrift, 2005, p 3).

Hence our co-authors have avoided conspiratory narratives, with *post hoc* rationalisations about inevitability, and are concerned to show what Harvey (2005) and Thrift (2005) both identify as jumbled and provisional experimentations, the savvy reworkings and adaptive relocations that take place. What operates under the umbrella of neoliberalism is a body of ideas but, as Harvey (2007) has shown, it is the 'political project' of corporate elite restoration that has mattered more: 'when neoliberal principles clash with the need to restore or sustain elite power, then the principles are either abandoned or become so twisted as to be unrecognizable' (Harvey, 2007, p 19). It seems that while the state is the espoused enemy, in reality state authority is needed to maintain the conditions in which elite interets are protected and extended.

This interplay between ideas, small events and strategising can be witnessed in our stories, and interestingly those who do the work are not necessarily named. Yes, some big names are there, but what we have mainly seen are those 'in the middle' who do corporate work: who act as conduits through which ideas, activities and languages flow, who venacularise choice, competition and consumerism into what is possible in the day to day. There are those who do this through political means (Burch et al, Saltman, Schirmer and Apple, Chapters 1, 2, 3); there are those who do this through established structures (Sinclair and Swalwell, Prosser, Lim, Chapters 6, 7, 8), reformed structures (Fitzgerald, Gaus and Hall, McGinity, Chapters 4, 5, 13) and new structures (Wilkins, Courtney, Higham, Chapters 11, 12, 14); and there are those who do this through professional means (Duggan, Gunter, Smyth, Chapters 9, 10, 15).

A number of our authors talk about changes within and to the middle classes, in ways that construct them as carriers of corporatised education – it enables them to access and sustain inbuilt advantage for their children, and to seek new forms of work and status that would previously have been denied to them. In addition, they can carry packages of ideas, practices and languages with them to other educational sites, where by giving back through using their skills as school/university governors (trustees, and so on), setting up new forms of schools, and demanding higher workforce standards to support their business plans, they can influence appointments, hardware and software purchases and curriculum design.

We need at this stage to exercise some caution, and so we wish to raise some important points about how our contribution should be read.

We want to begin with the danger of reducing what research is uncovering to corporate elites alone and to corporate elites as a homogeneous group. Faith organisations and charities are major providers of education, they often provide where the state is absent, and there is a need to consider corporatised networking within and between this. Apple (2006a, 2013) documents that corporate elites are not always ideologically uniform. Some are indeed deeply committed to marketisation and privatisation, with the core values underpinning their actions being grounded in a basic belief that 'private is necessarily good, and public is necessarily bad'. Yet there are strong elements of different values within some parts of this agenda. Neoconservative visions of faith, discipline, the nuclear family, and the power of 'sacred' texts and authority can also be found. Indeed, Ball's (2012a) mapping of international neoliberal networks reveals close connections between neoliberal and neoconservative foundations and funding sources both inside and outside multiple nations.

It is clear, then, that corporate identities that are also located in faith and neoconservative values such as family, engage in what is best thought of as 'missionary work', whereby there is a drive for benefaction along with the conversion of the unfortunate into preferred identities and practices. Pedagogy exercised by corporate elites is therefore conceptualised as the transmission of relevant skills and appropriate knowledge, with an emphasis on behaviour and commitment. Importantly, this is dressed up as enabling aspiration, where role models in the form of individuals and family dynasties espouse the importance of success through hard work. This generates temptation to at least emulate but possibly surpass, to imagine entry into this exclusive world, but at a very basic level to conform to the rules of the game through forms of simulation where you are – but are not – the same.

Hence we want to articulate a second warning regarding causation. By framing our approach to governance through Robertson and Dale (2013), we are recognising that there are a range of policy actors involved in a range of sites both at local and national levels (for example think-tanks, charities, political parties, universities) and at supranational levels (for example the European Union, the International Monetary Fund, the Organisation for Economic Co-operation and Development and the World Bank), where what we might identify and label as corporate ideas are generated, promoted and circulated (see Souto-Otero, 2015). As Goodwin (2009) identifies, we may map interconnections, but how influence is actually exercised is what matters, so our cases show the complexity of exchange relationships. Our research shows glimpses of how corporate influences work through people who position and invest – and reposition and disinvest – and who manoeuvre in order to control and possibly replace not only public education services but also the government systems that enable such services. Illuminative of this are major changes in the US, where our co-authors have shown the link between large and small corporate America, and the releasing of taxpayers' money to build corporate advantage. Certainly Buras' (2015) study of post-Hurricane Katrina reforms in New Orleans provides detailed analysis of the installation of charter schools without consultation, and based on corporatised alliances between political, economic and social elites.

We would also want to acknowledge how local resistances operate to reject marketised solutions through corporate deals (see Burch et al, Chapter 1), and corporate curriculum and cultures (see Smyth, Chapter 15). Fronting the issue of resistance is particularly important due to the ways in which corporate reforms have linked markets to equity and civil rights agendas, and where critical work has been labelled as destructive. In firing back, researchers make explicit that resistance is not based on a restoration agenda, but recognition that racial and other forms of discrimination endure within new structures. In addition, projects are revealing considerable evidence of community-based rebuilding, where collective memories are being used as a resource, rather than elided (Buras, 2015; Mirón et al, 2015).

It seems to us that the exchanges in which ideas, practices and identities are shaped and enabled are located in dynamic and threatening contexts, where corporate elites have sought to structure but have also had their worlds restructured by the fall of the Berlin Wall, 9/11 and the 'war on terror', and the financial crash in the first decade of the new millennium. Hence while, as Harvey (2007) states, the emphasis has been on 'liberating individual entrepreneurial freedoms' through 'private property rights, free markets, and free trade' (p 2), this has been at a time when the state has halted the roll-back in order to protect the security of money, private interests and nation state borders.

At the same time, we should be cautious of something else. We need to remember that resistance to elite agendas can also take authoritarian forms. Populism can be progressive; but it can also be deeply retrogressive. The fact that authoritarian forms of populism are increasingly influential in many nations in Europe, in the United States and elsewhere speaks to the importance of understanding what Stuart Hall called 'authoritarian populism' (Hall, 1980). Such movements may often function to support certain aspects of elite interests, but it would be unwise to reduce these movements and the people that are involved in them to simply puppets of dominant elite and corporate agendas (see, for example, Apple, 2006b). This may make our analyses more complicated; but reality itself is filled with contradictions and tensions.

Public education

Our essays are located in what we have traditionally called 'public education'. Following Wood and Flinders (2014) we identify that public education is a product of politicisation, where the political context not only recognises that education is a public good linked to citizenship and an inclusive and vibrant civil society, but also that it is a matter for public debate, provision and funding. Significant intellectual work has been done to discredit the politicisation of public services:

> Hierarchical, centralized bureaucracies designed in the 1930s or 1940s simply do not function well in the rapidly changing, information-rich, knowledge-intensive society and economy of the 1990s. They are like luxury ocean liners in an age of the supersonic jet: big, cumbersome, expensive, and extremely difficult to turn around. (Osborne and Gaebler, 1993, p 12)

What our data and analysis provide is an overview of how influential such analysis has been, through how politics is being taken out of public education, and how through such depoliticisation the space for corporatisation has opened up and is displacing other publics (see Schirmer and Apple, Chapter 3).

Research has identified the problematics with public services education, not only issues of gender, race and class discrimination, but also how claims made for more recognition and inclusion to be the core focus of reform were not taken forward quickly enough and in ways that were based on the real concerns of parents and communities (see Apple, 2006b; Fraser, 2014). Hence while corporate elites have sought to align corporate goals with political goals, with a foothold in politics through financing of parties and campaigns (Harvey, 2005), what we are talking about here is something much more substantial. We are concerned with how corporations are entering into government and acting as 'shadow governments' (Guttman and Willner, 1976), and potentially replacing representative forms of government with corporate forms of government. Indeed, investigative research has revealed forms of 'kleptocracy' (Dawisha, 2015), where greed is a prime driver and public assets are being stolen: 'some charter school operators around the country have taken advantage of the lack of regulation and oversight, which has led to numerous scandals involving embezzlement, cheating, and other illegal practices' (Au, 2014, p 147).

At a very basic level, we are witnessing the replacement of politics with forms of consumerism (Norris, 2011): we shop to boost the economy, rather than talking about what matters within economic relations. When corporate power is linked to structural advantages, then as our cases show (for example Sinclair and Swalwell, Prosser, Lim, Chapters 6, 7, 8) the deep cleavages within civil society become visible:

> In the UK, good results can be bought through private education or by buying housing near to 'good' schools – so the cycle of rising domination by the richest continues, generation on generation. In no other OECD country, apart from Chile, is a higher proportion of national income spent on private education by so few – for so few. Half of all A and A★ grades at A level in the UK are secured by the 7 per cent of students who are privately educated, and 4.5 times as much is spent on teaching them as on the average state-educated pupils. (Dorling, 2014b, p 38)

Politics is about choices, but it is different from consumerism, because the latter is based on securing satisfaction in ways that democracy cannot. In an election we vote but may not get what we want, and so we must be satisfied with that until the next election; but in shopping we can obtain immediate gratification. It seems that we are witnessing the replacement of citizenship with calculative individualism (Hartley, 2012). We require a service to be bespoke, but as the majority do not have the resources to purchase this, then we ask ourselves: how can we get what we need? When action is demanded from us we ask: what is in it for me? Such ways of thinking, speaking and acting are encouraged not only through corporate forms of agency and deliberation that make judgements about what is said and what is worth saying, but also through how the relationship of civil society to the structures of the state are changing.

Our co-authors shed light on, and provide forensic detail about, what it means to be thrust into these topsy-turvy changes, where you are told that you have agentic aspirations, but people's experiences suggest a more complex story. Within our accounts there is evidence of how those located in public services do take up corporate identities with risk-taking entrepreneurship. Hence we have seen analysis about: cutting through the rules and getting things done in regard to outsourcing student identity (Burch et al, Chapter 1), assessment (Saltman, Chapter 2) and employment rights (Schirmer and Apple, Chapter 3); improving professional training and development opportunities (Duggan, Gunter, Chapters 9, 10); adopting corporate personas to set up new educational services (Wilkins, Higham, Chapters 11, 14); and making existing schools and universities run more efficiently and effectively (Fitzgerald, Gaus and Hall, McGinity, Courtney, Chapters 4, 5, 12, 13). However, the precarious nature of the conditions in which the logic of capitalism is located (see Burch et al, Saltman, Chapters 1, 2), and the fabrications involved in the construction of corporate ideas and practices as the best location for equitable opportunities (Sinclair and Swalwell, Prosser, Lim, Chapters 6, 7, 8), means that even after all the major changes, most people and families are, it seems, still left 'Waiting for "Superman"' (Guggenheim, 2011).

Corporate and conservative America has rallied to the call in this 'Superman' film to rescue families from the failings of public education through the provision of choice, particularly through charter schools. Guggenheim (2011) focuses on the stories of five families, where the use of local lotteries for market-rationed school places has enabled parents and children to experience individualised competition, where success and failure are based on personal choices (Swalwell and

Apple, 2011). It seems that there is a need to fix public education in a particular way:

> The message of these films has become alarmingly familiar: American public education is a failed enterprise. The problem is not money. Public schools already spend too much. Test scores are low because there are so many bad teachers, whose jobs are protected by powerful unions. Students drop out because the schools fail them, but they could accomplish practically anything if they were saved from bad teachers. They would get higher test scores if schools could fire more bad teachers and pay more to good ones. The only hope for the future of our society, especially for poor Black and Hispanic children, is escape from public schools, especially to charter schools, which are funded mostly by the government but controlled by private organizations, many of them operating to make a profit. (Ravitch, 2012, pp 19-20)

It is generally regarded that such films have been an important wake-up call (see Swail, 2012), and they speak to an emerging right-wing globalised position that is about keeping the state out of educational provision. However, while the reform of public administration is regarded as necessary, the corporate agenda is being questioned. Darling-Hammond and Lieberman (2012) argue that children and families should not be subjected to a lottery in order to find a place in a good school. They go further and argue that if there are education systems that are doing better than in the US, then different strategies need to be enacted:

> … there is too little talk about what high-performing countries actually *do:* fund schools equitably; pay teachers competitively and comparably; invest in high quality preparation, mentoring, and professional development for teachers and leaders, completely at government expense; organize a curriculum around problem-solving and critical thinking skills; and test students rarely – and almost never with multiple-choice tests. Indeed, the top-performing nations increasingly rely on school-based assessments of learning that include challenging projects, investigations, and performances…. (Darling-Hammond and Liebermann, 2012, p 42, emphasis in original)

What is emerging is a demand for the reform of public education that is genuinely public and educative. Such arguments stretch beyond the US, where debates and campaigns are underway to shift from 'my school' and 'my university' towards 'our' public education.

Working for public education

Our co-authors have shown that the 'public' and 'publics' in regard to public education continue to matter. This includes, for example, local communities (Burch et al, Schirmer and Apple, Chapters 1, 3), indigenous peoples (Fitzgerald, Chapter 4) and children (Smyth, Chapter 15). In addition, our co-authors have made explicit the conditions and experiences that those who are involved in corporatised governance have gone through and continue to go through. As such, we have rallied to the call by Robertson and Dale (2013) to: 'consider … relational effects, and especially wider issues of obligation and responsibility' (p 441). Even those who have taken on board the agentic aspirations of corporate global entrepreneurship have often done so through major changes to their livelihoods (losing your job, Gunter, Chapter 10), through to changing their identities and purposes (chief executives, Courtney, Chapter 12), where the alternatives of unemployment were real and dangerous for themselves and their families.

It seems to us that our contribution is such that there is a need to examine a number of salient issues within research:

- **The public matters** – we accept that the public domain outranks markets (Judt, 2010; Marquand, 2004), and that it is more than a rhetorical device used to justify change based on constructions of 'public opinion'. Our claim is that the public is more than activites being undertaken in public, or that it has 'collapsed into a loose collection of selfish individuals' (Newman and Clarke, 2009, p 2). Issues are 'made public' (Newman and Clarke, 2009, p 2) because they matter and need to be connected to how civil society has aspirations that include – but are more important than – global economic competition (Carr and Hartnett, 1996; Dewey, 2011).
- **Publics matter** – we accept diversity within civil society, whereby we are working for recognition of difference and inclusion within the economy in ways that are different to consumerism and branding. Our claim is that the relationship between the state and public institutions, such as schools and universities, needs to be renewed and developed in ways that work for participation and

parity of esteem. This is where issues of intersectionality of class, race, gender, sexuality and age are just some of the key structural features of civil society that create injustices that limit access to education, and certainly limit/enhance access to corporate forms of the public as consumers in stratified markets (see Raffo et al, 2010).

- **Public education matters** – our co-authors have presented graphic cases of how the idea, as well as the reality, of public education is being discredited. Yet as Fitzgerald (Chapter 4) argues, 'we should not rule out the possibility that a new dream is possible'. Such a dream is a reality, whereby the changes outlined by our co-authors are more often failing the consumers that they are meant to benefit. In fact, such failures are integral to the marketised economy through new and more responsive products. As our stories show, there are spaces for outlining such failures and the damage that has been done, as well as to give notice to examples from the wider literatures about the successes of public education (see Darling-Hammond and Lieberman, 2012; Lubienski and Lubienski, 2014) and the ongoing potential for how children's participation can be enhanced (Smyth, 2006).

This requires us to recognise that the impact and influence of corporate elites is not only economic and social, but is also primarily political. The ways in which power is exercised to secure and prevent are based on more than the principle of: one person, one vote. Corporate elites not only have a range of resources that enable them to influence those who seek votes and to bypass the institutions that are run by those who are publicly accountable, but they can also be both global and local through networks that can be disconnected from territory and national state borders. Their role in the creation and dependence on a globally mobile 'middle' corporatised elite enables their influence to spread, even though they may be at one remove from the day-to-day aspects of change and outcomes.

While our research reveals evidence about corporatised governance, we know that some research is being financed and used to silence critical education policy. We are aware that we can operate in counter-hegemonic ways. What we mean here is that the job of researchers is more than projects and publications – though these are important in providing peer-reviewed primary research data that are publicly disseminated. In working with children, families, communities, schools and universities, we have to negotiate and agree our collaborations, and this enables us to take up positions with and alongside people (Apple, 2013; Gunter et al, 2014a). What we are seeking to do is to restore choice as a political process; where income, social status, race, gender and sexuality are not used to exclude. The rehabilitation of politics – or the interrelationship between individual choice (vote), shared choices (universal access to services) and funding choices (how scarce resources are raised and allocated) – is core to this agenda. Or how representative government systems operate in ways that may or may not satisfy people, and in doing so it will always come a poor second to private views (I am always right), consumerism (I can satisfy my goals through purchasing) and elitism (I am better than you).

Our stories illuminate what Flinders (2013) suggests is how 'large sections of the public have become politically decadent in their expectations about what politics should deliver, how politicians should behave and their own responsibilities within society' (pviii). Flinders goes on to argue that such decadence does not mean that the public or publics are uninterested or stupid or corrupt, but that there is a need for a more vibrant, honest and inclusive political culture. Our cases show evidence of this in action, and how those required to do corporate work often struggle with the change imperative alongside their deep commitment to public values.

Perhaps a useful starting point is through adopting the position taken by Arendt (2005), whereby 'politics is based on the fact of human plurality', and where political exchange relationships are located 'between' humans (pp 93-5). Sharing ideas, visions, facts and analysis is integral to political choices and politics is no space for assumptions of status based on structural advantages: 'freedom exists only in the unique intermediary space of politics' (Arendt, 2005, p 95).

All of this asks us, as critical scholars, to take up certain kinds of roles within and for intellectual work. We realise that 'public intellectual' could be a problematic position, but it has potential for researchers regarding the interplay between ideas and data, and for bringing the trends outlined in this collection into the public domain.

Here it is wise to listen to Pierre Bourdieu, when he reminds us that while our intellectual efforts are crucial, they 'cannot stand aside, neutral and indifferent, from the struggles in which the future of the world is at stake' (Bourdieu, 2003, p 11). Schools, universities and education in general play significant roles in constructing and defending a public sense of this world – and of our collective and individual responsibilities in it.

References

Adonis, A. (2012) *Education, Education, Education. Reforming England's schools.* London: Biteback Publishing.

Allen, K. (2013) *Coalition policy and 'aspiration raising' in a psychic landscape of class.* Paper to the Journal of Youth Studies conference, Glasgow University, April.

Allen, R. and Allnutt, J. (2013) *Matched panel data estimates of the impact of* Teach First *on school and departmental performance*, Institute of Education, DoQSS Working Paper No. 13-11. http://repec.ioe.ac.uk/REPEc/pdf/qsswp1311.pdf

Allen, R. and Burgess, S. (2010) *The future of competition and accountability in education.* London: RSA.

Altbach, P. (2004) Globalisation and the university: Myths and realities in an unequal world, *Tertiary Education and Management*, 10(1), 1-25.

Altbach, P. (2013) *The international imperative in higher education.* Rotterdam: Sense.

Anderson, G.L. and Donchik, L.M. (2016) Privatising schooling and policymaking: the American legislative exchange council and new political and discursive strategies of education governance. *Educational Policy*, 30(2), 322-64.

Angod, L. (2015) *Behind the ivy: How schools produce elites through the bodies of racial others* (Unpublished doctoral dissertation). Toronto, Canada: Ontario Institute for Studies in Education, University of Toronto.

Anyon, J. (1980) Social class and the hidden curriculum of work, *The Journal of Education*, 162 (1), 67-92.

Apple, M.W. (1990) *Ideology and curriculum* (2nd edn). New York, NY: Routledge, Chapman and Hall, Inc.

Apple, M.W. (1995) *Education and power* (2nd edn). New York, NY: Routledge.

Apple, M.W. (1996) *Cultural politics and education.* New York, NY: Teachers College Press.

Apple, M.W. (2004) Creating difference: neo-liberalism, neo-conservatism and the politics of educational reform. *Educational Policy*, 18(1), 12-44.

Apple, M.W. (2006a) *Educating the 'Right' Way: Markets, Standards, God, and Inequality* (2nd edn). New York, NY: Routledge.

Apple, M.W. (2006b) Interrupting the Right: on doing critical educational work in conservative times. In G. Ladson-Billings and W.F. Tate (eds) *Education Research in the Public Interest*. New York, NY: Teachers College Press, 27-45.

Apple, M. (2009) Series Editor's Introduction to Hidden Markets. In: Burch, P. (2009) *Hidden Markets*. New York: Routledge, ix-xiii.

Apple, M.W. (ed) (2010) *Global Crises, Social Justice, and Education*, New York: Routledge.

Apple, M.W. (2013) *Can Education Change Society?* New York: Routledge.

Apple, M.W. (2014) *Official knowledge* (3rd edn). New York: Routledge.

Apple, M.W. (2015) Reframing the question of whether education can change society. *Educational Theory*, 65(3), 299-315.

Archer, L. (2008) Younger academics' constructions of 'authenticity', 'success' and professional identity, *Studies in Higher Education*, 33(4), 385-403.

Archer, L., Hutchings, M. and Ross, A. (eds) (2003) *Higher education and social class: Issues of exclusion and inclusion*. London: RoutledgeFalmer.

Arendt, H. (2005) *The Promise of Politics*. New York, NY: Schocken Books.

Aronowitz, S. (2000) *The knowledge factory: Dismantling the corporate university and creating true higher education*. Boston: Beacon Press.

Atkinson, H. (2012) *Local Democracy, Civic Engagement and Community: From New Labour to the Big Society*. Manchester: Manchester University Press

Au, W. (2009) *Unequal By Design: High-Stakes Testing and the Standardization of Inequality*. New York: Routledge.

Au, W. (2014) Seeing students as humans, not products. In P.C. Gorski and K. Zenkov (eds) *The Big Lies of School Reform*. New York: Routledge, 143-152.

Au, W. and Ferrare, J.J. (2015) *Mapping Corporate Education Reform*. New York, NY: Routledge.

Bacchi, C. (2009) *Analysing Policy: What's the problem represented to be?* Frenchs Forest, NSW: Pearson Publishing.

Bagdikian, B. (1997) *The Media Monopoly*. Boston, MA: Beacon Press.

Bailey, P.J. (2013) The policy dispositif: historical formation and method, *Journal of Education Policy*, 28(6), 807-827.

Ball, S.J. (1993) Education markets, choice and social class: The market as a class strategy in the UK and US. *British Journal of Sociology of Education*, 14(1), 3-19.

Ball, S.J. (2003a) *Class Strategies and the Education Market: The Middle Classes and Social Advantage*. London: RoutledgeFalmer.

Ball, S.J. (2003b) The teacher's soul and the terrors of performativity. *Journal of Education Policy*, 18(2), 215-28.

Ball, S.J. (2007) *Education PLC*. Abingdon: Routledge.

Ball, S.J. (2008) New philanthropy, new networks and new governance in education. *Political Studies*, 56(4), 747-765.

Ball, S.J. (2009a) Privatising education, privatising education policy, privatising educational research: Network governance and the 'competition state'. *Journal of Education Policy*, 24(1), 83-99.

Ball, S.J. (2009b) Academies in Context: politics, business and philanthropy and heterarchical governance. *Management in Education*, 23(3), 100-03.

Ball, S.J. (2012a) *Global Education Inc.* Abingdon: Routledge.

Ball, S.J (2012b) Performativity, commodification and commitment: an I-spy guide to the neoliberal university, *British Journal of Educational studies*, 60(1), 17-28.

Ball, S.J. (2013) *Education, justice and democracy: The struggle over ignorance and Opportunity*. London: Centre for Labour and Social Studies.

Ball, S.J. (2015) Accounting for a sociological life: influences and experiences on the road from welfarism to neoliberalism. *British Journal of Sociology of Education*. DOI: 10.1080/01425692.2015.1050087

Ball, S.J. and Junemann, C. (2012) *Networks, New Governance and Education*. Abingdon: Routledge.

Ball, S. and Maroy, C. (2009) School's logic of action as mediation and compromise between internal dynamics and external constraints and pressures. *Compare*, 39(1), 99-112.

Ball, S.J. and Nikita, D.P. (2014) The global middle class and school choice: a cosmopolitan sociology. *Z Erziehungswiss*, 17, 81-93.

Ball, S.J. and Youdell, D. (2008) *Hidden Privatisation in Public Education*. Brussels: Education International.

Banchero, S. (2012) *School vouchers gain ground*. http://www.wsj.com/articles/SB10001424052702303624004577338131609745296

Barber, M. (2007) *Instruction to Deliver*, London: Politico's Publishing Ltd.

Barber, M., Moffit, A. and Kihn, P. (2011) *Deliverology 101, A Field Guide for Educational Leaders*. London: Sage.

Barr, M.D. (1999) Lee Kuan Yew: Race, culture and genes. *Journal of Contemporary Asia*, 29(2), 145-66.

Barr, M.D. (2006) The charade of meritocracy. *Far Eastern Economic Review*, 169(8), 18-22.

Barr, M.D. and Skrbis, Z. (2008) *Constructing Singapore: Elitism, ethnicity and the nation-building project*. Copenhagen: Nordic Institute of Asian Studies Press.

Barrow, L. and Rouse, C.E. (2008) School vouchers: recent findings and unanswered questions. *3Q/2008, Economic Perspectives*, 2-16.

Batson, J. (2008) *Her Oxford*. Nashville: Vanderbilt University Press.

Bauman, Z. and Lyon, D. (2013) *Liquid Surveillance*. Malden, MA: Polity Press.

BBC (British Broadcasting Corporation) (2012) *Q and A: Academies*, 10 May. www.bbc.co.uk/news/education-132740907-765 (URL no longer available)

Beck, J. (2002) The sacred and the profane in recent struggles to promote official pedagogic identities. *British Journal of Sociology of Education*, 23(4), 617-26.

Beck, J. and Young, F.D. (2005) The assault on the professions and the restructuring of academic and professional identities: a Bernsteinian analysis, *British Journal of Sociology of Education*, 26(2), 83-197.

Beckett, F. (2007) *The Great City Academy Fraud*. London: Continuum.

Beech, J and Barrenechea, I. (2011) Pro-market educational governance: is Argentina a black swan?, *Critical Studies in Education*, 52(3) 1-15.

Benn, M. (2012) *School Wars: The Battle for Britain's Education*. London: Verso.

Benn, M. and Downs, J. (2016) *The Truth About Our Schools*. Abingdon: Routledge.

Berliner, D. (2014) 'Effects of Inequality and Poverty vs. Teachers and Schooling on America's Youth', *Teachers College Record*, 116(1). www.tcrecord.org/ExecSummary.asp?contentid=17293

Bernstein, B. (1977) *Class, Codes, and Control, Volume 3*. London: Routledge and Kegan Paul.

Bernstein, B. (1990) *Class, codes and control: The structuring of pedagogic discourse*. London: Routledge.

Bhabha, H.K. (1994) *The Location of Culture*. Abingdon: Routledge.

Billot, J. (2010) The imagined and the real: identifying the tensions for academic identity, *Higher Education Research and Development*, 29(6), 709-21.

Blackmore, J., Brennan, M. and Zipin, L. (eds) (2010) *Re-positioning university governance and academic work*. Rotterdam: Sense Publishers.

Bleiklie, I. and Byrkjeflot, H. (2002) Changing knowledge regimes: universities in a new research environment, *Higher Education*, 44, 519-32.

Bloomberg LP (2014) *CQ Roll Call*, "Amplify CEO Joel Klein Interviewed on Bloomberg TV", 4 April.

Board Opposed to Private School Voucher Proposal (2013) *Channel 3000*, 22 February. www.channel3000.com/news/Board-opposed-to-private-school-voucher-proposal/-/1648/19046792/-/100trmd/-/index.html

Bobbitt, P. (2002) *The Shield of Achilles*. London: Penguin.

Bogle, A. (2014) What the failure of inBloom means for the student data industry. www.slate.com/blogs/future_tense/2014/04/24/what_the_failure_of_inbloom_means_for_the_student_data_industry.html

Boliver, V. (2011) 'Expansion, differentiation and the persistence of social class inequalities in British higher education', *Higher Education*, 61, 229-42.

Boliver, V. (2013) How fair is access to more prestigious UK universities?, *British Journal of Sociology of Education*, 64(2): 344-64.

Boorstin, D. (1961) *The image: Or, what happened to the American dream*. New York, NY: Atheneum.

Bourdieu, P. (1984) *Distinction*. Cambridge, MA: Harvard University Press.

Bourdieu, P. (1986) The forms of capital. In: J. Richardson (ed) *Handbook of Theory and Research for the Sociology of Education*. New York: Greenwood, 241-58.

Bourdieu, P. (1990) *In other words: Essays towards a reflexive sociology*. Cambridge: Polity Press.

Bourdieu, P. (1996) *The state nobility: elite schools in the field of power*. Stanford, CA: Stanford University Press.

Bourdieu, P. (1998) *Practical Reason: On the theory of action*. Cambridge: Polity Press.

Bourdieu, P. (2000) *Pascalian Meditations*. Cambridge: Polity Press.

Bourdieu, P. (2003) *Firing Back: Against the Tyranny of the Market 2*. New York, NY: New Press.

Bourdieu, P. and Passeron, J.C. (1990) *Reproduction in Education, Society and Culture* (2nd edn). London: Sage.

Bourdieu, P. and Wacquant, L.J.D. (1992) *An Invitation to Reflexive Sociology*. Chicago, IL: University of Chicago Press.

Brennan, J. and Naidoo, R. (2008) Higher education and the achievement (and/or prevention) of equity and social justice, *Higher Education*, 56: 287-302.

Bridgeland, J., Dilulio, J. and Morison, K. (2006) *The silent epidemic: perspectives of high school dropouts*. Washington DC: Civic Enterprises for the Bill and Melinda Gates Foundation.

Brighouse, H. and Schouten, G. (2014) To Charter or Not to Charter: What Questions Should We Ask, and What Will the Answers Tell Us?, *Harvard Educational Review*, 84(3), 341-65.

Brindle, D. (2013) Frontline founder: 'Social work needs life-changing professionals'. *The Guardian*, 11 September. www.theguardian.com/society/2013/sep/11/josh-macalister-social-work-frontline

Brooks, R. and Waters, J. (2015) The hidden internationalism of elite English schools. *Sociology*, 49(2), 212-28.

Brown, R. with Carasso, H. (2013) *Everything for sale? The marketisation of UK higher education*. Abingdon: Routledge.

Buckley, K.E. and Burch, P. (2011) The changing nature of private engagement in public education: for-profit and non-profit organisations and educational reform. *Peabody Journal of Education*, 86(3), 236-51.

Buras, K.L. (2015) *Charter Schools, Race, and Urban Space*. New York, NY: Routledge.

Burch, P. (2009) *Hidden Markets*. New York, NY: Routledge.

Bush, G.W. (2015) *No Child Left Behind Act of 2001 Executive Summary*, Retrieved 2/2/15 from LD Online ldonline.org

Caesar, S. (2013) 'Glendale district says social media monitoring is for student safety. *Los Angeles Times*, 14 September. http://articles.latimes.com/2013/sep/14/local/la-me-glendale-social-media-20130915

Cameron, D. (2009) *The Big Society*, Speech delivered in London, 10 November.

Cameron, D. (2011) *Speech on 'The Big Society'*. Speech delivered in Milton Keynes, 23 May. https://www.gov.uk/government/speeches/speech-on-the-big-soci

Carr, W. and Hartnet, A. (1996) *Education and the Struggle for Democracy*. Buckingham: Open University Press.

Carrasco, A., Seppänen, P., Rinne, R. and Falabella, A. (2015) Educational accountability in Chile and Finland: divergent principles framing school choice policies. In: P Seppänen, A. Carrasco, M. Kalalahti, R. Rinne and H. Simola (eds) *Contrasting Dynamics in Education Politics of Extremes*. Rotterdam: Sense Publishers, 53-80.

Carroll, W. (2009) Transnationalists and national networkers in the global corporate elite, *Global Networks*, 9(3), 289-314.

CBS News (2014) High schoolers protest conservative proposal, September 24, 2014. Arvada, CO. http://www.cbsnews.com/news/colorado-high-schoolers-protest-conservative-proposal/

Chang, R. (2011) Parents' background the edge for students at top schools: MM, *The Straits Times*, 25 January, p A3.

Chapman, C. (2013) Academies, federations, chains and teaching schools in England: reflections on leadership, policy and practice. *Journal of School Choice: International Research and Reform*, 7(3), 334-52.

Charity Commission (2016) *Teach First – Data for financial year ending 31 August 2015.* http://beta.charitycommission.gov.uk/charity-details?regid=1098294&subid=0

Chiapello, E. and Fairclough, N. (2002) Understanding the new management ideology: a transdisciplinary contribution from critical discourse analysis and new sociology of capitalism. *Discourse and society*, 13(2), 185-208.

Clark, M.M. (2014) Whose knowledge counts in Government literacy policies and at what cost?, *Education Journal*. No 186. 20 January, 13-16.

Clarke, J. (2008) Living with/in and without neo-liberalism, *Focaal*, 51, 135-147.

Clarke, J. and Newman, J. (1997) *The Managerial State: Power, Politics and Ideology in the Remaking of Social Welfare.* London: Sage.

Clegg, R., Kulas, O. M., Proffitt, E., Nisbett, K., Shidaker, S., Tuneberg, J. and Van Hoozer, S. (2013) *A curriculum audit of the Kenosha Unified School District.* Bloomington, IN: Phi Delta Kappa.

Clegg, S. (2008) Femininities/masculinities and a sense self: thinking gendered academic identities and the intellectual self, *Gender and Education*, 20(3), 209-21.

Cohen, M. (2012) *Argentina's Economic Growth and Recovery, 2001–2008.* Abingdon: Routledge.

Coldron, J., Crawford, C., Jones, S. and Simkins, T. (2014) The restructuring of schooling in England: The responses of well-positioned headteachers, *Educational Management Administration and Leadership*, 42(3), 387-403.

Collier, D. (2011) Understanding process tracing, *Political Science and Politics*, 44(4), 823–830.

Collini, S. (2012) *What are universities for?*, London: Penguin.

Collins, J.C. (2001) *Good to Great: Why some companies make the leap ... and others don't.* US: Collins Business.

Collins, J.C. (undated) *Getting from Good to Great in Higher Education.* https://net.educause.edu/ir/library/pdf/ffp0403s.pdf

Confessore, N. (2016) Koch Brothers' budget of $889 million for 2016 is on par with both parties' spending, *New York Times*, 26 January. www.nytimes.com/2015/01/27/us/politics/kochs-plan-to-spend-900-million-on-2016-campaign.html?partner=rss&emc=rss&_r=0

Connell, R. (1996) *Prepare for interesting times: Education in a fractured world,* Inaugural professorial lecture, University of Sydney, 6 August.

Connell, R. (1998) Social change and curriculum futures, *Change: Transformations in Education*, 1(1), 84-90.

Connell, R. (2007) *Southern Theory.* Cambridge: Polity Press.

Connell, R. (2010) Building the neoliberal world: managers as intellectuals in a peripheral economy. *Critical Sociology*, 36(6), 777-92.

Cookson, W. and Persell, C. (1985) *Preparing for power: America's elite boarding schools*. United States: Basic Books.

Cookson, W. and Persell, C. (1991) Race and class in America's elite preparatory boarding schools: African Americans as the "outsiders within", *Journal of Negro Education*, 60(2), 219-28.

Cookson, W. and Persell, C. (2010) Preparing for power: Twenty-five years later. In: A. Howard and R.A. Gaztambide-Fernández (eds) *Educating elites: Class privilege and educational advantage*. Lanham, MD: Rowan and Littlefield Education, 13-30.

Coopers and Lybrand (1988) *Local Management of Schools*. London: Coopers and Lybrand

Coughlan, S. (2016) Academy chain to scrap governing bodies. *BBC News*, 19 January. www.bbc.co.uk/news/education-35347602

Courtney, S.J. (2015a) Corporatised leadership in English schools. *Journal of Educational Administration and History*, 47(3), 214-231.

Courtney, S.J. (2015b) *Investigating school leadership at a time of system diversity, competition and flux*. Unpublished PhD thesis, University of Manchester, UK.

Courtney, S.J. (2015c) Mapping school types in England, *Oxford Review of Education*, 41(6), 799-818.

Courtney, S.J. and Gunter, H.M. (2015) Get off my bus! School leaders, vision work and the elimination of teachers. *International Journal of Leadership in Education: Theory and Practice*, 18(4), 395-417.

Courtney, S.J. and Gunter, H.M. (2017, in press) Privatising leadership in education in England. In: D. Waite and I. Bogotch (eds) *The International Handbook of Educational Leadership*. Hoboken, NJ: Wiley-Blackwell Publishers.

Croft, J., Sahlgren, G.H. and Howes, A. (2013) *School Vouchers for England*. London: Adam Smith Institute and Centre for Market Reform of Education.

Cross, S., Hubbard, A. and Munro, E. (2010) *Reclaiming Social Work London Borough of Hackney Children and Young People's Services*. www.safeguardingchildrenea.co.uk/wp-content/uploads/2013/08/Eileen-Munro-Review-of-the-Hackney-Model.pdf

Currie, J., Harris, P. and Thiele, B. (2000) Sacrifices in greedy institutions: are they gendered?, *Gender and Education*, 12(3), 269-91.

Dale, R. (1989) *The state and education policy*. Milton Keynes: Open University Press.

Darder, A. (2012) Neoliberalism in the academic borderlands: an ongoing struggle for equality and human rights, *Educational Studies*, 48(5), 412-26.

Darling-Hammond, L. and Lieberman, A. (2012) Educating Superman. In: Swail, W.S. (ed) *Finding Superman, Debating the Future of Public Education in America*. New York, NY: Teachers College Press, 31-45.

Davies, B. and Bansel, P. (2007) Introduction: neoliberalism and education, *International Journal of Qualitative Studies in Education*, 20(3), 247-59.

Davis, M. (2006) *Planet of Slums*. London: Verso.

Dawisha, K. (2015) *Putin's Kleptocracy: Who owns Russia?*, New York, NY: Simon and Shuster.

Dean, C., Dyson, A., Gallannaugh, F., Howes, A. and Raffo, C. (2007) *Schools, governors and disadvantage*. York: Joseph Rowntree Foundation.

Dean, J. (2016) *Crowds and Party*, London: Verso.

Deem, R. (1998) 'New managerialism' and higher education: The management of performances and cultures in universities in the United Kingdom, *International Studies in Sociology of Education*, 8(1), 47-70.

Deem, R. (2001) Globalisation, new managerialism, academic capitalism and entrepreneurialism in universities: is the local dimension still important?, *Comparative Education*, 37(1), 7-20.

Deem, R., Brehony, K. and Heath, S. (1995) *Active citizenship and the governing of schools*. Buckingham: Open University Press.

Deem, R., Hillyard, S. and Reed, M. (2007) *Knowledge, higher education, and the new managerialism*. Oxford: Oxford University Press.

Delanty, G. (1998) The idea of the university in the global era: from knowledge as an end to the end of knowledge? *Social Epistemology: A Journal of Knowledge, Culture and Policy*, 12(1), 3-25.

Delissovoy, N., Means, A. and Saltman, K.J. (2014) *Toward a New Common School Movement* Boulder, Co: Paradigm.

Department for Education (DfE) (2010) *The Importance of Teaching*. London: TSO.

Department for Education (2011) *Free Schools in 2013: how to apply*. London: TSO.

Department for Education (2013) *Governors' Handbook*. London: Crown Copyright

Department for Education (2014) *Number of academies and free schools*. https://www.gov.uk/government/publications/number-of-academies-and-free-schools

Department for Education (2015a) *Open academies and academy projects in development.* 12 June. https://www.gov.uk/government/publications/open-academies-and-academy-projects-in-development

Department for Education (2015b) *Free schools: open schools and successful applications.* 21 May. https://www.gov.uk/government/publications/free-schools-open-schools-and-successful-applications

Department for Education (2015c) *Free schools applications: criteria for assessment.* https://www.gov.uk/government/uploads/system/uploads/attachment_data/file/487713/Free_school_applications_criteria_for_assessment_-_mainstream_and_16_to_....pdf

Department for Education and Skills (DfES) (2005) *Higher standards, better schools for all.* London: HMSO.

Department of Statistics (2011) *Singapore census of population 2010 statistical release 1.* Singapore: Department of Statistics.

Desker, B. (2013) Will Singapore's collective spirit prevail?, *The Straits Times,* 9 August, p A24.

Dewey, J. (2011) *Democracy and Education.* Hollywood, FL: Simon and Brown.

Directorate General of Higher Education (DGHE) (2013) *Lecturers workloads guidance (LWGD).* Jakarta: DIKTI.

Doerr, N.M. (2012) Study abroad as 'adventure': Globalist construction of host-home hierarchy and governed adventurer subjects. *Critical Discourse Studies,* 9(3), 257-68.

Doerr, N.M. (2013) Do 'global citizens' need the parochial cultural other? Discourse of immersion in study abroad and learning-by-doing. *Compare,* 43(2), 224-43.

Donnelly, M. (2014) The road to Oxbridge: Schools and elite university choices, *British Journal of Educational Studies,* 62(1), 57-72.

Dorling, D. (2014a) *Inequality and the 1%.* London: Verso.

Dorling, D. (2014b) Division grows as inequality multiplies. *Times Higher Education,* 25 September–1 October, 2, 171, 34-41.

Downs, J. (2013) Trouble at two academy chains: AET banned from expanding and E-Act gets a warning. *Local Schools Network.* www.localschoolsnetwork.org.uk/2013/04/trouble-at-two-academy-chains-aet-banned-from-expanding-and-e-act-gets-a-warning/

Duhigg, C. and Dougherty, C. (2008) From Midwest to M.T.A., pain from global gamble, *The New York Times,* 1 November. www.nytimes.com/2008/11/02/business/02global.html?pagewanted=alland_r=0

Dyhouse, C. (1995) *No distinction of sex? Women in British universities 1870–1939.* London: UCL Press.

Edison Learning (2013) *Collaborative academies trust.* www.edisonlearning.net/who-wework-with/cat/collaborative-academies-trust.html

EducationInvestor (2011) DfE unveils list of approved free schools suppliers. www.educationinvestor.co.uk/ShowArticle.aspx?ID=2556andAspxAutoDetectCookieSupport=1 (URL no longer available)

Effendi, S. (2005) *GATS and the liberalisation of higher education.* Paper presented on the GATS: Neo-imperialism in education conference, Gadjah Mada University, September.

Ellis, V., Maguire, M., Trippestad, T.A., Liu, Y. Yang, X. and Zeichner, K. (2015) Teaching other people's children, elsewhere, for a while: the rhetoric of a travelling educational reform. *Journal of Education Policy*, 31(1), 60-80.

Emerson, C. (2006) *Vital signs, vibrant society.* Sydney: University of New South Wales Press.

Fairclough, N. (2003) *Analysing discourse: Textual analysis for social research.* London: Psychology Press.

Ferris, K.O. (2010) The next big thing: Local celebrity, *Society*, 47, 392-5.

Fitzgerald, T. (2010) Spaces in–between: Indigenous women leaders speak back, *International Journal of Leadership in Education*, 13(1), 93-105.

Fitzgerald, T. (2014) *Women leaders in higher education: Shattering the myths.* Abingdon: Routledge.

Fitzgerald, T. and Collins, J. (2011) *Historical portraits of women home scientists: The University of New Zealand 1911–1947.* New York: Cambria Press.

Fitzgerald, T., White, J. and Gunter, H.M. (2012) *Hard labour? Academic work and the changing landscape of higher education.* Bingley: Emerald.

Flinders, M. (2013) *Defending Politics.* Oxford: Oxford University Press.

Flores, T. (2011a) Unified OKs transformation plan, *Kenosha News*, 3 March. http://kenoshanews.com/news/unifi ed_oks_transformation_plan_335146617.html (URL no longer available)

Flores, T. (2011b). Unified layoffs affect nearly every school, *Kenosha News*, 3 May. www.kenoshanews.com/home/unified_layoffs_affect_nearly_every_school_136429303.html (URL no longer available)

Flores, T. (2011c) SEC charges Stifel with fraud, *Kenosha News*, 12 August. www.kenoshanews.com/home/sec_charges_stifel_with_fraud_207348082.html (URL no longer available)

Flores, T. (2012) KEA Leader: Teacher morale falls as class sizes rise, *Kenosha News*, 20 September. www.kenoshanews.com/news/kea_leader_teacher_morale_falls_as_class_sizes_rise_440076013.html (URL no longer available)

Flores, T. (2013) Proposed expansion of school vouchers to Kenosha disappoints Unified officials, *Kenosha News*, 18 February. www.kenoshanews.com/news/at_unified_choice_schools_waiting_lists_abound_473875489.html (URL no longer available)

Forbes, J. and Lingard, B. (2015) Assured optimism in a Scottish girls' school: habitus and the (re)production of global privilege, *British Journal of Sociology of* Education, 36(1), 116-36.

Forrester, D. (2013) 'Why I'm leading Frontline's social work education scheme', *Guardian Professional*, 23 August. www.theguardian.com/social-care-network/2013/aug/23/leading-frontline-social-work-education-scheme

Forsyth, H. (2014) *A history of the modern Australian university.* Sydney: University of New South Wales Press.

Francis, B. (2006) Heroes or zeroes? The discursive positioning of 'underachieving boys' in English neo-liberal education policy, *Journal of Education Policy*, 21(2), 187-200.

Fraser, N. (1997) *Justice interruptus.* New York: Routledge.

Fraser, N. (2014) Can society be commodities all the way down? Post-Polanyian reflections on capitalist crisis. *Economy and Society*, 43(2), 541-58.

Freebody, P., Ludwig, C. and Gunn, S. (1995) *Everyday literacy practices in and out of schools in low socio-economic urban communities* (Vol 1). Melbourne: Curriculum Corporation.

Freire, P. (1970) *Pedagogy of the oppressed.* New York: Continuum.

Frontline (2015a) *About Frontline.* London: Frontline. http://thefrontline.org.uk/about-frontline

Frontline (2015b) *Graduate child social worker scheme rolls out across England.* London: Frontline. http://thefrontline.org.uk/news/graduate-child-social-worker-scheme-rolls-out-across-england

Frontline (2015c) *Our supporters.* London: Frontline. http://thefrontline.org.uk/supporters

Frontline (2015d) *FAQs.* London: Frontline. www.thefrontline.org.uk/faqs

Frontline (2016) *Frontline leadership*, Frontline: London.

Gale, T. and Hodge, S. (2014) Just imaginary: Delimiting social inclusion in higher education, *British Journal of Sociology of Education*, 35(5), 688-709.

Gamson, J. (1994) *Claims to fame: Celebrity in contemporary America.* Berkeley, CA: University of California Press.

Garcia, N. (2015a) Jeffco board OKs budget with more money for teachers, charters. *Chalkbeat Colorado*, 18 June. http://co.chalkbeat. org/2015/06/18/jeffco-board-oks-budget-with-more-money-for-teachers-charters/#.VlFFLK6rTEY

Garcia, N. (2015b) Nine claims made in the Jefferson County school board recall explained. *Chalkbeat Colorado*, 21 October. http:// co.chalkbeat.org/2015/10/21/nine-claims-made-in-the-jefferson-county-school-board-recall-explained/#.VlE6hK6rTEY

Garcia, N. (2015c) Jeffco school board members who pushed controversial changes ousted in recall. *Chalkbeat Colorado*. http:// www.chalkbeat.org/posts/co/2015/11/03/jefferson-county-recall-election-2015/

Garside, J., Wintour, P. and McVeigh, K. (2015) HSBC files, *The Guardian*, 10 February, 1.

Gaus, N. (2015) *The Indonesian State university in flux: academics and the neo-liberal turn*, Unpublished PhD thesis: The University of Manchester, UK.

Gaus, N. and Hall, D. (2015) Neoliberal governance in Indonesian universities: the impact upon academic identity, *International Journal of Sociology and Social Policy*, 35(9/10), 666-82.

Gaztambide-Fernández, R. (2009a) *The best of the best: Becoming elite at an American boarding school*. Cambridge, MA: Harvard University Press.

Gaztambide-Fernández, R. (2009b) What is an elite boarding school? *Review of Educational Research*, 79(3), 1090-128.

Gaztambide-Fernández, R.A. and DiAquoi, R. (2010) A part and apart: Students of color negotiating boundaries at an elite boarding school. In: A. Howard and R.A. Gaztambide-Fernández (eds) *Educating elites: Class privilege and educational advantage*. Lanham, MD: Rowman and Littlefield Education, 55-78.

Gaztambide-Fernández, R., Cairns, K. and Desai, C. (2013) The sense of entitlement. In: C. Maxwell and P. Aggleton (eds) *Privilege, agency, and affect: Understanding the production and effects of action*. New York, NY: Palgrave Macmillan, 32-49.

Gaztambide-Fernández, R. and Howard, A. (2010) Conclusion: Outlining a research agenda on elite education. In: A. Howard and R.A. Gaztambide-Fernández (eds) *Educating elites: Class privilege and educational advantage*. Lanham, MD: Rowman and Littlefield Education, 195-209.

Gaztambide-Fernández, R. and Howard, A. (2013) Social justice, deferred complicity, and the moral plight of the wealthy. *Democracy and Education*, 21(1), Article 7.

Gee, J.P. (2004) *Situated language and learning: A critique of traditional schooling.* New York, NY: Routledge.

Geo Listening (n.d.) *About Us.* https://geolistening.com/about-us/

Gewirtz, S. (2002) *The Managerial School.* London: Routledge.

Gibbons, M., Limoges, C., Nowotny, H., Schwartzman, S., Scott, P. and Trow, M. (1994) *The New Production of Knowledge.* London: Sage.

Gill, S (1990) *American Hegemony and the Trilateral Commission.* Cambridge: Cambridge University Press.

Gillborn, D. and Kirton, A. (2000) White heat: racism, under-acheivement and white working-class boys, *International Journal of Inclusive Education*, 4(2), 271-88.

Giroux, H.A. (1992) *Border crossings: Cultural workers and the politics of education.* London: Psychology Press.

Giroux, H. (2002) Neoliberalism, corporate culture and the promise of higher education: The university as a public sphere., *Harvard Educational Review*, 72(4), 425-63.

Giroux, H.A. (2003) Selling out higher education, *Policy Futures in Education*, 1 (1), 179-200.

Giroux, H. (2010) Challenging the military-industrial-academic complex after 9/11, *Policy Futures in Education*, 8(2), 232-37.

Giroux, H.A. (2014) *Neoliberalism's war against higher education.* Chicago: Haymarket Press.

Glatter, R. (2011) Joining up the dots: academies and system coherence. In: Gunter, H.M (ed) *The State and Education Policy: The Academies Programme.* London. Bloomsbury.

Glatter, R. (2012) Persistent preoccupations: the rise and rise of school autonomy and accountability in England. *Educational Management Administration and Leadership*, 40(5), 559-75.

Goh, C.K. (2013) Meritocracy works but beware of elitism, *The Straits Times*, 27 July. www.straitstimes.com/breaking-news/singapore/story/guard-against-elitism-and-sense-entitlement-esm-goh-20130727

Goh, D.P.S. (2015) Elite schools, postcolonial Chineseness and hegemonic masculinities in Singapore. *British Journal of Sociology of Education*, 36(1), 137-55.

Goodwin, M. (2009) Which networks matter in education governance? A reply to Ball's 'New philanthropy, new networks and new governance in education', *Political Studies*, 57, 680-7.

Gorard, S. (2014) The link between Academies in England, pupil outcomes and local patterns of socio-economic segregation between schools. *Research Papers in Education*, 29(3), 268-84.

Gorski, P.C. and Zenkov, K. (eds) (2014) *The Big Lies of School Reform*. New York: Routledge.

Grace, G. (1995) *School leadership: Beyond education management*. Bristol: The Falmer Press.

Gramsci, A. (1971) *Selections from Prison Notebooks*. London: Lawrence and Wishart.

Gray, S.P. and Streshly, W.A. (2008) *From Good Schools to Great Schools*. Thousand Oaks, CA: Corwin Press.

Greany, T. (2014) *Are we nearly there yet? Progress and next steps towards a self-improving school system*. London: Institute of Education.

Greany, T. and Scott, J. (2014) Conflicts of interest in academy sponsorship arrangements: A report for the Education Select Committee. www.parliament.uk/documents/commons-committees/ Education/Conflicts-of-interest-in-academies-report.pdf

Greenhalgh-Spencer, H., Castro, M., Bulut, E., Goel, K., Lin, C. and McCarthy, C. (2015) Social class as flow and mutability: the Barbados case, *British Journal of Sociology of Education*, 36(1), 156-73.

Greenwald, G., MacAskill, E. and Poitras, L. (2013) *Edward Snowden: the whistleblower behind the NSA surveillance revelations*. www.theguardian. com/world/2013/jun/09/edward-snowden-nsa-whistleblower-surveillance

Grenfell, M. and James, D. (2004) Change in the field – changing the field: Bourdieu and the methodological practice of educational research, *British Journal of Sociology of Education*, 25(4), 507-23.

Griffiths, D. (2010) Academic influence amongst the UK public elite, *Sociology*, 44(4), 734-50.

Guggenheim, D. (2011) *Waiting for 'Superman'*. A Paramount Vintage and Participant Media in association with Walden Media and Electric Kinney Films production.

Guinier, L. and Torres, G. (2002) *The miners' canary: Enlisting race, resisting power*. Cambridge, MA: Harvard University Press.

GUK (2013) Speech delivered at the Independent Academies Association (IAA) National Conference. GOV.UK, 8 July. https:// www.gov.uk/government/speeches/lord-nash-speaks-to-the-independent-academies-association-iaa-national-conference

GUK (2015) Nicky Morgan speaks about the importance of school governance. GOV.UK, 27 June. https://www.gov.uk/government/ speeches/nicky-morgan-speaks-about-the-importance-of-school-governance

Gumport, P.J. (2000) Academic restructuring: organizational change and institutional imperatives, *Higher Education*, 39, 67-91.

Gunter, H.M. (ed) (2011) *The state and education policy: the Academies Programme*. London: Continuum.

Gunter, H.M. (2012) *Leadership and the reform of education*. Bristol: The Policy Press.

Gunter, H.M. (2015) The politics of education policy in England, *International Journal of Inclusive Education*, 19(11), 1206-12.

Gunter, H.M. (2016) *An Intellectual History of School Leadership Practcie and Research*. London. Bloomsbury.

Gunter, H.M. and Forrester, G. (2009) School leadership and education policy-making in England, *Policy Studies*, 30(5), 495-511.

Gunter, H.M., Hall, D. and Mills, C. (eds) (2014a) *Education policy research: design and practice at a time of rapid reform*. London: Bloomsbury.

Gunter, H., Hall, D. and Mills, C. (2014b) Consultants, consultancy and consultocracy in education policymaking in England, *Journal of Education Policy*, 30(4), 518-39.

Gunter, H.M. and McGinity, R. (2014) The politics of the Academies Programme: natality and pluralism in education policy-making, *Research Papers in Education*, 29(3), 1-15.

Gunter, H.M. and Mills, C. (2017) *Consultants and consultancy: the case of education*. Cham, Switzerland: Springer.

Gutiérrez, R. (2014) Improving education and the mistaken focus on 'raising test scores' and 'closing the achievement gap'. In: P.C. Gorski and K. Zenkov (eds) *The Big Lies of School Reform*. New York: Routledge, 17-28.

Guttman, D. and Willner, B. (1976) *The Shadow Government*. New York, NY: Pantheon Books.

Gvirtz, S. and Beech, J. (2008) *Going to School in Latin America*. Westport: Greenwood Press.

Haimson, L. (2014) inBloom, Inc. and data-sharing: the threat to student privacy and safety. Presentation given in Austin, Texas, March 2014. www.classsizematters.org/see-leonie-haimsons-powerpoint-presentation-on-inbloom-given-in-austin-texas/

Halffman, W. and Leydesdorff, L. (2010) Is inequality among universities increasing? Gini coefficients and the elusive rise of elite universities, *Minerva*, 48, 55-72.

Hall, S. (1980) Popular democratic vs. authoritarian populism: two ways of taking democracy seriously. In: A. Hunt (ed) *Marxism and Democracy*. London: Lawrence and Wishart, 150-70.

Hall, S. (1988). The toad in the garden: Thatcherism among the theorists. In: C. Nelson and L. Grossberg (eds) *Marxism and the Interpretation of Culture*. Urbana, IL: University of Illinois Press.

Hall, S. (2011) The neoliberal revolution, *Cultural Studies*, 25(6), 705-28.

Hall, S., Critcher, C., Jefferson, T., Clarke, J. and Roberts, B. (2013) *Policing the Crisis*. Basingstoke: Palgrave Macmillan.

Hall, S. and Massey, D. (2015) Interpreting the crisis, In: S. Davison and K. Harris (eds) *The Neoliberal Crisis*. London: Lawrence and Wishart Ltd, 60-71.

Hall, D. and McGinity, R. (2015) Conceptualizing teacher professional identity in neoliberal times: resistance, compliance and reform. *Education Policy Analysis Archives*, 23(88), 1-17

Hallow, L. (2011) 'We need to be optimistic': Unified superintendent encourages parents, teachers to stay positive, *Kenosha News*, 1 September. www.kenoshanews.com/home/we_need_to_be_optimistic_221238606.html (URL no longer available)

Hargreaves, D. (2010) *Creating a Self-Improving School System*. Nottingham: National College for School Leadership.

Hargreaves, D. (2012) *A self-improving school system: Towards maturity*. Nottingham: National College for School Leadership.

Harris, S. (2005) Rethinking academic identities in neo-liberal times, *Teaching in Higher Education*, 10(4), 421-43.

Hartley, D. (2012) *Education and the Culture of Consumption*. Abingdon: Routledge.

Harvey, D. (2005) *The New Imperialism*. Oxford: Oxford University Press.

Harvey, D. (2007) *A Brief History of Neoliberalism*. Oxford: Oxford University Press.

Harvey, D. (2011) *The Enigma of Capital*. London: Profile Books.

Harvey, D. (2014) *Seventeen Contradictions and the End of Capitalism* Oxford: Oxford University Press.

Hazelkorn, E. (2011) *Rankings and the reshaping of higher education: The battle for world-class excellence*. New York: Palgrave Macmillan.

Hellmueller, L.C. and Aeschbacher, N. (2010) Media and celebrity: Production and consumption of well-knownness, *Communication Research Trends*, 29(4), 4-35.

Herold, B. (2014) 'In Bloom's collapse shines spotlight on data-sharing challenges', *Education Week*, 2 May. www.edweek.org/ew/articles/2014/05/02/30inbloom.h33.html?cmp=ENL-EU-NEWS1

Herman, E. and Chomsky, N. (2002) *Manufacturing Consent*. New York, NY: Pantheon.

Higham, R. (2014a) 'Who Owns Our Schools?' An analysis of the Governance of Free Schools in England, *Educational Management, Administration and Leadership*, 42(3), 404-22.

Higham, R. (2014b) Free schools in the Big Society: the motivations, aims and demography of free school proposers, *Journal of Education Policy*, 29(1), 122-39.

Higham, R. and Earley, P. (2013) School autonomy and government control: School leaders' views on a changing policy landscape in England, *Educational Management, Administration and Leadership*, 41(6), 701-17.

Hill, D. (2009) Class, capital and education in this neoliberal and neoconservative period. In: S. Macrine, P. McLaren and D. Hill (eds) *Revolutionizing pedagogy: Education for social justice within and beyond global neoliberalism* London: Palgrave Macmillan, 119-42.

Hill, R. (2012) *The Missing Middle: The Case for School Commissioners*. London: RSA.

HM Government (2013) *Working Together to Safeguard Children: A Guide to Inter-Agency Working to Safeguard and Promote the Welfare of Children*, London: DfE.

Hoe, Y.N. (2011) MM Lee was describing "worst-case scenario": Dr Yaacob. *Channelnewsasia.com*, 29 January. www.channelnewsasia.com/stories/singaporelocalnews/view/1107702/1/.html (URL no longer available)

Holehouse, M. (2013) Tax questions for Michael Gove's £1,000-a-day advisers, *The Telegraph*, 24 April. www.telegraph.co.uk/news/politics/10014723/Tax-questions-for-Michael-Goves-1000-a-day-advisers.html

Hood, C. and Jackson, M. (1991) *Administrative Argument*. Aldershot: Dartmouth Publishing Company Limited.

Howard, A. (2008) *Learning privilege: Lessons of power and identity in affluent schooling*. New York: Routledge.

Howard, A. (2010) Elite visions: Privileged perceptions of self and others, *Teachers College Record*, 112(8), 1971-92.

Howard, A. and Gaztambide-Fernández, R. (eds) (2010) *Educating elites: Class privilege and educational advantage*. Lanham, MD: Rowan and Littlefield Education.

Hoyle, E. and Wallace, M. (2007) Educational reform: an ironic perspective, *Educational Management Administration and Leadership*, 35(1), 9-25.

Hursh, D. (2008) *High Stakes Testing and the Decline of Teaching and Learning*. Lanham, MD: Rowman and Littlefield.

InBloom (n.d.) *Frequently Asked Questions*. http://web.archive.org/web/20140208213302/https://inbloom.org/.

Ingram, N. (2011) Within school and beyond the gate: complexities of being educationally successful and working class, *Sociology*, 45(2), 287-302.

James, D. (2015) How Bourdieu bites back: recognising misrecognition in education and educational research, *Cambridge Journal of Education*, 45(1), 97-112.

Jencks, C. (1988) Whom must we treat equally for educational opportunity to be equal? *Ethics*, 98(1), 518-33.

Jessop, B., Brenner, N. and Jones, M. (2008) Theorising sociospatial relation,. *Environment and Planning D; Society and Space*, 26, 389-401.

Jones, A. (2011) Theorising international youth volunteering: Training for global (corporate) work, *Transactions of the Institute of British Geographers*, 36(4), 530-44.

Jones, O. (2014) *The Establishment, And How They Get Away With It*. London: Allen Lane.

Judt, T. (2010) *Ill Fares the Land*. New York: The Penguin Press.

Junemann, C. and Ball, S.J. (2015) *Pearson and PALF: The Mutating Giant*. Brussels: Educational International.

Kamenetz, A. (2013) News Corp.'s Big Test, *Fast Company.Com*, July–August.

Kang, T. (2005) *Creating educational dreams: The intersection of ethnicity, families and schools*. Singapore: Marshall Cavendish Academic.

Kaufmann, V., Bergman, M.M. and Joyce, D. (2004) Motility: mobility as capital, *International Journal of Urban and Regional Research*, 28(4), 745-56.

Kendall, L. and Reed, S. (2015) *Let it go: Power to the people in public services*, London: Progress, Labour Progressives; Local Government Association. www.progressonline.org.uk/content//uploads/2015/01/PROJ2931_PRO_Mag_Jan_27.1.15_pamphletWEB_spreads.pdf (URL no longer available)

Kenosha Unified School Board (2013) Regular Board Meeting, 29 January. http://www.kusd.edu/sites/default/files/document-library/english/rm20130129.pdf

Kenway, J. and Fahey, J. (2014) Staying ahead of the game: The globalizing practices of elite schools, *Globalisation, Societies and Education*, 12(2), 177-95.

Kenway, J. and Fahey, J. (2015) The gift economy of elite schooling: the changing contours and contradictions of privileged benefaction. *British Journal of Sociology of Education*, 36(1), 95-115.

Kenway, J. and Koh, A. (2013) The elite school as 'cognitive machine' and 'social paradise': Developing transnational capitals for the national 'field of power', *Journal of Sociology*, 49(2-3), 272-90.

Kenway, J. and Koh, A. (2015) Sociological silhouettes of elite schooling, *British Journal of Sociology of Education*, 36(1), 1-10.

Khan, S. (2010) Getting in: How elite schools play the college game. In: A. Howard and R.A. Gaztambide-Fernández (eds) *Educating elites: Class privilege and educational advantage.* Lanham, MD: Rowan and Littlefield Education, 97-112.

Khan, S.R. (2011) *Privilege: The making of an adolescent elite at St. Paul's College.* Princeton, NJ: Princeton University Press.

Khan, S.R. (2012) 'The sociology of elites', *Annual Review of Sociology*, 38, 361-77.

Kickert, W.J.M. (1997) Public governance in the Netherlands: an alternative to Anglo-American 'managerialism', *Public Administration*, 75, 731-52.

Kogan, M., Johnson, D., Packwood, T. and Whitaker, T. (1984) *School Governing Bodies.* London: Heinemann Educational Books.

Kolsaker, A. (2008) Academic professionalism in the managerialist era: a study of English universities, *Studies in Higher Education*, 33(5), 513-25.

Koyama, J.P. (2010) *Making Failure Pay.* Chicago: The University of Chicago Press.

Kwek, K. (2007) Students of top schools worry more about elitism. *The Straits Times*, 18 May, p H18.

Kynaston, D. (2014) What should we do with private schools?, *The Guardian, Review.* 6 December, 2-4.

Labaree, D. (2010) 'Teach for America and Teacher Ed: Heads they win, tails we lose', *Journal of Teacher Education*, 61(1-2), 48-55.

Lacroix, K. (2013) Association offers fresh start for Wisconsin teachers, *Milwaukee Journal Sentinel*, 2 September. www.jsonline.com/news/opinion/association-offers-fresh-start-for-wisconsin-teachers-b9985309z1-221866951.html

Lacroix vs. Kenosha Unified School District, No. 2013-CV-1889 (Wis. Cir. Ct. Kenosha Cty. 2013)

Lash, S. (2002) Foreword: individualization in a non-linear mode. In: U. Beck and E. Beck-Gernsheim (eds) *Individualization: Institutionalized Individualism and its Social and Political Consequences.* Sage: London, vii-xiii.

Lavender, P. (2011) Americans for Prosperity accused of voter suppression in Wisconsin recall elections, *The Huffington Post*, 3 August. www.huffingtonpost.com/2011/08/03/koch-brothers-americans-for-prosperity-wisconsin-recalls_n_913561.html

Layton, L. (2014) How Bill Gates pulled off the swift common core revolution. *The Washington Post*, 7 June. https://www.washingtonpost.com/politics/how-bill-gates-pulled-off-the-swift-common-core-revolution/2014/06/07/a830e32e-ec34-11e3-9f5c-9075d5508f0a_story.html

Lee, H.L. (2012) Speech by PAP Secretary-General Lee Hsien Loong at 2012 Party Conference, 2 December. http://news.pap.org.sg/news-and-commentaries/news-reports/pap-must-set-clear-direction-lee-hsien-loong.

Lee, K.Y. (2011) *Hard truths to keep Singapore going*. Singapore: Singapore Press Holdings.

Leo, E., Galloway, D. and Hearne, P. (2010) *Academies and Educational Reform: Governance, Leadership and Strategy*. Bristol: Multilingual Matters.

Leonard, M. (2014) Rage against the machine, *New Statesman*, 30 May–5 June, 24-27.

Levinson, B. and Holland, D. (1996) The cultural production of the educated person: an introduction. In: B. Levinson, D. Foley and D. Holland (eds) *The Cultural Production of the Educated Person: Critical Ethnographies of Schooling and Local Practice*. Albany, NY: State University of New York Press, 1-54

Lieberman, M.B. and Montgomery, D.B. (1998) First-mover (dis)advantages: retrospective and link with the resource-based view, *Strategic Management Journal*, 19, 1111-25.

Lim, L. (2013) Meritocracy, egalitarianism and elitism: A preliminary and provisional assessment of Singapore's primary education review. *Asia-Pacific Journal of Education*, 33(1), 1–14.

Lim, L. (2014) Ideology, rationality and reproduction in education: A critical discourse analysis, *Discourse: Studies in the Cultural Politics of Education*, 35(1), 61-76.

Lim, L. (2015) *Knowledge, control and critical thinking in Singapore: State ideology and the politics of pedagogic recontextualization*. New York, NY: Routledge.

Lim, L. and Apple, M.W. (2015) Elite rationalities and curricular form: "Meritorious" class reproduction in the elite thinking curriculum in Singapore, *Curriculum Inquiry*, 45(5), 472–490.

Lim, L. and Apple, M.W. (2016) *The Strong State and Curriculum Reform: Assessing the Politics and Possibilities of Educational Change in Asia*. New York: Routledge.

Lim, L. and Kwek, K. (2006) Why the elite envy?, *The Straits Times*, 20 June, 10.

Lipman, P. (2011a) *New political economy of urban education: Neoliberalism, race and the right to the city.* New York, NY: Routledge.

Lipman, P. (2011b) Contesting the city: neoliberal urbanism and the cultural politics of education reform in Chicago, *Discourse*, 32(2), 217-34.

Lipman, P. (2014) Capitalizing on crisis: venture philanthropy's colonial project to remake urban education, *Critical Studies in Education*, 56(2), 241-258.

Lorenz, C. (2012) If you're so smart, why are you under surveillance? Universities, neoliberalism, and new public management, *Chicago Journal*, 38(3), 599-629.

Loseke, D.R. and Cahill, S.E. (1986) Actors in search of a character: Student social workers' quest for professional identity, *Symbolic Interactions*, 9, 245-68.

Lubienski, C. (2014) Re-making the middle: Dis-intermediation in international context, *Educational Management Administration and Leadership*, 42(3), 423-40.

Lubienski, C.A. and Lubienski, S.T. (2014) *The Public School Advantage: Why Public Schools Outperform Private Schools.* Chicago: The University of Chicago Press.

Lundhal, L. (2011) The emergence of a Swedish school market. In: R. Hatcher and K. Jones (eds) *No Country for the Young.* London: The Tuffnell Press, 37-49.

Lynch, K., Grummel, B. and Devine, D. (2012) *New Managerialism in Education: Commercialization, Carelessness, and Gender.* New York: Palgrave Macmillan.

MacAlister, J., Crehan, L., Olsen, A. and Clifton, J. (2012) *Frontline: Improving the children's social work profession*, London: Institute for Public Policy Research. /www.ippr.org/files/images/media/files/publication/2013/03/frontline-childrens-social-work_Oct2012_9705.pdf?noredirect=1

Maclean, M., Harvey, C. and Chia, R. (2010) Dominant corporate agents and the power elite in France and Britain, *Organization Studies*, 31(3), 327-48.

Macrine, S.L. (2003) Imprisoning minds. In: K.J. Saltman and D.A. Gabbard (eds) *Education as Enforcement.* 2nd edn, 230-8.

Mahony, P., Hextall, I. and Menter, I. (2004) Building dams in Jordan, assessing teachers in England: a case study in edu-business, *Globalisation, Societies and Education*, 2(2), 277-96.

Malkin, M. (2014) Feeding the Edu-Tech beast, *Pittsburgh Tribune*, 13 January. http://triblive.com/opinion/featuredcommentary/5380653-74/google-district-common#axzz3xndcON3t

Mansell, W. (2015) Tory donor complains of misuse of public funds for free school. www.theguardian.com/education/2015/nov/10/tory-donor-misuse-funds-free-school-warwick-mansell

Marginson, S. (2008) Global field and global imagining: Bourdieu and worldwide higher education, *British Journal of Sociology of Education*, 29(3), 303-15.

Marginson, S. (2014) University rankings and social science, *European Journal of Education*, 49(1), 45-59.

Marquand, D. (2004) *Decline of the Public*. Cambridge: Polity Press.

Marr, A. (2015) The centre cannot hold, *New Statesman*, 20–26 March, 27-9.

Martínez, S. (2012) Inclusión digital en la educación pública argentina: El Programa Conectar Igualdad [Digital inclusion in Argentinean public education: The Program Connecting Equality], *Revista Educación y Pedagogía*, 24(62), 205-18.

Marx, K. and Engels, F. (1888) *Manifesto of the Communist Party*. Authorised English translation. London: William Reeves Bookseller Ltd.

Maxwell, C. (2015) Elites: some questions for a new research agenda. In: A. van Zanten and S.J. Ball with B. Darchy-Koechlin (eds) *Elites, Privilege and Excellence. World Yearbook of Education 2015*, Abingdon: Routledge, 15-28.

Maxwell, C. and Aggleton, P. (2014) The reproduction of privilege: young women, the family and private education, *International Studies in Sociology of Education*, 24(2), 189-209.

Maxwell, C. and Aggleton, P. (2015) The historical construction of elite education in England. In: C. Maxwell and P. Aggleton (eds) *Elite Education: International Perspectives*, Routledge: London, 15-28.

McAdam, D. (1989) The biographical consequence of activism. *American Sociological Review*, 54(5), 744-60.

McChesney, R. (2004) *The Problem of the Media*. New York, NY: Monthly Review Press.

McDarrison, K. (2013) Sign of the times: Protest at Kenosha Unified School District, continued. *The Wisconsin Happy Farm*. http://wisconsinhappyfarm.com/sign-of-the-times-protest-at-kenosha-unified-school-district-continued/

McGinity, R. (2014) *An investigation into localised policy-making during a period of rapid educational reform in England*. Unpublished PhD thesis. University of Manchester, UK.

McGinity, R. (2015) Innovation and autonomy at a time of rapid reform: An English case study. *Nordic Journal of Studies in Educational Policy*, 1(2), 62-72.

McGinity, R. and Courtney, S. (2016) A response to the passing of the Education and Adoption Bill: A dark day for public education in England, *The Local Schools Network*, 29 February. www.localschoolsnetwork.org.uk/2016/02/a-response-to-the-passing-of-the-education-and-adoption-bill-a-dark-day-for-education-in-england

McGinity, R. and Gunter, H. (2016) New practices and old hierarchies: A case study in capital and leadership. In: Thomson, P., *Pierre Bourdieu and Educational Leadership*, Routledge.

McGregor, K. (2013) We must not be ashamed of trying to attract outstanding graduates into social work, *Community Care*. www.communitycare.co.uk/2013/09/18/we-must-not-be-ashamed-of-trying-to-attract-outstanding-graduates-into-social-work/

McKelvoy, A. (2015) The network-ocracy: meet London's new smart sets including George Osborne, Mick Jagger and Stephanie Flanders, *London Evening Standard*, 24 March. www.standard.co.uk/lifestyle/london-life/the-networkocracy-meet-londons-new-smart-sets-including-george-osborne-mick-jagger-and-stephanie-flanders-10129917.html?origin=internalSearch

McNamara, O. and Murray, J. (2013) *The School Direct programme and its implications for research informed teacher education and teacher educators.* York: Higher Education Academy.

Means, A.J. (2015) Generational precarity, education, and the crisis of capitalism, *Critical Sociology*, 8 January.

Means, A.J. (in press) Algorithmic education, big data, and the control society: toward a decolonial and biotechnical commons. *Cultural Studies in Science Education*.

Mendéz, A. (2013) *El colegio: La formación de una elite meritocrática en el Nacional Buenos Aires* [The school: The formation of a meritocratic elite at the Nacional Buenos Aires]. Buenos Aires: Sudamericana.

Meszaros, I. (2015) *The Necessity of Social Control.* New York, NY: Monthly Review Press.

Michaels, E, Handfield-Jones, H. and Axelrod, B. (2001) *The War for Talent.* Boston, MA: Harvard Business.

Michels, R. (1958) *Political Parties.* Glencoe, IL: Free Press.

Miliband, R. (1973) *The State in Capitalist Society.* London: Quartet Books.

Mills, C.W. (1956) *The Power Elite.* New York, NY: Oxford University Press.

Minister of Education (1988) *Tomorrow's Schools: The Reform of Education Administration in New Zealand.* Wellington: Government Printer.

Ministry of Education (1997) *Desired Outcomes of Education*. Singapore: Ministry of Education.

Ministry of Education (2010) *Performance by ethnic group 2000–2009*. www.moe.gov.sg/media/press/2010/12/performance-by-ethnic-group-2000-2009.php (URL no longer available)

Ministry of Education (2011a) *Gifted Education Programme: Rationale and goals*. www.moe.gov.sg/education/programmes/gifted-education-programme/rationale-and-goals

Ministry of Education (2011b) *Integrated Programmes (IP)*. www.moe.gov.sg/education/secondary/other/integrated-programme

Mirón, L., Beabout, B.R. and Boselovic, J.L. (eds) (2015) *Only in New Orleans*. Rotterdam: Sense Publishers.

Molnar, A. and Boninger, F. (2015) *On the Block: Student Data and Privacy in the Digital Age – The Seventeenth Annual Report on Schoolhouse Commercializing Trends, 2013–2014*. Boulder, CO: National Education Policy Center. http://nepc.colorado.edu/publication/schoolhouse-commercialism-2014

Molnar, A., Miron, G. and Urschel, J.L. (2010) *Profiles of for-profit education management organizations: Twelfth annual report – 2009–2010*. Boulder, CO: National Education Policy Center. http://nepc.colorado.edu/publication/EMO-FP-09-10

Moran, M. (2008) Representing the corporate elite in Britain: capitalist solidarity and capitalist legitimacy. In: M. Savage and K. Williams (eds) *Remembering Elites*. Oxford: Blackwell Publishing, 64-79.

Morduchowicz, A. (2005) Private education funding and (de)regulation in Argentina. In: L. Wolff, J.C. Navarro and P. González (eds) *Private Education and Public Policy in Latin America*, PREAL, Washington, 39-65.

Moreno, I. (2015) In Colorado battleground county, conservative school board members face recall efforts. *US News*. 31 October. www.usnews.com/news/us/articles/2015/10/31/colorado-recall-targets-conservative-school-board-members

Mosca, G. (1939) *The Ruling Class*. New York, NY: McGraw-Hill.

Mourshed, M., Chijoke, C. and Barber, M. (2010) *How the world's most improved school systems keep getting better*. London: McKinsey.

Mullen, A. (2009) 'Elite destinations: Pathways to attending an Ivy League university', *British Journal of Sociology of Education*, 30(1), 15-27.

Munro, E. (2011) *The Munro Review of Child Protection: Final Report. A Child-centered System*, Cm 8062. London: DfE.

Munt, I. (1994) The 'other' postmodern tourism: Culture, travel, and the new middle classes. *Theory, Culture and Society*, 11(3), 101-23.

Murphy, K. (2011) Kenosha teacher backs governor in fight over collective bargaining, *Kenosha News*, 12 July. www.kenoshanews.com/home/kenosha_teacher_backs_governor_in_fight_over_collective_bargaining_178420122.html (URL no longer available)

Narey, M. (2014) *Making the education of social workers consistently effective: Report of Sir Martin Narey's independent review of the education of children's social workers*, London: Department for Education.

Narodowski, M. and Andrada, M. (2010) The privatization of education in Argentina, *Journal of Education Policy*, 16(6), 585-95.

Narodowski, M. and Nores, M. (2002) Socio-economic segregation with (without) competitive education policies: a comparative analysis of Argentina and Chile, *Comparative Education*, 38(4), 429-51.

Nash, J. (2014) Speech on 'Unlocking the power of academies' at the Academies Show. www.gov.uk/government/speeches/lord-nash-speaks-about-unlocking-the-power-of-academies

Nash, R. (1990) Bourdieu on education and social and cultural reproduction, *British Journal of Sociology of Education*, 11(4), 431-47.

NAO (2015) *Training new teachers*, London: Department for Education, National Audit Office. https://www.nao.org.uk/report/training-new-teachers/

New Schools Network (NSN) (2012) *The Free School Applicant's Handbook for 2013 Opening*. www.newschoolsnetwork.org/sites/default/files/SpecialFreeSchoolsHandbookJan2012.pdf

New Schools Network (NSN) (2016) *Your Team*. http://www.newschoolsnetwork.org/set-up-a-free-school/get-started/your-team

Newman, J. and Clarke, J. (2009) *Publics, Politics and Power*. London: Sage.

Ng, E.H. (2008) Speech by Dr Ng Eng Hen, Minister for Education and Second Minister for Defence, at the MOE Work Plan Seminar 2008. www.moe.gov.sg/media/speeches/2008/09/25/speech-by-dr-ng-eng-hen-at-the-moe-work-plan-seminar-2008.php (URL no longer available)

Nichols, J. (2012) *Uprising: How Wisconsin renewed the politics of protest, from Madison to Wall Street*. New York: Nation Books.

Nixon, J. (2011) *Higher education and the public good*. London: Continuum.

Noble, D. (1979) *America by design*. New York, NY: Oxford University Press.

Norris, T. (2011) *Consuming Schools: Commercialism and the End of Politics*. Toronto: University of Toronto Press.

Oakes, J. (1985) *Keeping track: How schools structure inequality*. New Haven, CT: Yale University Press.

Offe, C. and Wiesenthal, H. (1980) Two logics of collective action: theoretical notes on social class and organizational form. In M. Zeitlin (ed.) *Political Power and Social Theory*Bingley: JAI Press, 67-116.

Office for National Statistics (ONS) (2010) *Standard Occupational Classifications 2010*. SOC2012 Structure. Newport: ONS.

Ofsted (2011) *School Governance: Learning from the Best*. London: Ofsted.

Ofsted (2015) *School Inspection Handbook*. London: Ofsted.

Olson, M. (2011) Wirch recall group has received nearly $11,000. *Kenosha News*, 30 March. www.kenoshanews.com/home/wirch_recall_group_has_received_nearly_11000_118415117.html (URL no longer available)

Olssen, M. and Peters, M.A (2005) Neoliberalism, higher education and the knowledge economy: from the free market to knowledge capitalism, *Journal of Education Policy*, 20(3), 313-45.

Osborne, D. and Gaebler, T. (1993) *Reinventing Government*. New York, NY: A Plume Book, Penguin.

Pareto, V. (1935) *The Mind and Society*. New York, NY: Harcourt Brace.

Pemberton, S., Gordon, D. and Nandy, S. (2012) Child rights, child survival and child poverty: the debate. In: A. Minu and S. Nandy (eds) *Global Child Poverty and Well-being: Measurement Concepts, Policy and Action*. Bristol: Policy Press, 19-37.

Peretti, J. (2015) What I learnt about inequality after spending time with some of the richest people in the world. *Independent*, 1 February. www.independent.co.uk/voices/comment/what-i-learnt-about-inequality-after-spending-time-with-some-of-the-richest-people-in-the-world-10016438.html

Perry, D. (n.d.) *Academy Chains*. Specialist Schools and Academies Trust. https://docs.google.com/viewer?a=v&pid=sites&srcid=ZGVmYXVsdGRvbWFpbnxzdGV2ZW5qb2huY291cnRuZXl8Z3g6NGYxMGJhYjMxYzdiZmNjZA

Persson, J. (2015) Pearson, ETS, Houghton Mifflin, and McGraw-Hill lobby big and profit bigger from school tests. *Center for Media and Democracy*, 30 March. www.prwatch.org/news/2015/03/12777/reporters-guide-how-pearson-ets-houghton-mifflin-and-mcgraw-hill-are-profiting

Peshkin, A. (2001) *Permissible advantage? The moral consequences of elite schooling*. London: Routledge.

Pickles, K. (2001) Colonial counterparts: The first academic women in Anglo-Canada, New Zealand and Australia, *Women's History Review*, 10(2), 273-97.

Pietsch, T. (2013) *Empire of scholars: Universities, networks and the British academic world 1850–1939*. Manchester: Manchester University Press.

Pilkington, E. (2014) Kansas academic petitions judge to keep Koch brothers correspondence sealed, *The Guardian*, 23 December. www.theguardian.com/us-news/2014/dec/23/kansas-university-academic-koch-brothers-emails?CMP=share_btn_link

Prosser, H. (2015) Servicing elite interests: elite education in post-neoliberal Argentina. In: C. Maxwell and P. Aggleton (eds) *Elite Education: International Perspectives*. London: Routledge, 173-85.

Prosser, H. (2016) Economy of eliteness: consuming educational advantage. In A. Koh and J. Kenway (eds) *Elite Schools: Multiple Geographies of Privilege*. London: Routledge, 217-30.

Pusser, B., Kempner, K., Marginson, S. and Ordorika, I. (2012) *Universities and the public sphere: Knowledge creation and state building in the era of globalization*. Abingdon: Routledge.

Raffo, C., Dyson, A., Gunter, H.M, Hall, D., Jones, L. and Kalambouka, A. (eds) (2010) *Education and Poverty in Affluent Countries*. London: Routledge.

Rahim, L.Z. (1998) *The Singapore dilemma: The political and educational marginality of the Malay community*. Kuala Lumpur: Oxford University Press.

Randall, G.E. and Kindiak, D.H. (2008) De-professionalization or post- professionalization? Reflections on the state of social work as a profession, *Social Work in Health Care*, 47(4), 341-54.

Ravitch, D. (2010) *The Death and Life of the Great American School System*. New York, NY: Basic Books.

Ravitch, D. (2012) The myth of charter schools. In: Swail, W.S. (ed) *Finding Superman, Debating the Future of Public Education in America*. New York, NY: Teachers College Press, 19-30.

Ravitch, D. (2013a) *Reign of Error: The Hoax of the Privitization Movement and the Danger to America's Public Schools*. New York, NY: First Vintage Books.

Ravitch, D. (2013b) Is inBloom engaged in identity theft?, *Diane Ravitch's Blog*. 7 April. http://dianeravitch.net/2013/04/07/is-inbloom-engaged-in-identity-theft/

Ravitch, D. (2013c) Meet the Broad superintendents, Blog post, 15 August. http://dianeravitch.net/2013/08/15/meet-the-broad-superintendents

Ravitch, D. (2014) *Reign of Error, the Hoax of the Privatisation Movement and the Danger to America's Public Schools*. New York, NY: Vintage Books.

Rawls, J. (1971) *A theory of justice*. Cambridge, MA: Harvard University Press.

Reay, D. (2001) Finding or losing yourself? Working-class relationships to education, *Journal of Education Policy*, 16(4), 333-46.

Reay, D. (2002) Shaun's story: troubling discourses of white working class masculinities, *Gender and Education*, 14(3), 221-34.

Reay, D. (2005) Beyond consciousness? The psychic landscape of social class, *Sociology*, 39(5), 911-28.

Reay, D. (2008) Psychosocial aspects of white middle class identities: desiring and defending against the class and ethnic 'other' urban multi-ethnic schooling, *Sociology*, 42(6), 1072-88.

Reay, D. (2009) Making sense of white working class educational underachievement. In: K. Sveinsson (ed.) *Who Cares about the White Working Class?*, 22-8.

Reay, D., Crozier, G. and James, D. (2011) *White middle-class identities and urban schooling*. London: Palgrave Macmillan.

Reay, D., Crozier, G., James, D., Hollingworth, S., Williams, K., Jamieson, F. and Beedell, P. (2008) Re-invigorating democracy?: white middle-class identities and comprehensive schooling, *Sociological Review*, 56(2), 238-55.

Reay, D., David, M.E. and Ball, S. (2005) *Degrees of choice: Social class, race and gender in higher education*. Stoke on Trent: Trentham Books.

Reay, D., Hollingworth, S., Williams, K., Crozier, G., Jamieson, F., James, D. and Phoebe, B. (2007) A darker shade of pale? Whiteness, the middle classes and multi-ethnic inner city schooling, *Sociology*, 41(6), 1041-60.

Reckhow, S. and Snyder, J.W. (2014) The expanding role of philanthropy in education politics, *Educational Researcher*, 43(4), 186-95.

Reed, M. and Wallace, M. (2015) Elite discourse and institutional innovation: making the hybrid happen in English public services. In: G. Morgan, P. Hirsch and S. Quack (eds) *Elites on Trial,* Emerald Group Publishing, 269-302.

Resnik, J. (2008) The construction of the global worker through international education. In: J. Resnik (ed.) *The Production of Educational Knowledge in the Global Era*, Sense Publishers, Rotterdam, 147-68.

Resnik, J. (2012) 'The denationalization of education and the expansion of the International Baccalaureate', *Comparative Education Review*, 56(2), 248-69.

Rhoades, G. and Slaughter, S. (2004) Academic capitalism in the new economy: challenges and choices, *American Academic*, 37.

Rhodes, R.A.W. (2007) Understanding governance: ten years on. *Organization Studies*, 28(8), 1243-64.

Rich, M. (2014) New all-digital curriculums hope to ride high-tech push in schoolrooms, *The New York Times*, 3 March, p A13.

Rizvi, F. and Lingard, B. (2010) *Globalizing Education Policy*. London: Routledge.

Roberts, P. (2007) Neoliberalism, performativity, and research, *Review of Education*, 53, 349-65.

Roberts-Mahoney, H., Means, A.J. and Garrison, M.J. (2016) Netflixing human capital development: personalized learning technology and the corporatization of K-12 education, *Journal of Education Policy*. DOI:10.1080/02680939.2015.1132774.

Robertson, S., Bonal, X. and Dale, R. (2002) GATS and the education service industry: the politics of scale and global reterritorialization, *Comparative Education Review*, 46(4), 472-96.

Robertson, S.L. and Dale, R. (2013) The social justice implications of privatization in education governance frameworks: a relational account, *Oxford Review of Education*, 39(4), 426-45.

Robles, Y. (2015) Americans for Prosperity group plans to stay in Jeffco. *The Denver Post*, 29 October. http://blogs.denverpost.com/coloradoclassroom/2015/10/29/americans-for-prosperity-group-plans-to-stay-in-jeffco/5440/

Rock, D. (2008) The British in Argentina: from informal empire to postcolonialism. In: M. Brown (ed) *Informal Empire in Latin America: Culture, Commerce and Capital*. Malden: Blackwell Publishing, 49-77.

Rose, N. (1999) *Powers of Freedom: Reframing Political Thought*. Cambridge: Cambridge University Press.

Rothblatt, S. (2006) How élite?, *Oxford Review of Education*, 32(1), 127-45.

Rothblatt, S. (2007) *Education's abiding moral dilemma: Merit and worth in the cross-Atlantic democracies 1800–2006*. Oxford: Symposium Books.

Rothkopf, D. (2008) *Superclass: The global power elite and the world they are making*. New York, NY: Farrar, Straus and Giroux.

Rueschemeyer, D. (1983) Professional autonomy and the social control of expertise. In: R. Dingwall and P. Lewis (eds) *The sociology of the professions*. Hong Kong: MacMillan, 38-58.

Sahlberg, P. (2013) The PISA 2012 scores show the failure of 'market based' education reform, *The Guardian*, 8 December. www.theguardian.com/commentisfree/2013/dec/08/pisa-education-test-scores-meaning

Sallis, J. (1988) *Schools, Parents and Governors: A New Approach to Accountability*. London: Routledge.

Saltman, K. (2007) *Capitalizing on disaster: Taking and breaking public schools*. Boulder: Paradigm Publishers.

Saltman, K. (2009a) The rise of venture philanthropy and the ongoing neoliberal assault on public education: The Eli and Edythe Broad Foundation. *Workplace: A Journal for Academic Labor*, 16, 53–72.

Saltman, K. (2009b) Corporatization and the Control of Schools. In M. Apple, W. Au and L. Gandin (eds) *The Routledge International Handbook of Critical Education*. New York, NY: Routledge.

Saltman, K. (2010) *The Gift of Education*. New York: Palgrave Macmillan.

Saltman, K.J. (2016) *Scripted Bodies: Corporate Power, Smart Technologies, and the Undoing of Public Education*. New York: Routledge.

Savage, G.C. (2016) Think tanks, education and elite policy actors, *The Australian Education Researcher*, 43(1), 35-53.

Savage, M., Devine, F., Cunningham, N., Taylor, M., Li, Y., Hjellbrekke, J., Le Roux, B., Friedman, S. and Miles, A. (2013) A New Model of Social Class? Findings from the BBC's Great Class Survey Experiment, *Sociology*, 47(2), 219-50.

Savage, M. and Williams, K. (eds) (2008a) *Remembering Elites*. Oxford: Blackwell Publishing.

Savage, M. and Williams, K. (2008b) Elites: remembered in capitalism and forgotten by social sciences. In: M. Savage, M. and K. Williams (eds) *Remembering Elites*. Oxford: Blackwell Publishing, 1-24.

Scarbrough, B. (2013) *What is summer for?: Summer learning and the construction of educational (dis)advantage.* Paper presented at the meeting of the American Educational Research Association, San Franscisco, CA, April.

Schirmer, E. and Apple, M. W. (2016) Teachers, school boards, and the power of money: how the right wins at a local level, *The Educational Forum*, 80, 137-53.

Schleef, D.J. (2006) *Managing Elites: Professional Socialization in Law and Business Schools*. Lanham: Rowman and Littlefield.

'School Logbook, 1896-1926', Caledonian School, unpublished archival document.

Scott, J. (2009) The politics of venture philanthropy in charter school policy and advocacy. *Educational Policy*, 23(1), 106-36.

Shah, V. (2015) Ways of giving, *Business Life*. December 2015/January 2016, 30-2.

Sheehan, P. (2013) Callous capitalism: endless insecurity, *The Age*, 29 July. www.theage.com.au/comment/callous-capitalism-endless-insecuirty-20130728-2qsnk.html

Shore, C. and Wright, S. (1999) Audit culture and anthropology: neo-liberalism in British higher education, *The Journal of the Royal Anthropological Institute*, 5(4), 557-75.

Siegel, H. (1988) *Educating reason*. New York, NY: Routledge, Chapman and Hall.

Slaughter, S. and Leslie, L.L. (1997) *Academic capitalism: Politics, policies, and the entrepreneurial university,* Baltimore, MD: The Johns Hopkins University Press.

Smart, S., Hutchings, M., Maylor, U., Mendick, H. and Menter, I. (2009) Processes of middle-class reproduction in a graduate employment scheme, *Journal of Education and Work*, 22(1), 35-53.

Smith, D. (2014a) Americans for Prosperity throws its weight into Kenosha Unified School Board race, *Kenosha News*, 24 March. www.kenoshanews.com/news/americans_for_prosperity_throws_ its_weight_into_kenosha_unified_school_board_race_476239373. html (URL no longer available)

Smith, D. (2014b) Proposed charter bill worries Kenosha Unified principals, *Kenosha News*, 10 January.

Smith, J.M.A. (forthcoming) *Exploring the Complexities of Private Sector Influence: The Case of Student Data Privacy Policy*, unpublished dissertation, University of Southern California, Los Angeles.

Smyth, J. (2006) Educational leadership that fosters 'student voice'. *International Journal of Leadership in Education*, 9(4), 279-84.

Smyth, J. and Hattam, R. (2002) Early school leaving and the cultural geography of high schools. *British Educational Research Journal*, 28(3), 375-97.

Smyth, J., Hattam, R., Cannon, J., Edwards, J., Wilson, N. and Wurst, S. (2000) *Listen to me, I'm leaving: Early school leaving in South Australian secondary schools*. Adelaide: Flinders Institute for the Study of Teaching; Department of Employment, Education and Training; and Senior Secondary Assessment Board of South Australia.

Smyth, J. and McInerney, P. (2014) *Becoming educated: Young people's narratives of disadvantage, class, place and identity*. New York: Peter Lang Publishing.

Souto-Otero, M. (ed.) (2015) *Evaluating European Education Policy-Making*. Basingstoke: Palgrave Macmillan.

Spring, J. (2012) *Education Networks. Power, Wealth, Cyberspace, and the Digital Mind*. New York: Routledge.

Stahl, G. (2012) Aspiration and a good life among white working class boys in London, *Journal of Qualitative and Ethnographic Research*, 7(8-9), 8-19.

Stahl, G. (2013) Habitus disjunctures, reflexivity, and white working-class boys' conceptions of status in learner and social identities. *Sociological Research Online*, 18(3).

Stahl, G. (2014) The affront of the aspiration agenda: white working-class male narratives or 'ordinariness' in neoliberal times, *Masculinities and Social Change*, 3(2), 88-118.

Stahl, G. (2015) *Identity neoliberalism and aspiration: educating white working-class boys*. London: Routledge.

Stahl, G. and Dale, P. (2012) Creating positive spaces of learning: DJers and MCers identity work with new literacies, *Educational Forum*, 76(4), 510-32.

Stahl, G. and Dale, P. (2013) Success on the decks: working-class boys, education and turning tables on perceptions of failure, *Gender and Education*, 25(3), 357-72.

Steinkraus, D. (2011) Angry volunteers rally at Wirch recall drive, *The Journal Times*, 26 February. http://journaltimes.com/news/local/angry-volunteers-rally-at-wirch-recall-drive/article_6d6a3a8e-4231-11e0-a7df-001cc4c03286.html

Stevens, M. (2007) *Creating a class: College admissions and the education of elites*. Cambridge, MA: Harvard University Press.

Stiglitz, J.E. (2013) *The Price of Inequality*. London: Penguin.

Stone, D. (2001) Think tanks, global lesson-drawing and networking social policy ideas, *Global Social Policy*, 1(3): 338-60.

Stone, M.J. and Petrick, J.F. (2013) The educational benefits of travel experiences: A literature review, *Journal of Travel Research*, 52(6), 731-744.

Strauss, V. (2013) Privacy concerns grow over Gates-funded student database, *Washington Post*, 9 June. https://www.washingtonpost.com/news/answer-sheet/wp/2013/06/09/privacy-concerns-grow-over-gates-funded-student-database

Strauss, V. (2015a) Report: Big Education firms spend millions lobbying for pro-testing policies, *The Washington Post*, 30 March.

Strauss, V. (2015b) Study on Online Charter Schools: 'It is literally as if the kid did not go to school for an entire year', *The Washington Post*, 31 October. https://www.washingtonpost.com/news/answer-sheet/wp/2015/10/31/study-on-online-charter-schools-it-is-literally-as-if-the-kid-did-not-go-to-school-for-an-entire-year/

Stuart, G. (2014) *A New World of School Governance*. BELMAS/NGA Conference, 1 November.

Svampa, M. (2001) *Los que ganaron: la vida en los countries y barrios privados* [Those who won: life in country clubs and private neighborhoods]. Buenos Aires: Editorial Biblos.

SWTF (Social Work Task Force) (2009) *Building a safe, confident future – The final report of the Social Work Task Force*. London: Department for Education.

Swail, W.S. (2012) Preface. In: Swail, W.S. (ed) *Finding Superman, Debating the Future of Public Education in America*. New York, NY: Teachers College Press, ix–xii.

Swalwell, K. (2013) *Educating activist allies: Social justice pedagogy with the suburban and urban elite*. New York, NY: Routledge.

Swalwell, K. (2015) Mind the civic empowerment gap: Elite students and critical civic education, *Curriculum Inquiry*, 45(5), 491-512.

Swalwell, K. and Apple, M.W. (2011) Starting the wrong conversations: the public school crisis and 'waiting for superman', *Educational Policy*, 25(2), 368-82.

Swift, A. (2003) *How not to be a hypocrite: School choice for the morally perplexed parent*. London: Routledge.

Tan, J. (2008a) Whiter national education? In: J. Tan and P.T. Ng (eds) *Thinking schools, learning nation*. Singapore: Prentice Hall, 72-86.

Tan, J. (2008b) The marketisation of education in Singapore. In: J. Tan and P.T. Ng (eds) *Thinking schools, learning nation*. Singapore: Prentice Hall, 19-38.

Tan, K.P. (2008) Meritocracy and elitism in a global city: Ideological shifts in Singapore, *International Political Science Review*, 29(1), 7-27.

Tan, L. (2016). Confucius: Philosopher of Twenty-First Century Skills. *Educational Philosophy and Theory*, 48,(12), 1233-1243.

Tarc, P. (2010) *Global Dreams, Enduring Tensions: International Baccalaureate in a Changing World*, New York, NY: Peter Lang.

Taylor, T. (1977) *A New Partnership for Our Schools. Report of the Committee of Enquiry* (The Taylor Report). London: HMSO.

Teach First (2015a) Home page, Teach First: London. https://www.teachfirst.org.uk

Teach First (2015b) *Building a Movement for Change*, London: Teach First. https://www.teachfirst.org.uk/what-we-do/building-movement-change

Teach First (2015c) *Beyond Teach First,* London: Teach First.: https://graduates.teachfirst.org.uk/leadership-development-programme/beyond-teach-first

Teese, R. (2000) *Academic success and social power: Examination and inequality*. Melbourne: Melbourne University Press.

Teo, C.H. (2000) *Technical education: Staying on the correct side of the skills divide*. Speech by RADM (NS) Teo Chee Hean, Minister for Education and Second Minister for Defence at the opening of ITE Bukit Batok and the opening of the 14th National Skills Competition, 28 June. www.moe.gov.sg/media/speeches/2000/sp28062000.htm

Tharman, S. (2013) Singapore in 20 years: A meritocracy of equals. *The Straits Times*, 19 April. http://news.asiaone.com/News/Latest+News/Singapore/Story/A1Story20130419-417173.html

The Key (2013) *At Cost* (URL no longer available).

Thomson, P. (2005) Bringing Bourdieu to policy sociology: codification, misrecognition and exchange value in the UK context, *Journal of Education Policy*, 2 (6), 741758.

Thomson, P. (2009) *School leadership: Heads on the block?* London: Routledge.

Thomson, P. (2010) Headteacher autonomy: A sketch of a Bourdieuian field analysis of position and practice., *Critical Studies in Education*, 51(1), 5-20.

Thompson, J. (1990) *Ideology and Modern Culture: Critical Social Theory in the Era of Mass Communication*, Stanford University Press, Stanford.

Thrift, N. (2005) *Knowing Capitalism*. London. Sage.

Tooley, J. (2000) *Reclaiming Education*. London: Continuum.

Trow, M. (1976) 'Elite higher education': An endangered species?, *Minerva*, 14(3), 355–76.

Ujifusa, A. (2013) John White withdraws Louisiana student data from inBloom. *Education Week*, 26 April.

van Apeldoorn, B. and de Graaf, N. (2012) Corporate elite networks and US post-Cold War grand strategy from Clinton to Obama, *European Journal of International Relations*, 2(1), 29–55.

van Dijk, T.A. (1993. *Elite discourse and racism*. London: Sage Publications.

van Dijk, T.A. (2006) Ideology and discourse analysis. *Journal of Political Ideologies*, 11(2), 115–40.

van Slyck, A.A. (2006) *A manufactured wilderness: Summer camps and the shaping of American youth, 1890–1960*. Minneapolis, MN: University of Minnesota Press.

van Zanten, A. (2015) Educating elites: the changing dynamics and meanings of privilege and power. In: A. van Zante. and S.J. Bal. with B. Darchy-Koechli. (eds) *Elites, Privilege and Excellence. World Yearbook of Education 2015*, Abingdon: Routledge, 3-12.

van Zanten, A. and Ball, S.J. with Darchy-Koechlin, B. (eds) (2015) *Elites, Privilege and Excellence. World Yearbook of Education 2015*, Abingdon: Routledge.

van Zanten, A. and Maxwell, C. (2015) Elite education and the state in France: durable ties and new challenges. *British Journal of Sociology of Education*, 3 (1), 71-94.

Veblen, T. (1918) *The higher learning in America: A memorandum on the conduct of universities by businessmen,* New Brunswick, NJ: Transaction Publishers.

Wakeford, S. (2013) The motivations, expectations and experiences of secondary school students involved in volunteer tourism: a case study of the Rangitoto College Cambodia house building trip, Doctoral dissertation. Auckland, New Zealand: Auckland University of Technology.

Wakeling, P. and Savage, M. (2015) Entry to elite positions and the stratification of higher education in Britain, *The Sociological Review,* 63, 290-320.

Walford, G. (1990) *Privatization and privilege in education.* New York, NY: Routledge.

Weis, L. and Cipollone, K. (2013) 'Class work': Producing privilege and social mobility in elite US secondary schools, *British Journal of Sociology of Education,* 34(5–6): 707-22.

Weis, L., Cipollone, K, and Jenkins, H. (2014. *Class warfare: Class, race, and college admissions in top-tier secondary schools.* Chicago, IL: University of Chicago Press.

Whitty, G., Edwards, T, and Gewirtz, S. (eds) (1993) *Specialisation and Choice in Urban Education: The City Technology Experiment.* London: Routledge.

Wigdortz, B. (2012) *Success Against the Odds : Five lessons in how to achieve the impossible; the story of Teach First,* ebook. London: Short Books.

Wilkins, A. (2012) Push and pull in the classroom: competition, gender, and the neoliberal subject, *Gender and Education,* 24(7), 765–81.

Wilkins, A (2015) Professionalising school governance: The disciplinary effects of school autonomy and inspection on the changing role of school governors, *Journal of Education Policy,* 3(2), 182-200.

Wilkins, A. (2016) *Modernising school governance: Corporate planning and expert handling in state education.* Abingdon: Routledge.

Wilkinson, R. and Pickett, K. (2009) *The Spirit Level.* London: Allen Lane.

Williamson, B. (2015) Governing methods: policy innovation labs, design and data science in the digital governance of education, *Journal of Educational Administration and History,* 4(3), 251–71.

Windle, J. and Nogueira, M.A. (2015) The role of internationalization in the schooling of Brazilian elites: distinctions between two class fractions, *British Journal of Sociology of Education.* 3(1), 174–92.

Winter, R. (2009) Academic manager or managed academic? Academic identity schisms in higher education, *Journal of Higher Education Policy and Management,* 31(2), 121-131.

Winter, R. and Sarros, J. (2002) Corporate reforms to Australian universities: views from the academic heartland, *Australian Association for Institutional Research Journal*, 1(2), 1-26.

WisPolitics.com (2015) Former teacher: I know my own worth. Wispolitics.com, 24 February. http://quorumcall.wispolitics.com/2015/02/former-teacher-i-know-my-own-worth.html

Wolfe, D. (2013) Schools: The legal structures, the accidents of history and the legacies of timing and circumstance, *Education Law Journal*, 2, 100-113.

Wood, M. and Flinders, M. (2014) Rethinking depoliticisation: beyond the governmental., *Policy & Politics*, 4(2), 151-170.

Woods, C.E. (2014) *Anatomy of a Professionalization Project: The Making of the Modern School Business Manager*. London: Bloomsbury.

Woods, P., Bagley, C. and Glatter, R. (1998) *School choice and competition: Markets in the public interest?* London: Routledge.

Woods P., Woods, G. and Gunter, H. (2007) Academy schools and entrepreneurialism in education, *Journal of Education Policy*, 22(2), 232-59.

Ye, R. and Nylander, E. (2015) The transnational track: state sponsorship and Singapore's Oxbridge elite, *British Journal of Sociology of Education*. 3(1), 11-33.

Ylijoki, O.H. and J. Ursin (2013) The construction of academic identity in the changes of Finnish higher education, *Studies in Higher Education*, 3(8), 1135-1149.

Yong, C. and Zaccheus, M. (2012. Top schools' students tend to have friends like themselves: Poll. www.edvantage.com.sg/content/top-schools-students-tend-have-friends-themselves-poll (URL no longer available)

Zelaya, M (2012) La expansión de universidades privadas en el caso argentino [The expansion of private universities: the Argentinian case], *Pro-Posições* 23(2), 179-194.

Zemach-Bersin, T. (2008) Selling the world: Study abroad marketing and the privatization of global citizenship. In: R. Lewin (ed) *The handbook of practice and research in study abroad: Higher education and the quest for global citizenship*. New York, NY: Routledge, 303-320.

Zimdars, A., Sullivan, A. and Heath, A. (2009) Elite higher education admission in the arts and sciences: is cultural capital the key?, *Sociology*, 43(4), 646-66.

Index

Note: page numbers in italic type refer to figures.